RELIGIONS
of the World

Ronald J. Wilkins

A discussion of the origin of religious
awareness in human beings and its
expression in the world today.

W9-BIR-632

Religious Education Division
Wm. C. Brown Company Publishers
Dubuque, Iowa

Book Team

Publisher
Ernest T. Nedder

Editor
Sandra J. Hirstein

Production/Photo Editor
Patricia Murray Hail

Designer
Janet K. Conradi

Scripture text in this publication is from the *Good News Bible,* the Bible in Today's English Version. Copyright © American Bible Society, 1976.

Unless otherwise indicated, other Scripture material is from *Great Religions of the World,* © National Geographic Society 1971, 1978.

All photo credits are on page 252.

Editorial Consultants

for Sacred Scripture—Very Rev. Brendan McGrath, Professor of Theology, Loyola University, Chicago, Illinois; Past President, the Catholic Biblical Association of America

for Adolescent Religious Education—Mrs. Ruth Cheney, Program Services Associate for the Youth Ministry of the Episcopal Church; Chairman of the Screening Committee of the International Christian Youth Exchange

for Adolescent Psychology—Dr. William D. Wilkins, Professor, School of Leadership and Human Behavior, United States International University, San Diego, California; Consultant for the Office of Economic Opportunity, Washington, D.C.

for Social Sciences—Dr. Raymond Polin, Professor of Political Science, Graduate School, St. John's University, Jamaica, L.I., New York

Fully aware of religious education as a key factor affecting human relations the editors invited a Protestant and a Jewish scholar to review material presented in this book as it bears on their respective faith communities. These are Dr. Edward Zerin, Rabbi, and Dr. Martin E. Marty, Editor, *Christian Century.* While their personal views and religious beliefs obviously must differ from some of the views presented in this book, both feel that the content has been so handled as to increase intergroup understanding.

Copyright © 1984 Wm. C. Brown Company Publishers.
Manufactured in the United States of America.
All rights reserved.

ISBN 0–697–01928–4

Printed in the United States of America
10 9 8 7 6 5 4 3

Contents

Religion is the expression of a person's relationship with whatever God is for that person.

Preface

Human civilization developed over the course of many centuries. When primitive people discovered that their survival depended on mutual cooperation, they developed ways to survive and to live in peace with each other. They created an **economic** system that would provide food, water, and shelter, and a **political** system that would enable them to provide these necessities in an orderly and relatively equitable manner. The organization of people into political groups to provide the necessities of life is called human society. As time went on, people's economic and political systems became more sophisticated, but their purpose remained the same.

As people organize into political groups to provide life's necessities, they express who they are and what they believe about themselves and the world in which they live—in their **culture**—expressed by their art, literature, music, dance, folklore, and religion. It is this last expression which is the subject matter of *Religions of the World*.

The historical reality of religion cannot be denied. It has been a part of the human experience since the dawn of civilization and has had a significant impact on the way civilization has developed. Its beliefs and practices have played a major role in shaping human culture. ''Through their symbol system,'' says Gregory Baum, an authority on the sociology of religion, ''the religions have provided man with a vision of life, an orientation of their energies, and a hierarchy of values that eventually produced various forms of culture and society. And through its own institutions, the religions have affected the style of life of vast numbers of people, and have created attitudes and practices that eventually had a profound influence on culture and society.'' To see what this influence has been and is, *Religions of the World* examines these religions. It looks at their origins, their beliefs, their practices, and their current status in the world.

It is not enough, however, to look at the religions which have shaped, and are shaping, the cultures of the world. It is necessary, also, to look at the origin of religious awareness, and to define and describe religion as a human phenomenon. Only in this way can we understand why religion has had such a profound influence in shaping human culture and expressing human needs.

Any human institution or expression of culture is a product of its own past. Like human beings and their institutions and culture, religion has experienced change. It is different from the way it was, but its roots are buried deep in the soil of human development. To know its origin and its expressions in the past is to understand its expressions at the present time. *Religions of the World* discusses the origin of religious awareness and proposes a definition of religion which can serve as a hub around which discussions of religion, religious awareness, and the role of religion in modern society can revolve.

The goal of *Religions of the World* is not simply to define religion and its expressions as they are found in the world today. Its goal is to help you better understand **people.** In this age of global awareness and increasing global tensions, it is imperative that we better understand other people.

We can do so if we understand their religious orientation—which, to a large extent, determines their vision of life, their moral values, their motivations, their hopes and fears, their joys and sorrows, their individuality and complexity.

Your study of the religions of the world will not only increase your knowledge and enable you to understand other people better, however, it will enrich your life.

part one

The Origin of Religion

Religion is a response to the Mystery of Life

chapter 1
What Religion Really Is

Sooner or later, everyone faces the question of the relevancy of religion in his or her life. Whether they have been raised in a religiously-oriented culture or in a secularist or atheistic atmosphere, they ask themselves about religion. They wonder what religion is, why it is, whether it is necessary, whether it is natural to people, and whether it is for them. Eventually, everyone takes a stance concerning religion.

Why is this so?

Perhaps the first reason is sociological. People experience religion around them, see it in action, and wonder why it is part of human experience. Depending upon their personal experience, they have a favorable or unfavorable impression. They decide that religion is for them, or they decide that it is not for them. They live their lives accordingly.

The second reason seems to be experiential. People who have been brought up in a particular religion wonder about it. They ask what it really means, where it came from, why they belong to this religious community rather than that, how their religion compares with others, whether it is "true," and whether they should seek another or abandon the practice of any religion.

A third reason that people wonder about religion in their own lives might be called "influential." That is, they are influenced by what they experience. Some people, for example, wonder about religion in their own lives because of the influence of a religious person like Pope John Paul II whose charism is experienced globally. Others see many influential people around them practicing no religion or expressing a kind of disdain for or amused tolerance of religion. They wonder whether religion should affect their lives at all. Still others, because they are unable to answer serious religious questions, wonder if religion really is a psychological crutch, an invention, a racket, or a superstition left over from "unenlightened" days. All of these people are influenced to a greater or lesser degree by the views of religion held by those who have influenced their lives.

Perhaps the most common reason for people asking themselves about religion and its role in their lives, however, is that, at some point in their lives, they have asked them-

Opposite page—A Hindu woman, India

5

selves about the meaning of life. They have searched for answers to questions about life that go beyond the obvious, the measurable, the observable, or the scientific. They have searched for answers to the *mystery of life.* They wonder where life came from, where it is going, and what its purpose is. For them, as we shall see, religion provides the best answers.

Encounter with Mystery

Behind humanity's questions about life's meaning and purpose lies an encounter with mystery.

The mystery of life confronts people at various times in their lives. When they experience the power, the beauty, or the magnitude of the universe, they wonder where it came from, what its purpose is, what it means, and where it is going.

When they read about Unidentified Flying Objects, they ask: Are they real? Where are they from? How do they travel? Are the creatures in them super- or subhuman? How do they subsist or exist? How are they related to earth's creatures?

When a man and a woman experience the joy of true love, they wonder about its source, its meaning, its purpose and its uniqueness.

When a husband and wife experience the mystery of pregnancy and the wonder of birth, they ask themselves what shaped this tiny form, what force created this miracle, what life is expressed in this helpless baby.

The mystery of life confronts people most of all, however, when they are in the presence of death. For most people, death is the great mystery: the unexpected, the unknown, the point where mystery is master. Death raises the ultimate question: "What is life?" and that question demands an answer.

People's Response to Mystery

In response to the mysteries of life, people have, in various places and at various times, formulated different answers. Whatever the answer, however, it contained a response to the decisive question: "Where did life come from?"

Some have found an explanation in the idea of many gods each fulfilling a separate function and arranged in order of importance and power. Some believe in one God explaining that their God is a Person, while others explain their God in impersonal terms.

Some have found their answer without God. They explain life in terms of the harmonious unfolding of material

How Big Is the Universe?

The universe consists of all the matter, light, energy, forms of radiation, and other phenomena known or presumed to exist. It consists of everything that reasonable people believe to be present in time and space.

We do not know how big the universe actually is because our means of measurement are limited. However, all the stars, of which our sun is one, are part of the universe. The Milky Way, a circular galaxy in our universe, contains over 100 billion stars! This galaxy is about 100,000 light years in diameter. (A light year is the distance that light travels in a year, roughly 5.9 trillion miles.) The Milky Way, the most familiar of the galaxies, almost pales into insignificance when compared with the discovery, in 1982, that what had previously been thought of as two separate galaxies were really one whose center had been blocked from vision by the Milky Way. This "new" galaxy is 700 million light years long and from 100 to 200 million light years from the earth.

Some astronomers believe that there are as many galaxies in the universe as there are stars in the Milky Way! And most astronomers think that galaxies called quasars may be as many as 10 billion light years from the earth. Is it any wonder that people are awed by what they see in the heavens and wonder where it all came from?

The Valley of the Kings, Egypt

possibilities into more complex forms with even greater possibilities. They simply leave the question of the origin of these possibilities unanswered. They conclude that, since the existence of God cannot be proved, God does not exist.

Some people respond to the mystery of life by saying that there is no answer to the mystery. Others believe that life always was. They say it had no beginning. They believe that life is lived in a series of reincarnations—successive lives for a single person.

A sixth response to the mystery of life is held by those who believe that people's role and purpose in life is meaningless. They believe that life is a tragic mistake, a trick of fate, a barbarous cruelty, a stroke of bad luck. They believe that death is a merciful release from an unwanted existence.

Whatever the answer people have formulated, however, it is a response to the mystery of life. This response is what we call religion. What these responses are and how they are expressed is the subject matter of *Religions of the World*.

What Religion Is

Many people think of religion in terms of what they see. They equate religion with a set of dogmas (or doctrines), a form of worship, and a moral code. In reality, dogma is an attempt to verbalize what is believed. Worship is the externalization of

The Origin of Religion

human responses which seem appropriate to whatever a person believes is the ultimate answer to life's mystery. Morality, on the other hand, is the response to whatever a person thinks is proper conduct for a human person. When these are organized, ritualized, and agreed on by a group of people, those people form a community of believers, or a church. What they do is often called a religion.

Religion, however, is a term including the many ways people have of giving expression to what they think life is all about. Put in another way, **religion is the human response to whatever the answer to the mystery of life is for a particular person.** It is the attempt to express a relationship to that answer. It encompasses both those whose response is found in a God answer and those whose response is found in a no-God answer, because both responses are based on faith.

Are the answers of any religion provable? Not if you are looking for scientific proof that can be mathematically formulated and verified by sense observation. There is no physical or chemical data on God, on life after death, on heaven or eternity, just as there is no mathematical or chemical proof or neatly measurable data on honesty or loyalty or mother love. Religion deals with a dimension beyond scientific grasp. Science can tell us about the data of life that are measurable, but it leaves unanswered the questions of who created the universe, why it was created, how it originated and what is its destiny.

Science and mathematics unravel the *problems* of the universe; religion responds to the *mystery* of the universe. When a problem is unravelled, the mind is satisfied; but since mystery can never be unravelled, the mind is never satisfied but always restless. The more people solve the physical, chemical, and biological problems of the universe, the more they can apply nature to their own purposes. But no one is able to unravel the mystery of another person's freedom, or the mystery of why one individual and not somebody else was called to exist. People cannot bend mystery to their purposes; they can only give themselves to the purposes of that mystery which is greater than themselves.

Jidai Festival in Kyoto, Japan

Responses Are Based on Faith

Whether people root the mystery of life in one God, many gods, or no God, and whether they formulate their destiny as an afterlife, an endless cycle of repeated lives, or a meaningful life which ends with the grave—their "certainty" in these answers is not scientific but is based on an act of *trust.*

Through their various beliefs, people say in effect, "The mystery can be trusted. It is greater than I am. It has thrust me into life and will one day call me out of life. I do not know why, but I trust there is a reason. I am an intelligent being; intelligence needs a purpose. Without a purpose, life would be unintelligible—but an unintelligible life for an intelligent being would be a cruel contradiction of my own nature. I trust that life is not ultimately so cruel. I believe, therefore, that life (and death, too, as a part of life) makes sense."

The faith of people whose answer is God-centered was best expressed by the writer of Hebrews, a New Testament book. In it he says:

To have faith is to be sure of the things we hope for, to be certain of the things we cannot see. It was by their faith that people of ancient times won God's approval.

It is by faith that we understand that the universe was created by God's word, so that what can be seen was made out of what cannot be seen.

—Hebrews 11:1–3

Schwedgaon Pagoda ground in Rangoon, Burma

The faith of people whose answer is no-God-centered (or universe-centered, or reality-centered) might be expressed this way: "People are not all there is. They are sharers of existence with All That Is. In one way or another, a person confronts the *Not*-me—that which is not himself or herself—and says in effect, 'I can trust the *Not*-me. Reality is my friend.' Reality is not rooted in some kind of God. It is rooted in a Trustable Something which makes it possible to say: 'Life makes sense. It is not to be wasted. It is to be responsibly lived. Death does not cancel out the meaning of a responsibly lived life.' "

But, one may ask, what about those who say there is no answer to the mystery of life? Is not their "nonanswer" an answer? Is it not a response? It is not based on faith—on the belief that there is no answer? Of course it is, for faith is the ultimate ingredient of an inquiring mind. It must search for an answer to mystery, and it is not satisfied until it finds an answer—whatever it may be. The faith of people whose answer to the mystery of life is no answer might be expressed in this way: "I believe there is no answer to the mystery of life. That is my answer."

The Influence of Religion on Society Today

Even though religion has been a major factor in influencing the development of various human cultures, its influence has ebbed and flowed. It is strong in one place at a particular time influencing a particular people. It is weak in another, having little influence on the way people live. The reasons for this are as diverse and as complex as human nature itself. The influence of religion is related to the political, economic, and cultural philosophies of countries as professed and practiced by their leaders. This influence has in recent times involved the orientation of the communications media and the charisma of religious leaders. Finally, the influence of religion depends upon its credibility as it is professed and practiced as well as the religious commitment of the people in a particular society.

At the present time, religion does not play a very important role in the political, economic, or cultural expressions of most of the world's political leaders.[1] It is true that many of them give a passing glance to what is called "human rights" and do remain attentive to the religious concerns of people when these are thrust on them forcefully. For the most part, however, economic and political decisions are based on pragmatic, secular ends.[2] Individuals in power may be religious, it is true, but political reasons often override their religious convictions in the decision-making process.

This is natural considering the complexity of the world today. On the one hand there are countries with diverse religious expressions among their people. No single expression could be imposed on the total population. Likewise, when various nations are dealing with each other, the religious convictions of one cannot and should not dominate. Finally, many governments are not only areligious,[3] they are antireligious. They cannot be dealt with on religious grounds. They force other governments to deal with them on strictly pragmatic economic and political terms.

A second reason that religion does not play a major role in shaping world opinion today is the secularist orientation of

1. There are occasional exceptions to this rule. In some countries with strong Islamic rulers, for example, almost all decisions are based on the Koran, the sacred writings of Islam.

2. The philosophy that economic, political, and cultural matters should be conducted without regard to religious elements.

3. Meaning "not," "without," or lacking religion.

the media. Its steady downplaying of religion and religious concerns tends to create a secularist society: people's attention is focused on everything but religion. Religion becomes a minor concern—an individual's option rather than a community's force.

This, too, is natural. In countries where the media is controlled by an areligious or antireligious political group, the media cannot give attention to religious concerns, or present them in a biased or prejudicial way. In countries where the media is not controlled, those responsible for production are forced into a neutral position because of the many religious philosophies of the society in which the media operates.

This secularist philosophy is reflected in the literature, art, theater, movies, and TV presentations available to the public at large. While it is true that religious topics and materials with religious themes are occasionally presented, the great bulk of material is areligious, much of it dealing with materials that are contrary to the philosophy of many religious groups. Religion has become the concern of small groups and of individuals in society, rather than the concern of society in general.

Another reason that religion does not play an important role in the political, economic, and cultural expressions of society is that many religious leaders do not exert a great influence on society. When human society was made up of literally hundreds of small groups (tribes, peoples, nations, and so on) more or less isolated from each other, a strong religious leader could mold a society along religious lines. This is what happened in the past and accounts for the great influence religion had in shaping the cultures of many peoples. At the present time, human society is global. Religious leaders, even the most notable, influence only a small part of the global society and exert little more than moral pressure on world concerns. They contribute only one part to the total of influences which shape the expressions of world culture.

A fourth reason that religion plays a lesser role in shaping world culture at the present time is that many religions, especially in the more advanced countries, adhere to some beliefs and practices which are at variance with the experience and the learning of the people to whom they address themselves. They lose their credibility, not on the major issues of life, but on the lesser aspects of religious belief and practice which, ultimately, do not affect people's lives. Because of this, many people do not look to religion or religious leaders for guidance in the business of living.

Media People Predominantly Secularistic

TAMPA—A recent article in *Public Opinion* magazine reported on a poll of more than 200 journalists and broadcasters. The poll was conducted by professors Robert Lichter of George Washington University and Stanley Rothman of Smith College and included those who are responsible for news content from the *Washington Post,* the *New York Times,* the *Wall Street Journal, Time Magazine, Newsweek, U.S. News and World Report,* CBS, NBC, ABC and PBS news.

The poll found that those who are responsible for news content are mainly white males in their 30s or 40s. Ninety-three percent have college degrees and more than half have graduate degrees. Most of them come from upper middle class backgrounds from the northeast and the midwest.

Ideologically, a majority of the top journalists consider themselves liberal. They show ambivalence in their pro-business concepts as contrasted with their commitment to the welfare state.

Among these media elite a predominate characteristic is their secular outlook. Only eight percent go to church or synagogue weekly. But 86 percent seldom or never attend religious services.

The views of those who are responsible for news content on sexual matters was pronounced. In answers to questions on the subject, 84 percent strongly opposed state control over sexual activities. Ninety percent felt that a woman has the right to decide for herself whether to have an abortion. Eighty-five percent support the right of homosexuals to teach in public schools and 75 percent do not think that homosexuality is wrong.

Fifty-four percent do not regard adultery as wrong and only 15 percent strongly agree that extramarital affairs are immoral.

Source: *Florida Catholic,* 26 November, 1982, page 20.

A fifth reason why religion plays only a minor role in shaping world affairs is the religious commitment of individuals in society. Most people believe in some kind of God and do express some kind of relationship with that God. They do the best they can to live up to their religious convictions, but they hesitate to bring their religious convictions into political, economic, cultural, or social issues.

At the same time, some "religious" people are not really religious. They don't live up to the convictions they profess because it is not convenient for them to do so, or because they do not understand the depth of meaning inherent in the faith they say they profess. They take the easy way out. Confused by what they believe are the "uncertainties" of religious faith, they often opt for the line of least resistance and simply exist in a religion instead of really living it. They are sociologically religious. In other words, they grew up in a particular religion and continue in it simply because they were born into it or because it is socially correct or convenient for them to do so. Yet, they are religiously indifferent. They practice a form of religion without being convinced that, in the long run, it matters either way.[4] Their religion has little effect on their lives; hence, it does not affect the lives of those around them.

Two other aspects of the religious commitment of individuals, which mitigate the influence of religion on world culture, are religious infantilism and religious ignorance.

Pita Bread for sale outside the Damascus Gate in Jerusalem, Israel

The Origin of Religion

Generally, people who are religiously indifferent, or who are, at best, lukewarm in their practice of religion, are content to live their religious lives with only the barest notion of what their religion is or means. They are children, religiously, reacting as children react and content as children are content with their religious knowledge and practice. Religion occupies very little of their time and attention; it exists on the fringes of their life, rarely disturbed because it is not important to them. People, whose religious life is lived on an infantile level, feel they know enough about religion, and they make no effort to either improve their knowledge or to deepen their commitment.

This religious infantilism often creates a second problem: religious ignorance. Because they do not know enough about religion (their own or others') but believe they do, religiously ignorant people are apt to make snap judgments about religion, religious people, or their own or another's religion. They tend to be prejudiced or contemptuous of others' religious convictions, and show little respect for others' religious beliefs and practices.[5] This ignorance and prejudice tends to separate people into religious enclaves and prevent them from cooperating with each other, thus lessening the influence of religion on the formation of global culture.

Even though religion does not affect politics, economics, and culture to the extent it did in the past, it does have a strong influence on the lives of individuals. Some ninety percent of the people of the world acknowledge some religious or spiritual influence in their lives, and at least half of these testify that it has a significant influence. In this sense, religion does affect the cultural expression of these people which, in turn, affects the cultural expression of society.

Conclusion

As we have said, one of the enduring phenomena of human development is the practice of religion. It has been part of the human scene since the dawn of human consciousness.

4. What is said here about God-centered religious people applies equally to people who subscribe to a no-God answer to the mystery of life. Atheists, agnostics, pure materialists, and rationalists are just like other people. Some are deeply convinced of the reasonableness of their faith stance, some are run-of-the-mill, and some are strictly sociological atheists, agnostic, materialistic, or skeptics.

5. Religious prejudice, of course, is not confined to people who are considered religiously ignorant. Misplaced zeal on the part of conscientious people can sometimes blind them to the validity of another's religious conviction and can cause them to attack others, misrepresent their position, or persecute them. (Those who profess no religion can, of course, be equally prejudiced, disrespectful, and ignorant.)

To find out why, it is necessary to discuss the origin of religious awareness, the origins of religions, and the development of religious awareness and practices. Each of these will be discussed in the next two chapters.

Summary

1. Religion is natural to human beings. It is a response to the encounter with the mystery of life.
2. There are many responses to the mystery of life. These responses have given rise to many different religions.
3. Religion is the expression of a person's relationship with whatever God is for that person.
4. Religion does not play a major role in influencing the economic, political, and cultural directions in the world.

For Review

1. Your book states that sooner or later everyone faces the question of the relevancy of religion in his or her life. What reasons are given?
2. Your book contends that at the center of people's religious sense there lies an encounter with mystery. What does it mean by that?
3. What are some of the responses people have made to this encounter with mystery?
4. How does your book define religion? How does the definition differ from most people's conception of religion?
5. Why does your book contend that people who say that they do not believe in any kind of God are religious? Do you agree? Why? Why not?
6. Why does your book allege that religion does not exert as great an influence on human culture as it once did?

For Discussion

1. In an open forum, discuss the reasons given for the declining influence of religion in the shaping of human culture. Which has had the greatest effect?

2. Discuss why many people can be classified as children in their knowledge of religion. Give reasons for your viewpoint, based on experience.

3. Do you agree or disagree with the following statement: "Your understanding of [religious things]—should it not be, perhaps, elevated to a level proportionate to your scientific knowledge of law, of history, of letters, or of biology? Would there not be a grave danger for you if in the maturity of your own judgments or of your critical acumen, you should be content to remain in the things of faith like little children, in the notions that were taught you in the course of your elementary or intermediate studies?"

For Research

1. In an almanac, or some source dealing with such matters, find the names of four religious leaders who have an influence on world opinion.

2. Prepare a brief report on Socrates.

3. Try to find evidence for or against your book's contention that most governments in the world are either neutral, areligious, or antireligious in their political policies.

4. Make a survey among TV listings, radio programs, magazine and newspaper articles about religious matters. Note their number and place in relationship to other items.

Words You Should Know

If there are any words in the list below which you are not sure of, look them up in the Word List at the back of the book.

areligious	experiential	ritual
Church	galaxy	secular
diverse	infantilism	tangible
dogma	relevancy	worship
enclave	religion	

chapter 2

The Origin of Religion

If the definition of religion as a response to the mystery of life is accepted, it is possible to say that religion is natural to human beings. Religious systems, or religions, however, develop from an explanation for the mystery of life. One person, or a group of persons, formulate an answer, or give an explanation, that at once makes sense and gives security to others searching for an answer, who then become believers, or acceptors, of the explanation. Those who accept a particular answer or explanation usually form a group and express their beliefs in formulas, their worship in rituals, and their living in moral or ethical codes. They acquire a name which, however loosely, identifies them as a particular group of believers who live and worship in a particular way.

Exactly how religion began, however, cannot be definitely stated. There are many theories but no certainties. One theory which seems most plausible, at this moment in time, is that religion probably began when the prehuman species, that evolved into primitive people, became aware of forces outside of themselves that they could not explain or control.

It must be remembered that the religions people subscribe to at the present time were not always as they are now. Even those which originated at a rather well-defined point in history (for example, Buddhism, Judaism, Christianity, Islam) did not arise full blown—with the elaborate theology and ritual they now have—at the moment of their origin. They were not formed in isolation from the culture and religious awareness of the times and places in which they originated and developed. Each major living religion has its own prehistory: a period of time which shaped and molded the society from which it came.

In other words, the religions people now practice evolved from more primitive religious awareness, and this awareness evolved from still more primitive awareness. What this means is that religious awareness began somewhere; evidence leads us to believe that it developed as people developed. This evidence is part of what we call prehistory.

Opposite page—Hindu priest seated at the entrance of a painted temple, India

19

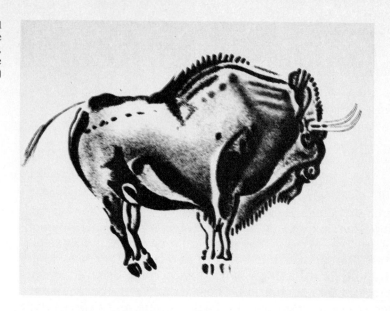

Standing bison bull wall painting of the Old Stone Age discovered in 1879, Spain. (Courtesy The Granger Collection)

Evidence from Prehistory

Prehistory is generally considered to be the time prior to *written* records—that is, for example, in Mesopotamia,[1] it was the time prior to 3400 B.C.; but in England it was the time before 55 B.C. Prehistory includes the archeological findings (bits and pieces of human tools, weapons, dwellings) and the careful speculation of archeologists, anthropologists, linguists, and historians as to what these mean.

No one can assert with absolute certainty what actually did happen—for no one has any *internal* record of the hopes and fears, needs and desires, or inner feelings of a prehistoric person or community. The kind of certainty reached in descriptions of prehistoric times is a *probable* certainty based on *external* information. Like detectives reconstructing an event from circumstantial evidence, present-day scientists piece together information from many sources, reconstructing a probable situation or condition and hypothesizing about what was, or could have been, done within the situation.

Experts on prehistoric religion have pieced together the elements of rather systematic religious practices which indicate a gradually developing religious sense among primitive people. Using information gained from archeologists (ruins of ancient temples, bones arranged in special patterns in caves,

1. An ancient country in Asia located between the Tigris and Euphrates rivers. Modern Iraq includes much of this area.

The Origin of Religion

artifacts that could only have some significance beyond use in everyday activities) and combining it with known facts about early societies like those of the early American Indian, the Maori, and the aborigines who are found in Australia and remote parts of the Philippines, these experts have been able to reconstruct the probable religious situation among early people.

If the *evidence* available from prehistory indicates a *developed* religious sense and elaborate religious practices, common sense dictates that that religious sense and those practices developed from earlier religious awareness. The question arises, therefore: Where did the first religious awareness stem from? The answer, admittedly speculative, is nevertheless reliable.

How Religion May Have Emerged

Those who examine the evidence of religion among early people surmise that they emerged from animal awareness to human self-awareness and experienced phenomena in their world that cried out for explanation. They sought answers to the mysteries of the world in which they lived. Their answers, simplistic by our standards, were their attempt to find reasons for the phenomena they experienced.

What seems to have happened was this. Survival was apparently the major preoccupation of the first people. Three things threatened this survival: the forces of nature, like earthquakes, floods, forest fires, thunder and lightning; the scarcity of food; and the experience of death. (Animals give us a clue to the fear of these things that exists in subhuman species.) Experiencing these things as they did, early people concluded that they were the result of the actions of invisible powers or spirits that controlled the forces or caused the scarcity of food or brought death, or that the phenomena of nature were themselves forces, powers, or spirits. To cope with these forces, powers, or spirits, primitive people tried to develop ways to overcome the spirits, offset their power, or placate the power or spirit that threatened their survival. **These ways seem to be the beginnings of religion—they were responses to the mystery of life faced by the first human beings.**

The acceptance of a spirit world to explain the existence of hostile forces was reinforced by people's experience of dreams. Because sleep and death resembled each other so much, and because people experienced dreams in which they "lived" in another world, primitive people believed that, during sleep, their own spirits went to live in this other world and then returned to awake the body which housed the spirit.

Believing firmly in the spirit world, early people explained the mysteries of their world in terms of the spirits who controlled the phenomena they experienced. The things they benefited from—such as the sun, or the plants and animals that provided food were controlled by friendly spirits. The things which threatened them were controlled by hostile spirits—or powers or gods, as they were called. Early people, therefore, established rituals, practices, ceremonies, prayers, songs, and chants to keep the friendly spirits friendly and to ward off the hostile spirits. As time went on (and this took many centuries), ceremonies became more elaborate and were scrupulously followed to curry the favor of friendly spirits or to circumvent the hostility of unfriendly spirits. Evidence for these ceremonies, rituals, and practices comes from prehistoric times.

What the Evidence Reveals

At the present time, scientists are not able to determine *exactly* from what prehuman or subhuman species people actually evolved. Evidence at this time seems to indicate that people may have evolved from a prehuman species which roamed East and South Africa over 5.5 million years ago. Whatever people's actual ancestry is, it is conjectured, at this time, that the first true human (hominid) lived over 3.5 million years ago. From this species, or a similar one perhaps, modern people evolved.[2] It is known that the Peking Man (who lived in Northern China) lived 700,000 years ago, and that the Swanscombe Man (who lived in England) existed at least 300,000 years ago, and modern people existed 50,000 years ago.

We do not have much evidence of the development and civilizing process of human beings in the Far East and in Africa. What evidence we do have comes from Europe and the Middle East. It is from this that we postulate our theories about the origin of religion and formulate our definition. What is said about the origin of religion, based on current European evidence, can probably be said about its origin in other parts of the world.

2. Continued research and discoveries lead scientists to revise their theories about the origin of human beings and to update their estimates of years, places of origin, and classifications. For example, in 1982, discoveries from a site in Israel indicate that human beings may have been in the Middle East 500,000 years earlier than in Africa.

The Origin of Religion

RELIGION AND PEOPLE DEVELOP CONTEMPORANEOUSLY

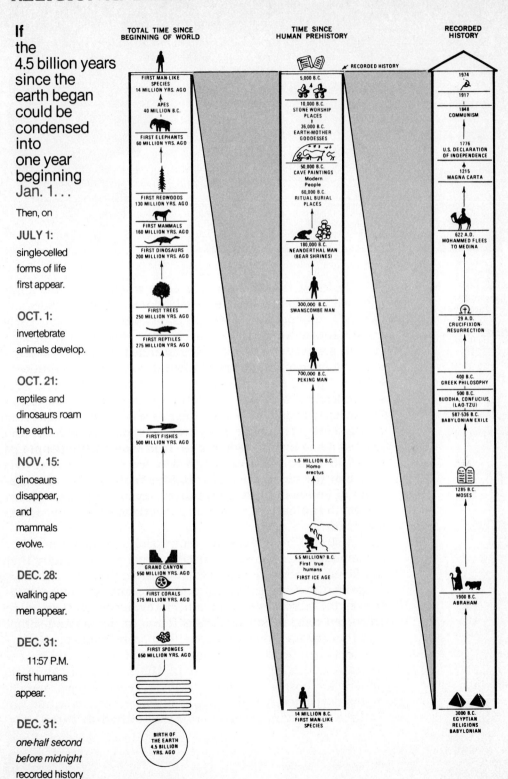

If the 4.5 billion years since the earth began could be condensed into one year beginning Jan. 1...

Then, on

JULY 1:
single-celled forms of life first appear.

OCT. 1:
invertebrate animals develop.

OCT. 21:
reptiles and dinosaurs roam the earth.

NOV. 15:
dinosaurs disappear, and mammals evolve.

DEC. 28:
walking ape-men appear.

DEC. 31:
11:57 P.M. first humans appear.

DEC. 31:
one-half second before midnight recorded history begins.

TOTAL TIME SINCE BEGINNING OF WORLD

FIRST MAN-LIKE SPECIES 14 MILLION YRS. AGO

APES 40 MILLION B.C.

FIRST ELEPHANTS 60 MILLION YRS. AGO

FIRST REDWOODS 130 MILLION YRS. AGO

FIRST MAMMALS 160 MILLION YRS. AGO

FIRST DINOSAURS 200 MILLION YRS. AGO

FIRST TREES 250 MILLION YRS. AGO

FIRST REPTILES 275 MILLION YRS. AGO

FIRST FISHES 500 MILLION YRS. AGO

GRAND CANYON 550 MILLION YRS. AGO

FIRST CORALS 575 MILLION YRS. AGO

FIRST SPONGES 650 MILLION YRS. AGO

BIRTH OF THE EARTH 4.5 BILLION YRS. AGO

TIME SINCE HUMAN PREHISTORY

RECORDED HISTORY

5,000 B.C.

10,000 B.C. STONE WORSHIP PLACES

36,000 B.C. EARTH-MOTHER GODDESSES

50,000 B.C. CAVE PAINTINGS Modern People

60,000 B.C. RITUAL BURIAL PLACES

180,000 B.C. NEANDERTHAL MAN (BEAR SHRINES)

300,000 B.C. SWANSCOMBE MAN

700,000 B.C. PEKING MAN

1.5 MILLION B.C. Homo erectus

5.5 MILLION? B.C. First true humans FIRST ICE AGE

14 MILLION B.C. FIRST MAN-LIKE SPECIES

RECORDED HISTORY

1974

1917

1848 COMMUNISM

1776 U.S. DECLARATION OF INDEPENDENCE

1215 MAGNA CARTA

622 A.D. MOHAMMED FLEES TO MEDINA

29 A.D. CRUCIFIXION-RESURRECTION

400 B.C. GREEK PHILOSOPHY

500 B.C. BUDDHA, CONFUCIUS, (LAO-TZU)

587-536 B.C. BABYLONIAN EXILE

1285 B.C. MOSES

1900 B.C. ABRAHAM

3000 B.C. EGYPTIAN RELIGIONS BABYLONIAN

Utensils on grave, San Blas, Panama *(above left)*; Head of man (2,000 years old) found in a bog at Tollund, Jutland *(right)*

We know that those who lived in what is now called Europe were driven south and east by successive ice ages between 1 million and 100 thousand years ago. The early inhabitants of Northern Europe struggled for survival through various glacial periods which finally ended about 50,000 years ago. Evidence of this struggle is found in the caves of southern France, Spain, Austria, Germany, Yugoslavia, southern Russia, Palestine, and the Tigris-Euphrates "fertile crescent." These early people were about five feet in height, stocky and resourceful. They made tools and weapons out of stone and hunted game over a wide range. **It is from these people of 180,000 to 50,000 years ago that we have our first evidence of the emergence of religious feeling. The arrangement of bones in high mountain caves or deep in gorges in the earth indicates a rather advanced ceremonial or ritual for death.**

Also in these caves are found skulls of bears or other "ceremonial" animals, arranged so neatly and exactly that hardly any other conclusion can be drawn than that such arrangements were purposeful and had some religious significance. In these caves and others, evidence of even more advanced religious awareness is found in the art and sculpture that points directly to *some form* of religious practice.

Between 50,000 years ago and 10,000 years ago, as the ice caps which covered all the northern parts of the world (much like those in Greenland today) receded and warmer climates developed, people sought out caves which, while unsuitable for living, were admirably suited to ceremonial

The Origin of Religion

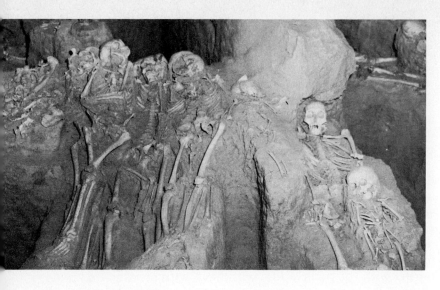

Indian burial plats at
Dickson Mounds State
Park, Illinois

gatherings for primitive worship and early forms of magic. In
these caves they painted graphic images of the deer, bison, and
mammoth in such profusion and in such form as to suggest
something more than a mere artistic urge or a simple pastime.

In these "special caves" (for early people sought shelter
in other, more suitable caves or constructed rude shelters in
which to live) are found not only very careful representations
of the animals people depended on for food, but representations of antlered sorcerers, skin-draped dancers, mutilated
hands or limbs of humans (indicating some puberty ceremony), and statuettes apparently related to religious rites.

It must be remembered that religious awareness—com-
pounded of those vague stirrings or feelings about a power beyond—developed over many thousands of years and was as
far removed from the advanced religious awareness of modern times as modern people are from their early ancestors.

Evidence for a further development in the evolution of
religious awareness in people is found in the carved figures of
women (about ten inches in height) found so profusely in the
caves mentioned above. These statues, dating from the late
Paleolithic period (50,000–10,000 B.C), seem to be directed toward another concern of early people: survival of the tribe,
the clan, or the group.

During this age there seems to have arisen an urge to
venerate the feminine "divine principle of survival." That
these figures were religious objects can hardly be denied, for
they do not fit into the practical side of early people's lives,
which are characterized by crude knives, fire circles, protec-

tive walls, and animal-skin clothing. These female figures are too closely allied to the later Babylonian myth and ritual associated with the goddess Ishtar to be dismissed as anything but religious.

Here again we have evidence of people reflecting, searching for meaning, looking, however crudely or simply, for a principle outside themselves to explain the mysterious, the unknown, and the uncontrollable, and searching for a way to control their environment—if only on the survival level.

Further evidence of the existence of early religion is the burial ceremony which antedates the animal shrines or statuettes of women. Death in people was not indifferently observed. Animal bones were thrown carelessly away; human remains, except where there were natural disasters, were always buried carefully and with much ritual. As in later times, for example, the time of the pyramids in Egypt, the dead were buried with the tools of life: with food, with ornaments "necessary" for the journey through death (suggesting the idea of immortality), and with companions for the journey.

Religion at the End of the Prehistoric Period

The final stage in the development of prehistoric people—from about 10,000 to 5,000 B.C.—indicates a rapidly developing cultural, economic, social, and religious awareness. During this age, there were objects and structures which are precise indications of cults devoted to the worship and the propitiation of powers, forces, or deities that operate in the sky, fertilize the earth (and people), and roam the spirit world "under" the earth.

Dating from this period, scientists have found, especially in France and Spain and later in England, arrangements of stones that could suggest places of worship as well as, or mixed with, means of calculating the movements of heavenly bodies. Flat stones, tables stones, circular arrangements of stones, and carefully arranged standing stones brought to the place at great labor, may indicate a rather advanced, elaborately ritualized form of worship, probably of the sun, the moon, the stars and other heavenly bodies. In the case of the famous Stonehenge ruins in England, there is evidence that an extremely accurate prediction of eclipses and other heavenly phenomena could be made by observing the heavenly bodies from certain definite positions within the stone circles.

These evidences of early religious feeling and of systems of nature worship among prehistoric people must not be con-

The Origin of Religion

fused with later religious awareness or practice. Religions of later periods, especially in the West after the great Greek philosophers, became more systematic and presented coherent rationales for their religious beliefs and practices. Early people did not do so—though there is evidence of a gradual development. What they were doing was working out a scheme for survival, a scheme which included not only fashioning weapons or artifacts for overcoming the forces they knew they could overcome, but also finding ways of coping with the forces they could not see but could feel—the forces, dimly conceived at first, that they "knew" they had to overcome or bargain with if they were to survive.

These early religious manifestations are forerunners of later religious awareness, systematization, and worship. Just as people had moved up the evolutionary ladder only after centuries of effort, so did they move up the religious ladder.

Stonehenge, a prehistoric monument on Salisbury Plain, Wiltshire, England

A Treasure from the Ice Age

. . . EXHIBIT SHOWS THE SKILLS OF CRO-MAGNON MAN

It was a startlingly different world. Vast areas of the Northern Hemisphere were covered with the ice. Across the ice-free parts of Europe and Asia, consisting largely of tundra and great treeless steppes, herds of mammoths, bison, reindeer and horses freely roamed. For long periods, winters were cruelly cold, and even in summertime the average temperature was 12° to 15° C (54° to 59° F.). Still, under these difficult conditions, during a period of 25,000 years before the dawn of civilization, the Ice Age Cro-Magnon people not only thrived, but created a surprisingly sophisticated culture that totally belies the popular image of them as savage, club-swinging brutes.

Nowhere is this cultural richness more apparent than in the artworks that these paleolithic hunters left in caves in France and Spain. When the first of these subterranean galleries was discovered in Spain nearly a century ago, Europe's savants, still reeling from the shock of Darwinian evolution, refused to believe that the find was anything more than a hoax. Since then, nearly a hundred richly decorated prehistoric caves have been found in Spain and France, and the existence of paleolithic painting has been established beyond doubt. The ancient artisans also left behind tiny sculptures of exquisite beauty, meticulous carvings on mammoth bone, and other stunning objects. Like the tableaux on the cave walls, some portray paleolithic man's animal neighbors. Others, often rendered in an almost contemporary style, show the Cro-Magnon people themselves.

Despite the abundance of these ancient works, the contemporary world has seen little of them. Many of the originals are carefully locked away in the vaults of various European cities, and some have never been publicly displayed. Nor are the caverns always accessible. France's celebrated Lascaux cave with its paintings of running bison and horses is now closed to all but a few selected scholars; contamination and changes in humidity and temperature caused by sightseers in the few decades after the cave was discovered in 1940 caused more damage to the fragile paintings than had occurred during the previous 16,000 years. . . .

The dazzling collection [assembled in Manhattan] includes, for example, a tiny, 6.4-cm-long (2½ in.) curving sculpture of a horse carved out of a mammoth tusk; it hardly seems possible that this graceful piece, fashioned more than 30,000 years ago, is one of the oldest *objets d'art* ever found. No less remarkable are the voluptuous "Venus" statuettes, some of them coiffed in Stone Age chic, that date back some 27,000 years. Even the wall paintings, some of them on a larger-than-life scale, show a mastery of form and perspective that was not seen again for almost 6,000 years.

These magnificent works reflect far more about Cro-Magnon man than his artistic ability. Indistinguishable from modern man either in brain capacity or physical appearance, he was clearly using his artistic skills to embellish a culture of a richness and complexity that is only beginning to be plumbed by scholars.

What that culture was like remains an enigma. What, for instance, is the significance of the Venus figures, with their exaggerated sexual features? What role did the great cave paintings play in the lives of those ancient people? Whatever the answers, it is clear the art is exceptionally complex, more than simple "hunting magic," as some turn-of-the-century scholars thought. Every indication is that Cro-Magnon man was deeply involved in rituals, ceremonies, myths, perhaps even a kind of religion.

[American Museum of Natural History curator Alexander] Marshack, a former science writer who has devoted 15 years to paleolithic studies, has suggested even bolder ideas. In his writings, notably *The Roots of Civilization,* he says that what looks like random scribbling on cave walls and even on some artifacts may actually represent many different symbol systems. These could have been used to record the passage of the seasons and astronomical observations and to indicate periods of rituals and ceremonies. If these controversial yet hardly dismissable ideas are correct, Cro-Magnon man may well have been experimenting with the precursors of writing, arithmetic, calendar making and other "civilized" skills.

Marshack asks the key question: "Did these traditions prepare the way for the artistic and symbolic traditions of the civilizations that began to develop not long after the ice melted, about 10,000 B.C.?" No one can say for sure whether paleolithic man did in fact light that intellectual spark. But it is undeniable, as Marshack notes, that the complex art comes from "persons like us, with our brains and our capacity, and that no visitors from space were required to teach them."

Source: This story was published in the June 5, 1978 issue of TIME. Copyright 1978 Time Inc. All rights reserved. Reprinted by permission from TIME.

Characteristics Common to All Prehistoric Religions

From what is now known about prehistoric human societies, religion played a very important role in every early society and affected the style of life, the structure of the society, and the relationship of members of the society with one another.

In spite of the fact that these early societies were isolated from each other, having little, if any contact with each other (and often concealing their beliefs and practices from any with which they came in contact), all prehistoric religions had certain characteristics which were common to all.[3] Among these common characteristics are the following.

1. Belief in spirit-forces or invisible powers

All prehistoric people believed that everything was controlled by unseen nonmaterial or spiritual forces or powers, often arranged in hierarchies of power and divided into friendly or hostile powers. There were spirits controlling every conceivable aspect and experience of life: they made trees grow, clouds move, fires burn, the earth quake, the thunder clap, the lightning flash, the waters move, people sicken, the crops grow or fail, the hunt succeed or not, the tribe prosper, and so forth. The good or evil experienced by every person or tribe was the direct result of the work of these invisible forces or powers, which acted not only on earth but in the sky and under the earth as well.

2. Close ties to a particular area or locality

Prehistoric religions were not universal. They did not try to be transcultural. They were closely tied to the territory in which the people lived, to the values perceived as necessary for survival, and to the mores of the close-knit society which practiced them.

3. A prescientific world view

The world of prehistoric people was circumscribed by where the people lived. They had no notion of a much larger world where things other than those with which they were familiar existed. Their world was governed by mystical forces that were capricious and unpredictable. They did not conceive of a world governed by predictable, natural forces.

---

3. Most of these characteristics are found to a greater or lesser degree in many contemporary societies that are prescientific and preliterate.

The Origin of Religion

4. Concern with survival

Prehistoric religions primarily focused on ensuring the success of those practical matters which affected the survival of the tribe. Their rituals centered on the hunt, the growth of crops, success against enemies, and the birth of healthy children.

5. Manipulation and coercion of the world of the spirits

Actions directly associated with religion—as distinct from merely cultural practices—became a part of all early human societies. These "acts of worship," or liturgies, were directed to particular gods or spirits of unknown and uncertain power who affected people's lives and their life situations. The actions were designed to ward off evil spirits and to call on friendly spirits for assistance.

These actions were designed to force the gods or spirits to act in accordance with the wishes or desires of individuals or tribes. They were performed, for the most part, by some individual in the tribe who seemed to possess special powers or influence over the spirit or force, or one who had a special relationship with the spirits or forces. They were participated in by individuals or members of the tribe who performed particular rituals or actions, sang particular incantations, or recited particular words at the direction of the leader or witch doctor. Such ritualistic actions, designed to force the gods or spirits to action, are called magic—the art of producing a desired effect through the use of various techniques, incantations, or potions designed to control the spiritual forces or powers controlling the universe.

6. Concern about death

All prehistoric people believed that human spirits lived in another world after death—the result of the relationship they saw between sleep-and-dreams and death. They developed elaborate burial ceremonies designed to make a dead person's passage to and existence in that world happy and prosperous. Many early tribes, believing that the spirits of the dead might return to haunt the living, developed magical actions or burial ceremonies to prevent such spirits from returning to disturb the tribe, or rituals designed to confuse the spirit of the dead person so that it could not find its way back to the tribe. Other rituals were designed to honor the dead and preserve the memory of heroes, kings, or leaders. In almost all cases, these acts were special religious acts—ways of dealing with the mystery of death.

7. Moral systems

Every prehistoric society had rules governing their way of life according to the particular needs of the tribe and their religious beliefs. Their moral codes included laws designed to protect the life of the tribe, such as laws prohibiting murder, adultery, stealing, lying, and so forth, and taboos and required actions based on religious beliefs.

Taboos, or positively forbidden actions, were the most powerful of the determining factors affecting a person's or a tribe's way of acting. They were always associated with the mysterious, or sacred, or spiritual, or totem forces affecting the life of the individual or tribe, and were forbidden because they were thought to automatically produce evil. A person who performed such a taboo action was required to undergo tribal purification, a system designed to ward off the evil effects of the action. Taboos and ritual purification were serious business; they were not merely superstitions as such. They were deeply associated with the religious beliefs of the tribe, and were revered and observed as sacred obligations to insure the survival of the tribe.[4]

8. Theology

All early societies developed a system of explanations for their religious beliefs and practices. These explanations were primitive according to our understanding of the world around us, but they were explanations that made sense to those who accepted them, and laid the foundation for later theological systems with which we may be familiar.

9. Scripture

Though no records of prehistoric writing have been found, early religions in their later stages did have a body of sacred writing that was generally accepted as the sacred word or, at least, the will of the gods. Such writings originated in the word-of-mouth stories and poetry which preceded them and included the myths, explanations, words, songs, incantations, rituals, moral codes, and general theology of the tribe. They

---

4. The term "taboo" comes from the Polynesian word for negative force, *tabu; Noa* was the Polynesian name for positive force. Both were manifestations of "power"—called *mana*—in whose presence people lived. If they experienced *tabu* they had to resort to some practice—sacrifice, priestly action, magic—to offset the power of this "negative" mana.

The term "totem" is applied to a natural object, a bird, animal, or natural phenomenon with which a primitive family or tribe considered itself closely related. The image of the totem often became the emblem or symbol of the tribe or family.

were passed on from generation to generation, more or less intact, and formed the fabric of beliefs and practices of the primitive tribe.

10. Prophecy

There is present, in almost all early religious societies and certainly in all known early religions, an aspect of "prophetic witness." By this is meant the presence of a person, particularly gifted, certainly charismatic, who, having experienced some extraordinary religious experience in himself or herself, exerts through words and actions, a profound and rather lasting effect on the religious life of the society which the person addresses.[5]

Aztec calendar

11. Sacrifice

Gifts signify a relationship between the giver and the receiver. Archeological discoveries reveal that in early societies, gifts were offered to the powers, forces, spirits, or totems of the tribes were offered in the form of food, items of tribal value, or sacrificed animals. When the sacrifice was tribal, the slain animal was divided and parts were offered to the power, force, spirit or totem, and the rest was eaten by the tribal members to signify their participation in the offering, and their oneness with the spirit, force, power, or totem.

12. Designated places of worship

Archeologists have discovered that in all early societies special places, areas, caves, rooms, or structures were set aside for religious ceremonies. Whether it be in the caves of Europe, the excavations in Africa, or the digs of the Middle East, the pattern is the same: people have been preoccupied with religious concerns in a very special way. They set aside certain places and things to express their beliefs in words and actions to show their relationship to whatever God was for them.

It is significant that these features are common to nearly all known early religions, even when the communities were isolated from others by oceans, mountains, impassable waters, dense forests, or their own fears of the unknown. This suggests that early religions have common features, not because of an exchange of ideas with people in other parts of the world, but because religion fulfills a basic need of human nature itself.

---

5. It is well to note that this prophetic witness contains a mysterious "I am sent" element which seems to come from beyond the person's own human condition, or even his or her own wish or inclination. In fact, some religions distinguish the "true" prophet from the "false" precisely on the basis of whether he or she is overly eager to be a prophet or not.

The Origin of God-Centered Religions

It is relatively simple to explain the origin of religious awareness. It is not so simple to explain how people came to believe in a God or gods—as distinct from impersonal forces in nature or mysterious powers acting in the world of people.

There are many theories about how God-centered religions and religious practices began, but no certainties. The major theories listed below present only fragments of an as yet incompletely deciphered puzzle. Some of these theories are in partial agreement with others. Some seem to be only half-true. None of them alone seems adequate to explain the origin of God-centered religion, and all of them together still do not give a final coherent answer. The fact that most people believe in a God—or Force or Supreme Power, or whatever other term is used to verbalize the concept—indicates that the idea of a God began somewhere. The theories of how this idea began fall into two general categories: (a) the individual coping with life's mysteries; and (b) the various communities of people responding to life's mysteries.

Pyramid of the Sun and Moon, Mexico

The Origin of Religion

The Individual Coping with Life's Mysteries

The theories of how individuals arrived at the notion of a God can be summarized in the following manner:

1. Psychological response

People who are insecure, uneducated, or unsophisticated may react in an infantile manner, seeking security in dependence upon another person. Perhaps early people, unable to explain or cope with the forces around them, "invented" a god as a super-parent to give them a sense of security amidst the instabilities of life.

2. Socioeconomic needs

The earliest societies were constantly confronted with the problems of survival—particularly with the problem of food and the problem of death. Because they experienced natural forces as powers outside of themselves capable of helping or hurting them, early people believed in spirits of good and evil and invented rituals to charm the good spirits and rites to ward off evil spirits—the former to provide them with food, the latter to prevent the visiting of misfortune upon them.

3. Naturism

The forces of nature (sun, moon, tornadoes, floods, earthquakes, oceans) were believed to be controlled by powers in nature (supernatural forces?) or to be powers in their own right. The almost universal evidence that early people worshipped the sun, the moon, even special trees or mountains, indicates some prehistoric concern with these as gods or at least as residences or places of gods. This evidence supports the notion that people's religious beginnings can be found in their sense of awe and mystery with forces they could not explain or control.

4. Animism

From their experience with animals and dreams, early people were led to believe that all things had "souls." When a person died, early people believed the "soul," like the souls of animals and other living things, went somewhere else. Because of the world people knew and from their belief that souls lived on, they concluded that the world was "full" of souls and "gods." The forces people had to deal with were not abstract physical forces (as we now think of them) but "real" forces with souls. The "souls" were present everywhere—and each had a "location"—in a mountain or woods or object in the sky.

People's religious practices were bent on placating, or on asking for protection or favor of, the "soul" or god of the particular thing or place.

5. Animatism

In contrast to the idea that there were many souls everywhere—the visible and invisible world being infested with souls—the animatism theory states that people experienced one single lifeforce, at once powerful and without precise form, not limited to a place or specific type of action, but all-pervasive, a force continuously encountered outside themselves, capable of producing good and evil.

6. Shamanism

Those who believed in this form of religion believed that the powerful spirits of their world could only be controlled or influenced by a particular "shaman." A shaman was a person of the tribe who acted both as doctor and priest and worked with what people believed to be the supernatural world that controlled the world in which they lived. Nothing was done without first consulting the shaman, or witch doctor, as we now call them.

7. Primitive monotheism

The Divine Presence may have in the beginning manifested itself as One—but people's minds were not able to grasp this unity; their belief degenerated into a belief in many gods or divine forces. There is some evidence for this theory in the religion of certain primitive peoples existing today, who believe in many gods, who carry with them legends or memories of a time when their people believed in only one God.

The belief in a God, or in a hierarchy of gods, developed over many centuries from these vague concepts of spirits inhabiting and controlling nature. As human beings became more sophisticated in their understanding of nature, they moved away from the general life-force concept to a more particularized force, to the acceptance of real spirits, and finally to the belief in particular spirits or gods. It was a natural progression of awareness, or knowledge similar to people's growth in knowledge or awareness in other areas of human experience.

Communities of People Responding to Life's Mysteries

The above theories about the origin of God-centered religions stress the notion of each individual person confronting mysterious forces outside himself or herself, and attempting to cope with these forces as well as explain them. People knew that they did not control the sun, the winds, good fortune or bad—but they sensed that someone, or something, had to. Their religious practices gave concrete expression to this belief.

But religion as we know it cannot be explained in terms of individual people alone, for people live in community. They share their views of life with other persons; they join in common expressions of what they commonly formulate as their common belief. The following theories of the origin of God-centered religions are speculations about the community aspect of early people's attempts to confront the mysterious forces greater than they.

View of the ruins of Machu Picchu, Peru

1. Totemism

The most widespread of the theories based upon community experience is the theory of origin called *totemism*. Totemism is the worship of an animal who is brother or sponsor of the tribe. We find the first confirmed totems in the bear shrines in Switzerland and Austria during the middle interglacial period, 180,000 to 50,000 B.C.

It can be said without too much hesitancy that totemism does not explain the origin of religion; rather, it presents a stage in the development of religion. But it is an important stage, for it points directly to the use of emblems, representations, and figures in later stages. Totem signs and figures remain to the present day in almost all societies; and the higher forms of religion, whose records are fairly continuous, are often

Comets, Evil Don't Mix, Indians Told

Brasilia, Brazil—Soldiers, settlers, and Indian pacifiers have been asked to cooperate in explaining to Brazil's superstitious Indian tribes that the appearance of the comet Kohoutek will not result in a tragedy or bring evil to their lives.

The National Indian Foundation [Funai] asked for help to "tranquilize" the Indians by explaining the nature of the comet before it appears.

Funai officials said they feared the comet might cause a revival of old rituals and cults as occurred during an eclipse of the sun in 1964.

During that eclipse, members of one tribe hid their faces, screaming and weeping, while warriors sent burning arrows toward the obscured sun to help it light up again. When the sun reappeared the warriors were hailed as heroes.

Another tribe, surprised during a meal by the eclipse, thought they were being punished by the gods for eating too much and promptly made themselves vomit the food. The tribe then went on a fast.

Source: Reprinted from the *Chicago Tribune*.

The Origin of Religion

nothing more than refinements of early totemism, or reactions to or rejections of the more primitive or crude forms of totemism. Perhaps at this point, if oversimplifying, we might point out that the Hebrew first commandment was aimed precisely against the basic totem idea—the worship of images or signs as gods rather than the worship of the "God of Abraham, of Isaac and of Jacob"—Yahweh, the saving God who was above all gods.

2. Scientism

Today, when science has succeeded in explaining by natural causes many things that formerly were mysterious or appeared to have only "super" natural causes, some persons claim that early religion arose as a kind of magic, a primitive substitute for science. According to this theory, because prehistoric people experienced forces they could not cope with, they tried to influence or counterbalance these forces by potions, spells, words, music, and actions, all designed to force the spirit or power into doing the people's will. Perhaps because of some success in restoring health by using certain herbs or substances, these people felt that certain actions or things had the power in themselves to produce the intended results. This power was interpreted, not as chemical or psychological, but as magical or spiritual.

3. Religious formulators

Every society experiences people who are more religiously inclined than others. Among these are those who embrace religion as a way of life. They interpret experiences religiously for the group to which they belong, formulate doctrines and rituals for the group, "translate" myths and folklore into religious stories, and prepare and recite prayers for the group or tribe to which they belong either in their own name, in the name of the tribe or group, or in the name of the god with whom they seem to have a special relationship. They are the formulators of the religion for the group.

It goes without saying that within totemistic societies there were some persons who were more oriented toward the "mysteries" of the society than others. These became the medicine men, the shamans, the priests. In some cases they had at one time or another done something wonderful, had "predicted" something, or had seemed to possess a force or quality beyond that of other members of the tribe or clan. In other cases they had experienced some extraordinary event in a dream, in sickness, or after prolonged fasting and hardship. Occasionally a particular person had a "vision" or a call which singled him or her out. In any case there arose wise

Weighing of the heart of
the scribe Ani in the
afterlife, c. 1450 B.C.
(Courtesy The Granger
Collection)

people, magicians, sorcerers, or leaders who spoke for the tribe to the "totem" or who even had their personal totem. These special persons not only spoke to the totem; they spoke *for* the totem and delivered messages about the whats and whys of tribal blessings or misfortunes. From these very early practices there arose a priestly class which in higher forms of religion took on more elaborate, less magical, ritualistic liturgies for the people.

4. Revelation

Some experts in the history of religion believe that God-centered religions developed from revelation. That is, they believe that God could and did reveal Himself to people gradually over many centuries, using the natural phenomena of the universe and people's natural intellectual powers to make Himself known in natural ways. They believe that this revelation is still going on as people propose more and more sophisticated answers to the mystery of life.

I, the Lord, am your God . . . You shall not have other gods besides me. You shall not carve idols for yourself in the shape of anything in the sky above or on the earth below or in the waters beneath the earth; you shall not bow down before them or worship them.

For I, the Lord your God, am a jealous God . . .

—Exodus 20:2–5

An overwhelming number of people throughout the history of people have believed in a God, or a Power, or a Presence outside of, beyond, and in control of the universe and all that's in it. Most people alive today so believe.

The nature of the God of these people determines, to a large extent, their response to their God. This, in turn, determines their religion. What these religions have been and are, shall be discussed in this book.

The Development of the God Aspect in Religion

The question of God—whether He is or is not—does not depend upon the above theories. Only one of two opposites can be true: either God is or He is not. If He is, no theorizing about

The Origin of Religion

how people came to know Him will change the fact. If He is not, no formula or pronouncement by anyone will "make" Him.

Without settling upon a final theory about how the notion of God first arose, what general statements can be made about the *development* of this notion once it did arise?

We might begin by recalling what we know of people's general awareness of what we call reality. People become aware of reality only through their own experience. For example, long before the physical theory of gravity was formulated, people were generally aware of its existence: things they threw into the air came down; if they fell, they hit with more or less force depending upon the distance of the fall. Everything in people's store of knowledge was arrived at through the painful process of experience, either directly or through their thought processes. They observed and drew conclusions. They reflected. They thought about things and tried to relate them to their own world of awareness.

In other words, the development of people's knowledge of reality is like their development in other areas. At first, when the animal that was to become human finally did emerge into a reflective animal, his reflections were simple—"crude," in the sense of extremely primitive or rudimentary—and his awareness was limited. After all, there is no evidence for believing that people, as people, evolved full-blown, complete with all their facilities as we know them now. Just as we are scientifically convinced that the human body evolved over thousands of years, we have every reason for thinking that people's mental abilities have developed. Just as their ability to cultivate food developed over millennia, so did their processes of thought.

Thus, people's concept of God—the Utterly Other—developed from the very primitive society-related concept of a deity or a set of gods or spirit forces to the sophisticated notion of God that we find in many philosophies today.

This should not surprise us. Just as giants in the field of art, literature, science, and medicine have arisen in various ages and various countries, (all of whom have contributed to the store of human knowledge in art, literature, science, and medicine), so have outstanding persons arisen in the field of religion, speculating on the "problems" of religion to sharpen people's notions of God.

In religion, as in any other field, three classes of "devotees" can be distinguished: the *intensely* religious, the *average,* and the people who have *little* interest in religion. And,

If the thought comes to you that everything you have thought about God is mistaken and that there is no God, do not be dismayed. It happens to many people. But do not think that the source of your unbelief is that there is no God. If you no longer believe in the God in whom you believed before, this comes from the fact that there was something wrong with your belief; and you must strive to grasp better that which you call God. When a savage ceases to believe in his wooden God, this does not mean that there is no God, but only that the true God is not made of wood.

Leo Tolstoy
Russian Novelist
(1828–1910)

of course, within these groups there are gradations from one end to the other—so much so that little difference can be seen between the highest grade of one division and the lowest grade of the next division.

Among those in the highest grade of religious awareness—those whose special interest and inclination is religion-oriented—we find particularly sensitive people whose acuteness and direction of thought stand out over and above even the very best of their companions. Among these are such recognized leaders as Gautama Buddha (c. 563–483 B.C.), Confucius (551–497 B.C.), Abraham (c. 1850 B.C.), Moses (c. 1280 B.C.), Jesus the Christ (4 B.C.–A.D. 29), and Mohammed (A.D. 570–632). All of them have contributed in one way or another to people's knowledge of and relationship with God. What their contributions have been, we shall discover as we discuss the major religions of the world.

The Origin of Religion

Summary

1. Religion began as a result of early people's awareness of forces or powers outside of themselves that seemed to control their destiny.

2. Prehistory gives evidence of practices that cannot be interpreted as other than religious.

3. Most prehistorical religions have common characteristics which illustrate that religion is a natural response to people's experience of reality.

4. The kind of God people have believed in has developed until certain people or groups have accepted a particular kind of God presented by the major formulators of their religious concepts.

For Review

1. What is the difference between religion and a religious system or Church? What is the meaning of "religious awareness"?

2. Why is it impossible to say how religion began?

3. What seems to be the probable origin of religion? Summarize the evidence that leads to that assumption.

4. Why did early people believe in a spirit world? Is there any evidence that people still believe in a spirit world?

5. Why did early people believe in life after death?

6. Be able to name and explain at least five of the characteristics common to almost all prehistoric religions.

7. How did the notion of a God—or Supreme Power—seem to develop?

8. Why does your book contend that religion is natural to people? Do you agree? why? why not?

9. Be sure that you can define prophetic witness, fetishism, animism, and mana.

For Discussion

1. Discuss how the theories about the origin and development of religion fit into the theory of evolution.

2. Discuss whether it is reasonable that people's ideas of God should develop gradually.

3. In an open forum, discuss the ramifications of the following true episode: One time a man who billed himself as the world's leading atheist stood on a stage before hundreds of people and said: "If there is a God, I command Him to strike me dead in ten seconds." He pulled out his watch and counted the seconds. After one minute, he announced triumphantly, "There is no God. If there were He would be so mad at me He would have struck me dead."

4. Discuss why some people do not believe in God.

5. Discuss at length the believability of the material presented in "Psychological response," on page 00.

6. Discuss why some people are uncomfortable when the subject of religion is brought up. Why do you suppose that many people are reluctant to discuss religion?

7. Assume for the moment that we know nothing about the physical, chemical, or geological forces that produce nature's phenomena. How would you explain the existence or experience of various things that happen in nature? Take a particular instance (for example, an earthquake) and try to explain it without the help of modern scientific knowledge.

For Research

1. Prepare a report on one of the following: totemism; common superstitions and their probable origins; the development of magic and its use in present-day societies; fetishes of early people; American Indians' happy hunting ground; prehistoric cave findings in Europe; excavations in Africa.

2. Make an informal survey among your friends to find out if any of them believe in the influence of evil spirits in people's lives. Report your findings to the class. Cite examples, if possible, of the interest in this subject in movies and TV.

3. Prepare a brief report on Leo Tolstoy.

4. At the direction of your teacher, read excerpts from *The Source* and *Hawaii* by James Michener, *The Curve and the Tusk* by Stuart Cloete, *The Spiral Road* by Jan de Hartog, or selected passages from the *Iliad*, the *Odyssey*, or *Bulfinch's Mythology* concerning primitive people's preoccupation with the life-force, the causes of death, and the attempts to ward off evil forces. Prepare a report on your reading.

5. From sources available to you, make a chart of evolution concentrating on the period from the emergence of upright animals to the positive identification of human beings. (See, for example, *Evolution* and *Early Man*, two publications in the *Life Nature Library*, published by Time Incorporated, New York.)

Words You Should Know

If there are any words given below that you are not sure of, look them up in the Word List in the back of the book.

anthropologist	linguist	puberty
archeologist	magic	rationale
artifacts	mammoths	speculative
charismatic	placate	taboo
circumvent	postulate	totem
curry	prehistory	transcultural
hypothesis	primitive	

chapter 3

The Growth of Religious Awareness in the Western World

Because the principle studies of prehistoric and early historic peoples have been made in what is known as the Western world, our discussions on the origin, growth, and development of early religions are centered on the early religions of the Western world.[1]

Our knowledge of the prehistoric religions of the people of the Western world is based on the interpretations of religious artifacts of those periods made by archeologists, anthropologists, and religious historians. Our knowledge of the religions of early historic peoples of the Western world is based on *written* records. These consist of clay tablets, inscriptions on temple walls and statues, historical accounts compiled by palace scribes, and written copies of earlier legends and myths. These records give us a fairly accurate picture of the development of the religious awareness among the peoples of the Western world, clues to the development of the living religions of the Western world, and an understanding of people's continuous search for an answer to the mystery of life.

All three of these can be demonstrated through an examination of three ancient religions—Babylonian, Egyptian, and Greek—each of which shows not only the continuity and development of people's religious awareness, but also that religion, as such, is not the invention of this or that person or group, but is a response to the mysteries of the kind of world in which the people who accepted the interpretation of these mysteries lived.

---

1. The Western world is generally understood to be the geographical areas west of China and Japan and certain areas of Southeast Asia. What we know of prehistoric and early historic religions in the Orient, Africa, North and South America, and the islands of the Pacific Ocean leads us to believe that their origin and growth were much the same as in Europe and the Middle East.

Opposite page—Statues of Rameses II, each thirty feet high, lining the walls of the Great Temple at Abu Simbel (Courtesy UPI)

The Egyptian cosmos, depicting Geb (Earth), Shu (Air), and Nut (Heavenly Vault), who carries the barges of the sun on her star-studded back (Courtesy The Granger Collection)

In order to understand ancient historic religions, it is important to remember that the beliefs, rituals, and cultures associated with each were developments and refinements of earlier religious awareness. They did not spring whole and entire at some point in the history of the people who lived in Babylonia, Egypt, and Greece. They developed as the civilization of these areas developed.

The process of people becoming civilized (that is, living in an ordered society in established territories) was long and arduous. The first human beings were nomadic: they went where they could find food and shelter. As time went on, they learned to herd animals and cultivate foods for future use.[2] When they began to settle in places favorable to the preservation of their herds and the cultivation of food, they staked out the territory as their own and took means to preserve and protect it from others. Clans, tribes, and peoples with similar tastes and backgrounds banded together and became, in the course of time, a nation or a people with common purposes and goals, and eventually, with a common philosophy or explanation for the mysteries of life they experienced.

Accepting the world of the gods as a reality, they explained the mysteries of life they now encountered with a whole new set of gods—or spirits—who controlled the world in which they now lived. As time went on, these gods became the gods of their tribe or territory, and former gods (still living, of course, in the places from which they came), who no longer needed to be courted for favors, receded from memory and finally disappeared altogether from their religious practices.

As centuries passed, a new religious awareness sprang up among these people of the Western world, not simply because of the new life experiences of people, but because people, becoming more and more sophisticated, were able to explain in more refined ways the mysteries of the world around them. As they became more aware that the world in which they lived could be controlled, they abandoned their nature gods almost entirely and developed religious beliefs and practices associated with what they could not control—the "heavens." As time went on, the religious beliefs and practices of these people became a part of their civilizations and helped shape the economic, political, and cultural world in which each civilization developed.

2. History tells us that the people in Egypt, Babylon, and India were raising dairy cattle for family use and for trade with their neighbors before 5,000 B.C.

The Origin of Religion

Religious Awareness Shown in Religious Ceremonies

The best way to trace the development of religious awareness in people is to examine what people have believed. We can do this by looking at the religious ceremonies of historic religions.

These ceremonies had two major parts: the ritual, or actions of the religious leaders and the people, and the story of the origin of the world as the people understood it. Both dealt with the people's understanding of the role and activity of the gods who controlled the world the people experienced. Both the ritual and the story were believed to have some kind of power in themselves to bring about a desired result—a magic which forces the god or gods to the will of the people. (Only later were ritual and story separated from magic in the more sophisticated civilizations. They continued to contain this magical concept in many religions, and still do in some religions to the present day.)

The origin, or creation, stories in these religions were not just any stories. They were solemn, imaginative, and often, to our way of thinking, fantastic stories which explained the roots of reality as the people understood that reality. These special kinds of religious stories dealing with the origin or creation of the world are called myths.[3]

Winged being offering a branch with pomegranates. From the palace of Ashur-nasir-apal II (885–860 B.C.) King of Assyria, at Kalhu, modern Nimrud (Courtesy The Metropolitan Museum of Art. Gift of John D. Rockefeller Jr., 1931)

Myths always dealt with supernatural persons and events: they were stories of the actions of the gods or near-gods living in a supernatural world. They were ritualistic stories which attempted to explain the unknown origins of the world, of people, and of people's relationship to the world of the gods. They answered the question about where life (that is, people, the world, and things in the world) came from.

A study of the myths of early historic religions reveals two things about religion. The first is that religion is a response to mystery—the presence of myths in all early religions indicates that a religious sense is common to people. The second is the developing refinement of myths from early historic religions to later historic religions. This indicates a developing religious awareness in people.

Myths are not falsehoods; they are descriptions of the world—its origins, its forces, its challenges—as primitive and early people experienced it. Modern people, of course, do not accept myths as literally true, though primitive and early people probably did. Modern people accept myths for what they mean: they tell us how ancient peoples explained their world.

3. From the Greek word *muthos,* meaning story.

Though early myths have in common a concern with the origins of the world and the activities of the gods in relation to people, they differ from each other in important ways. This is natural since people in ancient lands did not all live in the same kind of world. Each group of people explained in picture-language to their children how *their* kind of world was put together by *their* kind of god.

For example, according to the *Eddas*, a collection of stories of the origin of the world from ancient Norway, Sweden, Denmark, and Iceland:

. . . there was once no heaven above nor earth beneath, but only a bottomless deep, and a world of mist in which flowed a fountain. Twelve rivers issued from this fountain, and when they had flowed far from their source, they froze into ice, and one layer accumulating over another, the great deep was filled up.

Southward from the world of mist was the world of light. From this flowed a warm wind upon the ice and melted it. The vapours rose in the air and formed clouds, from which sprang Ymir, the Frost giant and his progeny, and the cow Audhumbla, whose milk afforded nourishment and food to the giant. The cow got nourishment by licking the hoar frost and salt from the ice. While she was one day licking the salt stones there appeared at first the hair of a man, on the second day the whole head, and on the third the entire form endowed with beauty, agility, and power. This new being was a god, from whom and his wife, a daughter of the giant race, sprang the three brothers Odin, Vili, and Ve. They slew the giant Ymir, and out of his body formed the earth, of his blood the seas, of his bones the mountains, of his hair the trees, of his skull the heavens, and of his brain clouds, charged with hail and snow. Of Ymir's eyebrows the gods formed Midgard (mid earth), destined to become the abode of man.

Odin then regulated the periods of day and night and the seasons by placing in the heavens the sun and moon, and appointing to them their respective courses. As soon as the sun began to shed its rays upon the earth, it caused the vegetable world to bud and sprout. Shortly after the gods had created the world they walked by the side of the sea, pleased with their new work, but found that it was still incomplete, for it was without human beings. They therefore took an ash tree and made a man out of it, and they made a woman out of an alder, and called the man Aske and the woman Embla. Odin then gave them life and soul, Vili reason and motion, and Ve bestowed upon them the senses, expressive features, and speech. Midgard was then given them as their residence, and they became the progenitors of the human race.

Norwegian Stave Church

The Origin of Religion

The mighty ash tree Ygdrasill was supposed to support the whole universe. It sprang from the body of Ymir, and had three immense roots, extending one into Asgard (the dwelling of the gods), the other into Jotunheim (the abode of the giants), and the third to Niffleheim (the regions of darkness and cold). By the side of each of these roots is a spring, from which it is watered. The root that extends into Asgard is carefully tended by the three Norns, goddesses, who are regarded as the dispensers of fate. They are Urdur (the past), Verdandi (the present), Skuld (the future). The spring at the Jotunheim side is Ymir's well, in which wisdom and wit lie hidden, but that of Niffleheim feeds the adder Nidhogge (darkness), which perpetually gnaws at the root. Four harts run across the branches of the tree and bite the buds; they represent the four winds. Under the tree lies Ymir, and when he tries to shake off its weight the earth quakes.

Asgard is the name of the abode of the gods, access to which is only gained by crossing the bridge Bifrost (the rainbow). Asgard consists of golden and silver palaces, the dwellings of the gods, but the most beautiful of these is Valhalla, the residence of Odin. When seated on his throne, he overlooks all heaven and earth. Upon his shoulders are the ravens Hugin and Munin, who fly every day over the whole world, and on their return report to him all they have seen and heard. At his feet lie his two wolves, Geri and Freki, to whom Odin gives all the meat that is set before him, for he himself stands in no need of food. Mead is for him both food and drink. He invented the Runic characters, and it is the business of the Norns to engrave the runes of fate upon a metal shield. From Odin's name, spelt Woden, as it sometimes is, came Wednesday, the name of the fourth day of the week.

Odin is frequently called Alfadur (All-father), but this name is sometimes used in a way that shows that the Scandinavians had an idea of a deity superior to Odin, uncreated and eternal.[4]

Even peoples who lived in the same general geographical area of the world had different myths to explain *their* world. For example, consider the differences between the Babylonian (an empire in Southwest Asia which flourished around 2000 B.C.) and Egyptian myths of early historic times.

The Babylonians lived in a geographic area that was unsettling and unpredictable. Though the land was rich and fertile, there were frequent storms and memories of severe floods. People looked upon the world with anxiety and suspicion. For

4. Thomas Bulfinch, *Bulfinch's Mythology*, (New York: Dell Publishing Company, 1959), pages 240–242.

The Origin of Religion

them, maintaining human life was a struggle. In addition, wars, social strife, cruelty, and slavery were part of the real world they experienced. Hence, their gods were expressions of this kind of world-view. They were unpredictable, warlike, and had a thumbs-down attitude toward people. Their religious rituals reflected their relationship with these kinds of gods.

The Egyptians, on the other hand, lived in a more stable world—the sun always shone, the Nile always provided fertile strips of land, enemies were few, and social upheavals were rare. Egyptian myths reflected this kind of world. Their gods were tranquil, their death rituals portrayed a certainty of securing a tranquil afterlife, and their liturgies were pompous and serene. Their creation myths clearly portray the world-view, the real experience of these people.

What do these early myths tell people of our time who are concerned about their own religious stance? First of all, they show the fundamental root-concepts of the gods, the world, the afterlife, and the meaning of life that were prehistoric and early people's first glimmerings of light in their spiritual evolution. Second, they give a frame of reference for understanding the origins of the beliefs of some modern religions. Third, by contrasting ancient myths with modern theologies, people can see the direction of people's spiritual evolution and perhaps sense the prophetic direction of the future of people's search for an answer to the mystery of life.

The three ancient historic religions, presented in the following pages, were selected because they demonstrate the development of people's religious awareness from primitive times, and because they are the three that most affected the development of the major living religions of the Western world. They were a major force in forming the culture and the mentality of the region in which Judaism, Christianity, and Islam were to have their beginnings.

The Religion of Babylonia

The seeds of future religious development in the West were sown in the Fertile Crescent, extending from the Mediterranean Sea through the valley of the Tigris and Euphrates rivers to the Persian Gulf. In this region, also called Mesopotamia, the city of Babylon played such a dominant role that the entire region is sometimes called Babylonia (just as in later times the name "Rome" came to stand for the entire Roman Empire dominated by the city of that name).

Babylonian religion flourished as far back as 3000 B.C. and continued even into biblical times. Abraham, the "father" of the Jewish people, came from the Babylonian city of Ur around 1850 B.C. Some of his Jewish descendants were forced to return to Babylon from Palestine more than a thousand years later in 587 B.C.

The Babylonians' lives were full of turmoil and uncertainty. Their religious beliefs, their myths and rituals, and their moral life reflected this uncertainty and struggle. Subject as they were to unpredictable natural phenomena, to invasion, to pestilence, war and violent death, the Mesopotamians had a somewhat dark view of life; this was expressed in a body of myths, a set of rituals, magical practices, incantations, a priesthood, and eventually a system of theology.

Babylonian myth "explained" the universe as Babylonians saw it. It "answered" basic questions about the beginning of the world, the origin of the gods, the existence of a spirit world, the role of the gods in their dealings with people, the meaning and effect of death, and the nature of the afterlife.

Like all those who went before them, the Babylonians constructed tales to put order into a universe that, to their minds, was essentially disorderly, and governed by forces greater than themselves. Their chief god was Apsu the Water-God, who with the she-dragon Tiamat (who lived in and con-

The Ancient Near East

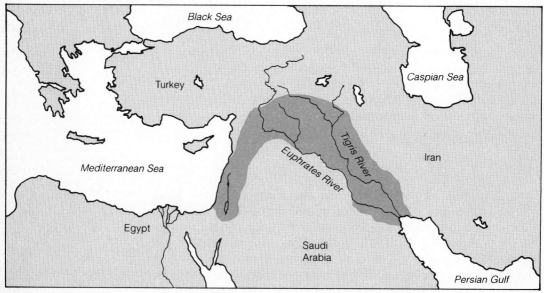

◼ = The Fertile Crescent

The Origin of Religion

trolled the waters which frequently flooded the valley) begot Anu, the lord of the heavens and the highest of the gods; Enlil, lord of the middle air; and Ea, ruler of the moisture that irrigated the earth.

The most important deity in Babylonian religion, however, was Marduk, the son of Ea, who championed the gods in the plot by the evil she-god Tiamat to destroy the gods. Marduk defeated Tiamat, split her in half and thus formed the sky and the earth. Marduk also destroyed Kingu, the consort of Tiamat, and from Kingu's blood people were formed who will continually send up sacrifices to the gods.

As preposterous as these myths sound, they tell us that for the Mesopotamians life was struggle, bloodshed, violence and tribulation. They also tell us that life had to be made orderly by effort. In order to bring some order into society, codes of law were framed governing every aspect of real life in Babylon. The most famous code of law was that of King Hammurabi (about 1700 B.C.), who codified all the laws which had been inherited from more ancient civilizations, added necessary laws to fit his own people, and presented them as coming directly from heaven, from the sun-god, Shamash.

The Babylonians were concerned about people's fate after death, but they took a dim view of their chances in the next life, because only the gods had a good chance of living in the land of the dead. "When the gods created mankind, for man they set aside death; life they retained for their own keeping," runs an old Babylonian saying. It reflects the pessimism, the doubt, the anxiety of all Babylonian life. It also gave birth to searching inquiry for answers to the mystery of life. Unlike the Egyptians, whose myths and rituals promoted the *status quo*, the Babylonians continually searched for answers or solutions to the negative forces which beset them on every side. Their rites and ceremonies were constructed to affect the power, to appease the god, or to achieve favor.

These rites and ceremonies (liturgies) were presided over by a priestly clan who soon had specific functions or particular rites which belonged to them only. Rites took on the qualities of magic, whose purpose was to ward off evil planned by the gods.

Because death held no security in a peaceful afterlife for the Babylonians, this life was all that mattered. Life became a game of winning at least some of their contests with the gods. Although there were sacrifices in the temple to the Babylonian gods, magic and divination became the practical religious expression of the Babylonians—divination to determine the "will of the gods" (or the direction of the power or divine force) and magic to coerce the gods or the forces into doing the human will.

An important development in Babylonian religion, and one directly connected with the practice of divination, was the growth of astrology or the study of the stars or heavenly bodies. Elaborate charts of the heavens and the variations in placement of the stars and planets were constructed and studied to see if favorable conditions existed for undertaking an action. Because the stars and planets were the dwelling places of the gods, Babylonians believed the position of the stars, and their relationship with each other, would "tell" something about the will of the gods, or at least indicate their disposition.

This form of "divining" the will of the gods (as well as other forms of auguring: casting oil on water or seeking the wisdom of a seer, a witch, a prophet or a priest) was accompanied by "insurance for success" in the form of magic. Spells and incantations, mutilation and voodoo dolls (putting pins into figures of enemies), are ancient practices that carry down to the present day in many quarters of the world. They are the forebearers of such "civilized" practices as reading one's horoscope determining one's "sign," not walking under a ladder, omitting the thirteenth floor in hotels, skipping on or over cracks in the sidewalk, and knocking on wood.

To us, these ancient practices may be amusing or they may be mere superstition. To the serious Babylonians, they were attempts to answer the perennial question about life's meaning. Had things been tranquil, or the Babylonians less dissatisfied, humanity might have remained in the grip of ancient myths that now seem to provide such feeble answers. It is to their credit that they were *not* satisfied, that they continued to search for answers, that they scanned the heavens and the earth and the waters, that they were restless and inquiring. From them came the force that was to give birth to the cultural heritage of the entire Western world.

The Early Egyptian Religion

The most striking features of Egypt, even in the present day, are the pyramids, the sphinxes, the desert sands, and the Nile River. Considered as curiosities or as evidence of a now dead glorious civilization, these things give us our clearest insights into Egyptian religion.

The pyramids are tombs of the near-divine pharaohs. These and lesser tombs, as well as burial texts and architec-

An Excerpt from the Babylonian Creation Myth

When the sky above was not yet real,
And firm ground did not exist,
There was nothing but their father Apsu,
The river-god who was from the
    beginning,
And Tiamat, destructive seagoddess,
    who was their mother.
These two waters merged as one body,
And the gods were formed within them.
In this fateful womb, where destinies
    began,
A god was born, most powerful and
    wisest of gods.
In the heart of Apsu was he created—
Marduk was his name.
Four were his eyes, four were his ears;
When he moved his lips, fire blazed forth.
He was the tallest of the gods, gigantic
    was his size.

Tiamat, the sea-goddess of chaos,
    prepared for battle
Against the gods, her offspring.
Marduk, wisest of the gods, came forth to
    face Tiamat.
Bow and quiver he hung at his side.
In front of him he discharged lightning.
With a blazing fire he filled his body,
And then, to trap Tiamat,
He made this net—the four winds—
Stationed so that nothing of her might
    escape.
When Tiamat heard this,
She was like one possessed.
Out of her senses, in fury Tiamat cried
    aloud.

Then Marduk (wisest of the gods)
And Tiamat began the fight.
Locked in battle, they wrestled back and
    forth.
When Tiamat opened her mouth to
    swallow him up,
He drove in an Evil Wind
And she could not close her lips.
As the fierce wind filled her belly,
Her body was bloated and her mouth was
    wide open.
He shot an arrow, tearing her belly,
Cutting her insides, ripping her heart.
Then the lord paused to view her dead
    body,
That he might carve the monster up
And create something artistic.
He split her like a clam into two parts:
Half of her set up as a ceiling to the sky.
He constructed fixed posts for the gods
and stars in the sky.

"I will compress blood and make bones,"
    he said.
"I will create a savage and call him Man.
He will be made a servant to the gods
While they relax in leisure."
From the blood of a guilty god was
    fashioned mankind.
He imposed service on them and freed
    the gods for leisure.
"Let them bring food to feed the gods
    and goddesses!
Don't let them forget to support their
    gods!"

Source: Paraphrased and condensed from James B. Pritchard, *Ancient Near Eastern Texts Relating to the Old Testament*. (Princeton: Princeton University Press, 1969) pp. 60–69. Reprinted by permission of Princeton University Press.

Egyptian god Osiris
(Courtesy Field Museum
of Natural History,
Chicago)

ture, tell us the great truths of the early Egyptian religion. Perhaps the most significant characteristic of this Egyptian religion was its fixity. For almost 3,000 years (before Menes in 3100 B.C. until long after the Romans had conquered Egypt), Egyptian religion remained set in its rites, its beliefs, and its theology. No other civilization exhibits such stability. This is directly due to the stability of life along the Nile River, which was as regular in its fertilization and movement as a natural force could be, to the deserts which stretched on either side of Egypt and so kept enemies at bay, and to the regularity of the heavenly bodies clearly visible over the desert sky.

In other words, the Egyptians lived a stable form of existence—they did not experience the natural or manmade upheavals of other early civilizations. Their lives, aside from the normal internal problems of their society, were secure.

The Egyptian gods tell nearly all we need to know about Egyptian religion. Their two chief gods were Re, the sun god, and Osiris, the god of life everlasting. There were other gods, of course, but they were satellite gods whose purpose was to serve the two main gods.

Long before the Nile Valley was settled, the forebearers of the Egyptians lived in the highlands to the west of the Nile River. As these lands became arid, the people moved to the swampland around the Nile, cultivated the land, founded cities, and soon gave birth to a flowering civilization. By the year 3100 B.C. under the kingship of Menes, Egyptian civilization had reached a degree of sophistication unmatched in other lands. They had settled into a way of life and a religion that was to last long after the Roman invasions three thousand years later.[5]

Because the general flow of Egyptian life was stable, the emphasis in religious rites and myths was centered upon death rituals and stories. Almost all Egyptian religious ceremony centered upon elaborate burial rites designed to insure safe passage to the land of Osiris and peace and happiness there forever.

The mummification and burial rites, which lasted seventy days for royalty, required a priesthood divided into several levels or hierarchies according to their various duties. Since the burial rites "insured" safe passage, it was important that each action, each word, be done according to a strict rite.

5. The last known reference to Isis, goddess and sister-wife of Osiris, was in A.D. 451. Nubians were permitted to bring sacrifices to her temple on an island in the Nile. Obviously the Egyptian religion remained long after that, probably until Islam was firmly established.

The Origin of Religion

Although burial rites dominated Egyptian religious practice ("salvation by rite"), the whole superstructure of Egyptian religion was based upon its elaborate myths; for if there were no gods to be appeased, what would be the sense of ritual to appease them? As obvious as this seems, it is crucial, not only to an understanding of Egyptian religion but to an understanding of any religion.

Obviously, therefore, the question that comes to mind is: Since there are gods, where did they come from? Some kind of answer is found, of course, in the elaborate myths of all early religions.

In Egypt, the creation myths eventually presented an amalgam of all the simple myths of pre-Egyptian society. Although Re and Osiris were preeminent in Egyptian mythology and religious systems, other gods were "created" according to the need to explain real situations faced by the Egyptians. Where did the earth and people come from? Egyptian myths give the answer: from Atum and Ptah, both creating gods who came into existence at some unspecified time in the remote past of the world of the gods.

The Egyptians "knew" that Atum (later Atum-Re) generated from his own body two other gods, Geb and Nut, the god and goddess of earth and sky, and Shu, the god of the air, who held them apart. Wondering about the origin of Atum, the "creator" of earth and heaven, the ordinary Egyptian learned that this god was the result of the thought of Ptah. People, then, were fashioned by the gods, in one account as the tears of Re; in another, on the potter's wheel of a god named Khaum.

Egyptian god Ptah (Courtesy Field Museum of Natural History, Chicago)

From the vantage point of disinterested or curious study, many questions arise as to how all these gods could be consistent with each other. These questions may have arisen in ancient Egypt, too. (In fact, for a brief period about 1370 B.C., the pharoah Amenhotep IV—Akhenaton—attempted unsuccessfully to do away with the syncretism[6] of Egyptian myth and promote a single all-powerful deity, Aton.) But the only thing that really counted in Egypt was the death ritual which provided a safe, eternal journey to the land of Osiris. Thus, it was around this god that most Egyptian myth centered.

The various manifestations of the physical universe had gods to preside over them—important gods for important duties, lesser gods for less important duties, city gods, village gods, temple gods, home gods—a veritable storehouse of gods who kept the visible universe and the social order intact.

6. An attempted reconciliation or fusion of opposing beliefs or practices.

The Gods of Early Egypt

The ancient Egyptians thought that the world was full of gods, but they did not limit their veneration to living beings such as men, animals and certain trees. For example, they even worshipped the Amon-Re Temple in Thebes as a goddess. . . . Many animals such as falcons, bulls, rams, crocodiles, cats, baboons, hippopotamuses, snakes, etc., were considered as divine beings or as reincarnations of such, and consequently they were not only spared, but well fed during their life-time, and embalmed and buried after their death. The Apis-Bull in Memphis and the Ram in Mendes are two examples of this worship. It was also common for gods to be represented as animals, or as having animal heads. Thus the goddess of the heaven was pictured as a cow and the sun god as a beetle. Thoth, the god of the moon and of learning, had the head of an ibis; Re, the head of a sparrow-hawk; Anubis, the god of the dead, the head of a jackal; the goddess Bast, that of a cat, and Sobk, that of a crocodile.

In many places there existed local cults of deities who were considered protectors of a definite city. But only a few of these cults succeeded in extending

Rameseś Sarcophagus, Valley of the Kings, Egypt

their following to wide enough regions as to eventually encompass the entire Nile valley. On the other hand, gods did exist, who from time immemorial were recognized by the entire kingdom. These were mainly the cosmic gods. The sun god of Heliopolis, Re, who for a long time was considered as the chief god of the kingdom also occupied first place among the celestial beings. It was believed that he sailed across the heavens in a golden bark and fought with the cloud-snake, Apophis. During the Middle Kingdom, he was merged with the Theban god of the air and the wind, Amon, who was the husband of the goddess Mut. In Heliopolis, a different sun-god, Atum, was venerated along with his spouse Jusas; in Abydos, Anher . . . was considered the sun-god, while in Hermonthis near Thebes, the falcon-headed Month, functioned both as sun-god and war-god. Chonsu was the moon god. Ptah, the great god of Memphis to whom the Apis-Bull was sacred, was married to the lion-headed, warlike Sechmet, the sender of plagues. At a later time, Ptah, who was also the protector of artists, was merged with Sokar, the grave-god. From other gods there emerged: Geb, the god of earth; Nut, the goddess of heaven; Upuaut, the "opener of the way," who was also the local god of Siut. From Koptos, there emerged the fertility-god, Min, . . . whereas the Nile-god, Chnum became the protector of Nubia. The bandy-legged dwarf demon, Bes, probably originated in the lands of the Red Sea where incense is traditionally burned because he is often represented on the toilet objects of ladies. Among the most important goddesses were: Maat, the heavenly mistress of justice and truth; Hathor, the heavenly goddess of Dendera, who was also the guardian of the cemeteries of the dead. According to some researchers, Neith of Sais, originally was a Lybian war-goddess, who at a later time became an "opener of the way." Nephtys was the sister and wife of Set.

But the most famous of all the Egyptian gods were Osiris, Isis and their son Horus.

. . . Many different versions of the Isis and Osiris myth exist. But basically it follows this pattern. Osiris, the king of Egypt is locked up in a coffin by his wicked brother Set (known as Typhon by the Greeks) and is thrown into the sea. The coffin is washed ashore in Byblos (near present-day Beirut). Isis, who is both Osiris' wife and sister searches everywhere for the coffin. She finds it and hides it. But Set, who had also been looking for it locates it while Isis is away. He cuts up the body into fourteen pieces and scatters it into the marshes. With Anubis' assistance, Isis recovers the pieces and reassembles them. Osiris is brought to life again for a sufficiently long period of time for Isis to bear her husband the child Horus. After Horus grows up, he victoriously defeats Set in battle. The earth-god then enters the picture and brings peace to Egypt by dividing the land between Set and Horus. (According to the temple texts of Edfu, Set was eventually driven out of Egypt by Horus.) Osiris next leaves earth and becomes lord of the underworld. At a later time these three gods were venerated not only in the Nile country but throughout the Mediterranean area.

Source: Harold L. Friess, editor, *Non-Christian Religions, A to Z* (New York: Dunlap, 1963) pp. 72–74.

This seems to be the essence of Egyptian religion. It reflected an orderly view of the world (every day the sun god, Re, rode across the clear blue sky; the Nile provided regular irrigation for cultivating food; burial rituals insured eternal safety) and explained people's place. With few exceptions Egyptian rites, myths, magic, and prayer continued unchanged for generation after generation. They withstood the normal developments of time and passed from the world scene only after Islam had taken over the land—about A.D. 700.

The Religion of the Ancient Greeks

Perhaps the greatest single influence in the development of Western civilization was the emergence of Greek culture. No other culture has had as great an influence on the development of Western society.

The Greek's development of philosophy, mathematics, science, sculpture, architecture, political thought, and religious awareness, and their influence on current and subsequent civilizations marked a definite turning point in the development of human society.

As far as religious awareness is concerned, Greek philosophical thought enabled it to move away from fear, force, power, and magic to a more rational approach which led, eventually, to understanding religion as a relationship with whatever God is for a particular person.

Although it is somewhat of an oversimplification, the development of religious awareness in Western civilization might be put this way:

1. Prehistoric people gave first expression to a *sense* of mystery in life.

2. Ancient Babylonian and Egyptian people *systematized* the mystery of life through myth-making.

3. Ancient Greek people *humanized* the mystery by systematically cultivating a people's-eye view of life rather than a god's-eye view of life.

The people we know today as Greeks are descended from people who probably came from all parts of prehistoric Europe and Asia Minor. There is no doubt that the last glacial period drove the inhabitants of the north into the Mediterranean coastlands, and successive invasions by the Aryan tribes from the East helped to form the ethnic group which became the Greeks of the Golden Age (fifth and fourth centuries B.C.).

The Origin of Religion

Ceremonial Sun Chariot of the Aryans, who spread from Denmark to India

History provides us with evidence of a civilization, called Minoan, located on the island of Crete (about 50 miles south and east of the mainland), which flourished about 1600 B.C. This civilization (they had five-story buildings and inside plumbing, which was not to become common again until the late A.D. 1800s) was taken over by the Mycenaean civilization, so-called because it was centered in Mycenae, a city in the southeastern section of the mainland. Mycenae was the home city of Agamemnon, the famous king who led the Greeks in the battle against Troy.[7]

The difference between the Minoan and the Mycenaean civilization seems to have been that the Minoans were peace-loving, while the Mycenaeans were inclined to war, invasion, and conquest.

It was because of this "war philosophy" that the Mycenaeans were eventually conquered by the northern Greek tribe called Dorians. Weakened by the efforts of the ten-year Trojan War, the Mycenaean civilization gave way to a barbaric civilization which brought on what is called the Dark Ages of Greece. It was not until about 750 B.C. that the Greece of historical influence began to arise.

7. A city on the northwest coast of modern Turkey. This story is told in the most famous epic poems of all time, the *Iliad* and the *Odyssey*, supposedly written by a Greek poet, Homer, who lived in the eighth century B.C.

It was from the pre-Dorian times that the legends celebrated in Greek history and mythology came. But it was from these times and from the Dorian ages that the historical Greek religion came: ancient myths and Dorian myths intermingled in the later Greek religious myths that attempted to explain the mysteries of the world and the world of the gods and spirits.

The myths of the early Greeks, like the myths of other early peoples, told of the creation of the world, the origin of the lesser gods, and the nature of the afterlife (the usual features of religious myths of that period of human development). The religious practices of the early Greeks consisted of magical acts, incantations, animal sacrifices, prayers, and ritual washings and ceremonies much like the religious practices of other early peoples.

As Greek thought developed, particularly during the Golden Age, however, Greek religion developed. It was significant in that it "humanized" religious thought and practice by the gradual evolution of the Greek gods from natural forces into supermen, and by the tendency to answer the question "What is the meaning of life?" with people-oriented responses rather than with myth-oriented responses.

The usual epic mythological stories about the gods and their battles became mingled with legends about ancient Greek heroes into a kind of divine-human "gods of the round table" mythology, with the gods living on top of Mount Olympus. Zeus the Mighty, Hera, Apollo, Athena, Aphrodite, Artemis, Hermes, and Poseidon are familiar names even in our own times.[8] Magnificent temples stand today even in their ruins as mute evidence of the strength and force of Greek devotion to these gods and goddesses and what they stood for. Eventually, Greek gods, even the sky god and mother-earth goddess, were no longer mere forces, indifferent or hostile to the people. They had human characteristics (though on a vaster "heroic" or "olympian" scale). They thought and acted in the same way that people do in the human world.

The second element of the Greek genius for "taming" the mystery of the universe to something people could cope with was their questioning instinct. They attempted to understand life piece by piece, step by step, and to build everyday explanations rather than mythical ones by accumulating a careful catalogue of what was already known. They then used known information to gain further information.

8. All of these gods and goddesses have Roman counterparts, whose names are equally familiar.

The Origin of Religion

The development of the Greek city-states and the establishment of schools such as at Athens, set the Greeks to speculating on all areas of their lives: government, politics, society, war, mathematics, biology, religion, and so forth. Great philosophers turned their minds to explaining the "reasonableness" of religion. They began to draw conclusions about deities and religious practice in a systematic, rational way that has become standard in most Western religions.

Philosophy is not religion, but it is a useful tool for understanding the *content* of what religion responds to as the mystery of life. What philosophers such as Socrates and Plato

Hellenistic sculpture of Artemis the Huntress, known as the Diana of Versailles (Courtesy The Granger Collection)

Grave relief: Girl with Pigeons, 455–450 B.C., from the Island of Paros (Courtesy The Metropolitan Museum of Art, Fletcher Fund, 1927)

really accomplished was the clearing away of the accretions of centuries and the establishing of a concern for basic principles about life. In place of many gods—undiscriminated, amorphous, of undetermined origin, purpose or location, often animal and violent—they put a principle of good or singleness of duty. Where they found magic, witchcraft and incantations designed to coerce the gods, they sought natural explanations of the "mysteries" of the universe. When they found people subject to the fate decreed by the gods, they urged them to begin ordering their own lives to the greatest good: virtue for its own sake, social well-being, harmony, beauty, and peace. They delivered people of the Western world from a deity-fated universe (in which the whims of an animal god, an Atum or Osiris or Zeus, decided people's destiny) to a people-centered universe, where the idea of a single deity, a creative force or an all-powerful but not vengeful God, could begin to make sense.

With the emergence of Greek thought, the search for an answer to the mystery of the universe in the Western world narrowed. People, prepared slowly and naturally over the course of thousands of years, were ready to accept the idea that a God—the Utterly Other, the Almighty—had created the world with people as the highest form of creation and had destined them for things greater than this earth offered.

This thought, however, was not to burst on the world. It, too, was prepared for and found its acceptance slowly. How it was prepared for and how it is expressed in Western religions are described in the next part of this book. How religious awareness developed and how it is expressed in the East are described in a subsequent section.

Summary

1. The history of religious awareness in the Western world reveals a trend toward greater and greater sophistication in understanding and expression.

2. Archeological studies of early historic religious practices reveal people's concern about the mystery of life, survival, continuity of the tribe, death, and life after death.

3. Early myths reveal the kind of god people believed in, their relationship with this god (or gods), and the kind of world-view held by the people of the time.

4. Early myths reflect the kind of world exprienced by the people of prehistoric and early historic times.

The Origin of Religion

5. The Greeks provided the greatest move to a more sophisticated religious awareness in the West through their questioning and searching for natural causes to ordinary experiences of life.

For Review

1. Why is it to be expected that the religious awareness of people should develop and become more sophisticated?
2. What is the common meaning of the word "myth"? How does this meaning differ from the religious meaning of the word? Explain in detail.
3. What was the role of myth in primitive and early historic religions? What shaped the content of the myth in various primitive and early religions? Illustrate. What do these myths say to modern people?
4. What three concerns seemed to be central to all primitive and early historic religions? How do we know this?
5. Contrast the Babylonian and Egyptian views of the origin of the world, the gods, and life after death.
6. How did the practice of astrology begin?
7. What was the central concern of early Egyptian religion?
8. What role did the Greek view of religion play in the development of religious awareness in Western civilization? Explain. How did the Greek view of the gods differ from the view of the gods of people who lived before them? Why did this development take place?
9. Be sure that you can define pyramid, sphinx, Trojan horse, and superstition.

For Discussion

1. Discuss why some people consult the stars or pay visits to astrologers. Is there any evidence that the stars or the planets affect things on the earth?
2. Discuss the relationship of the Santa Claus story or the legends about a historical figure such as George Washington, Evangeline, or Hiawatha, to the myths of ancient religions.

3. Discuss why some religions seem not to have developed beyond a certain stage. Could it be because the answers to the mystery of life provided by their religious leaders satisfied them?

4. Discuss the reasons for some religions simply dying out.

For Research

1. Prepare a report on the religion of Rome. Include material on the cult of the emperor.

2. Prepare a report on one of the following topics: the development of ancient civilization; the pyramids and the Sphinx; Egyptian religion and culture; the Golden Age of Greece; the influence of Rome in spreading Greek culture; the myths of Greece and Rome; the laws of Hammurabi; the Acropolis; the Trojan War; the Iliad and the Odyssey; or the theology of Amenhotep IV (Akhenaton).

3. Make a list of the major Greek gods and their role in the universe as the Greeks conceived that role. After each, put the name of the Roman god who fulfilled the same role.

4. Prepare a summary of various myths of ancient religions, giving the place where the myth was used, the general content, and a probable cause for the myth's content and formulation.

5. Find out what you can about the origin of the Olympic games.

Words You Should Know

If there are any words listed below that you are not sure of, look them up in the Word List at the back of the book.

accretions	divination	rational
amalgam	hierarchies	satellite
amorphous	horoscope	seer
astrology	mummification	subsequent
auguring	myth	tribulation

part two

The World's Living Religions

The living religions of the West are basically revelational. They trace their origins to a particular person in a particular place.

The living religions of the East are basically behavioral. Their origins are shrouded in mystery and their stress is on right conduct.

The God Seekers

For the purposes of this study, the world's living religions have been divided into two major parts—the religions of the Western world and the religions of the Eastern world. The religions of the so-called "Third World" have not been included in a separate category because, for the most part, they are either Western or Eastern, except in those areas where early, prescientific, preliterate religions still flourish. These are, generally, in isolated pockets in Africa and in some of the islands of the Pacific and the Caribbean.

The Western world, as we said, is that part of the world which lies, roughly, west of the easternmost shore of the Mediterranean. The Eastern world is that which lies east of the 60° meridian. The land area in-between is referred to as the Middle East. The Third World is made up of those countries which are deprived economically and educationally. They are located in Africa and the Near East mostly.

When we speak of the Western religions, we are referring to those that arose in the Middle East (Judaism, Christianity, Islam) and are practiced in the Western world and in the Moslem countries. When we speak of the Eastern religions, we are referring to those that arose and are practiced in India, China, and Japan, and are practiced in Southeast Asia and the Far East.

One more thing needs to be said about the differences between the East and the West, and that is the mind-set or philosophical outlook of the people in each. The mind-set of the West, nurtured as it has been by the great Greek philosophers, is, basically, earth-bound, pragmatic, scientific, and deductive. The mind-set of the East is cosmic, passive, spiritual, and inductive. Each has its own way of looking at reality that is peculiar to the way it thinks about the world, people, things in the world, and the spiritual, or nonmaterial universe. This mind-set, or way of looking on things, has influenced not only religion itself in each area, but the beliefs and practices of the religion that flourish in each area.

Although there are many living religions by which people in the Western world live, there are three—Judaism, Christianity, and Islam—which have played a dominant role in shaping the contemporary culture of the West. These three were selected for discussion, not only because space does not allow for a discussion of each of the hundreds of religious expressions found in the Western world, but also because these three typify the development of religious awareness in the Western world.

Many things distinguish these Western religions from the ancient religions discussed in the first part of this book. The first is that each has a known starting point, and each is dominated by a single person, or founder.

This does not mean they have no roots which go back before their founder, even to prehistoric times. After all, every founder must have materials with which to build. It means that these religions did not just "happen" or "evolve" into being by a slow process of social accumulation. Each was formed by a definite individual.

There are differences among the three founders, of course, as we shall see. Moses founded the Israelite religion by codifying a centuries-old collection of Hebrew traditions into a unified Law of God. Jesus is remembered as having founded the Christian religion by claiming to be the sum and substance and fulfillment of what Moses had founded. Mohammed founded the Islamic religion by passing along to humanity messages which he claimed were from the angel Gabriel, writing them down in a Holy Book called the Koran.

Since their founding, of course, each of these major living religions has developed to a greater complexity and branched into subdivisions. In this brief survey of the living religions of the world, we are not interested in the causes or the nature of the complexities or the subdivisions. We are only concerned with the nature and purpose of the religious awareness which finds its expression in the living religions of the Western world.

Before beginning a study of the living religions of the world, it might be useful to put the study in its proper perspective. Religion is very much alive in the world, even though its influence in some parts of the world is on the decline. It influences the lives of most people the world over, whether it is expressed in the sophisticated nuances of advanced societies or contains a goodly share of what we have called primitive, or early, beliefs and practices. It enables people to express a relationship with whatever God is for the people who practice its various expressions.

As Huston Smith, an eminent scholar who spent much of his life studying and explaining the world's religions observed:

I write these opening lines on a day widely celebrated throughout Christendom as World-Wide Communion Sunday. The sermon in the service I attended this morning dwelt on Christianity as a world phenomenon. From mud huts in Africa to igloos in

Christian pilgrim at Holy Sepulchre Church, Jerusalem

Labrador Christians are kneeling today to receive the elements of the Holy Eucharist. It was an impressive picture.

Still, as I listened with half my mind the other half wandered to the wider company of God-seekers. I thought of the Yemenite Jews as I watched them six months ago in their Synagogue in Jerusalem: dark-skinned men sitting shoeless and cross-legged on the floor, wrapped in the prayer-shawls their ancestors wore in the desert. They are there today, at least a quorum or ten morning and evening, swaying backwards and forwards like camel-riders as they recite their Torah, following a form they inherit unconsciously from the centuries when their fathers were forbidden to ride the desert-horse and developed this pretense in compensation. Yalcin, the Muslim architect who guided me through the Blue Mosque in Istanbul, has completed his month's Ramadan fast that was beginning while we were together, but he too is praying today, five times as he prostrates himself toward Mecca. Swami Ramakrishna in his tiny house by the Ganges at the foot of the Himalayas will not speak today. He will continue the devotional silence which, with the exception of three days each year, he has kept for five years. By this hour U Nu is probably facing the delegations, crises, and cabinet meetings that are the lot of a Prime Minister, but from four to six this morning, before the world broke upon him, he too was alone with the eternal in the privacy of the Buddhist shrine that adjoins his home in Rangoon. At that, Dai Jo and Lai San, Zen monks in Kyoto, were ahead of him an hour. They have been up since three this morning, and until eleven tonight will spend most of the day sitting cross-legged and immovable as they seek with intense absorption to plumb the Buddha-nature that lies at the center of their being.

What a strange fellowship this is: the God-seekers of every clime, lifting their voices in the most diverse ways imaginable to the God of all men. How does it all sound to Him? like bedlam? Or, in some mysterious way, does it blend into harmony? Does one faith carry the melody, the lead, or do the parts share in counterpoint and antiphony when not in solid chorus?

We cannot know. All we can do is try to listen, carefully and with full attention, to each voice in turn as it is raised to the divine.*

*Huston Smith, *The Religions of Man*, (New York: Harper & Row, 1958), pp. 1–2.

The Living Religions of the Western World

"God is One"

chapter 4

Judaism

Today, as Israel and the Arab nations observe an uneasy truce in their perennial conflicts over a strip of land on the eastern shores of the Mediterranean Sea, prayers for victory to Yahweh (the Jewish name for their God) and Allah (the Moslem name for their God) arise from both sides—and from many parts of the world.

It is not within the purpose of this book to discuss the Israeli-Arab conflict or to pass judgment on either side. (Perhaps only a Jew or a Moslem will completely understand the nature of the conflict.) Its purpose is to help you understand Judaism and Islam as expressions of religious awareness.

The Essence of Jewish Faith

The heart of Jewish religious faith is best expressed in the "Shema," a Jewish liturgical prayer recited at morning and evening services, which expresses Israel's strong faith in and love of God. It is taken from the Book of Deuteronomy, and goes like this:

Hear, oh Israel, the Lord our God, the Lord is One. You shall love the Lord your God with all your heart, with all your soul, with all your might. These words which I command you this day shall be in your heart. You shall teach them diligently to your children. You shall talk about them at home and abroad, night and day. You shall bind them as a sign upon your hand and they shall be as frontlets between your eyes and you shall inscribe them on the doorposts of your homes and upon your gates.

—Deuteronomy 6:4–9

The cry, "Hear, O Israel, the LORD is our God, the LORD alone!," resounding through the world for over 3,000 years as the morning and evening prayers of every devout Jewish person, proclaims the essence of Judaism. It harkens back to the desert of Sinai, where Moses, coming down from the mountain, brought to his travel-weary gathering of escaped Egyp-

Opposite page—A Jewish man with phylacteries and prayer shawl worn for morning weekday prayers

tian slaves **the Torah which would make them one people bound in solemn covenant to Yahweh.**[1] And the commands contained in verses 7 to 9 have been followed faithfully. Each year the works of the Lord are relived and made present to the Jewish people in the celebration of the Jewish feast days.

Today there are about fourteen and one-half million Jews in the world. There are about three million in Asia, mostly in Israel, four million in Europe, and seven million in the Americas, of whom nearly six million live in the United States and 350,000 live in Canada. Although Judaism is divided into three major movements—Orthodox, Conservative, and Reform—and each has subdivisions which give particular expression to Jewish law, Judaism is one in its basic tenets.

Many Jews believe that God created the Jewish people by His Torah. The essence of Judaism is, therefore, God, the People, and the Torah. For the Jew, however, ''God'' does not mean just any god, but the One and Only God who chose a particular People.

The People are not just any motley group of individual people, but a collected, gathered, chosen family with a close-knit mutual concern for one another which imitates the concern God Himself has for them. The Torah is not merely a set of laws or a cultural system of teaching, but the God-given pattern which creates the People.

The Jewish religion is unique. It is about *this* God who chose *this* People to live *this* Way. Other religions may express people's approach to God; but the Jewish people see their history as revealing God's approach to people.

To understand this uniqueness of the Jewish religion, it must be looked at under four readings: Jewish history; God; people; and Jewish expressions of their relationship to God.

Jewish History

The history of Jewish beginnings can be told in two ways: (1) through the Bible and the traditions surrounding it; and (2) through external historical evidence supplied by archeologists and students of other ancient cultures. When these two versions are compared, it is apparent that the ''inside story'' and the story told by outside evidence are just not the same story. They do not exactly contradict each other, but neither do they entirely agree with each other; they have a completely

---

1. The Hebrew word *Torah* cannot be translated simply as ''Law.'' It includes Law and teachings, summarizing a whole way of life.

different point of view. The Bible in Jewish tradition says in effect, "This is the story of God's people and how God brought them together as His people." The external evidence found by secular historians says in effect, "This is the story of how a number of Hebrew tribes got together and came to think of themselves as God's people."

To adequately understand Jewish history, we must know both versions of the story, for each sheds light on the other. When they are put together in one composite story, the inside story is more completely understood.

The roots of Judaism go back before the time of Moses to the Mesopotamian world of about 1900 B.C., where the highly complex system of nature-gods and city-gods held sway over Babylonian culture. Among the many people who lived in this region were groups of wandering tribes called Habiru. These were not one single people but a set of loosely-related tribes of seminomads. Around 1900 B.C. there was a great migration of many of these clans from the area around the Persian Gulf across the Fertile Crescent.

The biblical book of Genesis tells us that a clan leader, named Abraham, moved his clan away from the city of Ur because he was called by the voice of *El Shaddai* (roughly translated "God of the Mountain," or perhaps "God Mighty as a Mountain") away from a land of many pagan gods to a land where Abraham and his descendants could worship Him as the One and Only God. This God and Abraham made a mutual covenant (Genesis 12).

Archeological and other secular historical discoveries have not unearthed evidence of any man named Abraham, but they do reveal some general information about the clans and their religious beliefs. Each clan had its own particular clan-god who was not stationed at any particular geographic location or city, but who accompanied the clan in its wanderings and was its faithful protector. Each clan did not believe that its god was the only god in the world, but that its god was the only one who remained loyal to and protected the particular clan. This was a kind of reaction against, or adaptation of, the Mesopotamian system of nature-gods and gods stationed at particular cities.

If the biblical Abraham's *El Shaddai* was typical of these clan-gods, then we do not as yet have the One and Only God of Jewish tradition. We have an intermediate understanding, a step in this direction, a step up from absolute polytheism (belief in many gods), but not yet the final stage of absolute monotheism (belief in only one God). If we could translate this clan-god concept into modern words, perhaps it would sound something like this: there may be many gods in the world, but a man (or tribe) can only be faithful to one.

Learning to Believe in One God

As the story is told in the Bible, Abraham's God was not just a clan-god but in fact, *the* God. However, most Scripture scholars realize that the book of Genesis was written centuries after Abraham lived (based on centuries of oral and written tradition and legend), and was edited and reedited many times before it reached its final form around the year 500 B.C. (1,400 years after Abraham lived and 800 years after the time of Moses). Very likely, the writers who put the story of Abraham into its final written form read back into his life their own more sophisticated understanding of God.

Jewish people, who consider the Bible to be God's inspired Word, recognize that God's general pattern of operation in the world is to bring about progress by slow evolution— leading people step by step not only into a growing awareness of such earthly things as agriculture, science, and mathematics, but also into a growing awareness of Himself. Christians and Jews understand the clan-god idea as a divinely, inspired step up from absolute polytheism. They believe that God led His people through many more stages (which we shall shortly examine) to the final stage of awareness of His absolute unity and holiness. Looking back from this vantage point, they see the early notion as the beginning of the later, more complete one. Hence, in a real sense, many Jewish people believe Abraham was called by the One God even though he himself may not consciously have realized it. The book of Genesis tells his story in poetic language, revealing not exactly what Abraham experienced but *what his descendants recognized behind his experience.*

The Bible picks up the story of the Jews centuries later. After centuries of wandering, many groups had come to settle in Egypt along the northern branches of the Nile. A series of political upheavals in the country found them at the bottom of the social ladder, reduced to slavery. Perhaps it was this unity in a common suffering that gave these groups a sense of being more than just a collection of individual isolated clans.

It was around the year 1285 B.C. that a powerful Hebrew leader, Moses, was able to instill in some of his lower class brethren a sense of their own unity and their dignity as free men. Escaping from Egypt under circumstances that they celebrated as miraculous, Moses' group solemnly entered into a national covenant with Yahweh in the desert at Mount Sinai and expressed its new-born code of laws as the Commandments of Yahweh.

The Lord said to Abram, "Leave your country, your relatives, and your father's home, and go to a land that I am going to show you." (Genesis 12:1)

The rock fortress, Masada, where thousands of Jewish zealots committed suicide rather than submit to Roman armies in the first century, Israel

The Bible, in the book of Exodus, portrays Yahweh as the One and Only God, the God of Abraham, Isaac, and Jacob, the God whom Abraham had called by the name *El Shaddai*. Again, most Scripture scholars point out that the book of Exodus probably had its beginnings in epic songs celebrating the desert escape; but additions and refinements, and newer, more complex laws were added to it over the succeeding centuries so that the book of Exodus as it has come down to us, shows evidence of a "reading back into" ancient events certain insights which actually come from a later period in Jewish religious evolution.

It may very well be that Yahweh, as Moses conceived of Him, was not the One and Only God in the whole world, but was the one national God of the newly-united Israelite[2] tribes. He led them to enlarge their notion of a clan-god to a national God.

Christians and Jews who take an evolutionary view of God's action upon people's understanding see in Yahweh-of-Mount-Sinai the second step up from Mesopotamian polythe-

2. The people unified around the tradition of escape from Egypt named themselves Israelites after Israel, Abraham's grandson, who had twelve sons. In Jewish circles, a "Hebrew" is one who lived before the Exodus; an Israelite is one who swore the Covenant with God; a Jew is one who lived the Jewish way of life after the period spent in Babylon.

The World's Living Religions

ism. Just as it made more religious sense for the wandering tribes to be faithful to one god wherever they went rather than worshipping a different local god stationed at each new place they came to, so it made more religious sense for the Israelite people to worship one God in common rather than for each tribe to have its own clan-god—for in their miraculous flight from Egypt, they had escaped as one people and sensed one power behind their escape.

The third stage in the evolution of Jewish monotheism took place through the inspired preaching of the prophets— men of various temperaments and characters and walks of life who, over many centuries in the Promised Land, felt called to purify the Jewish people's understanding of what had taken place in the Covenant founded at Mount Sinai.

It was the prophets who made determined efforts to root out of the Jewish people the last vestiges of polytheism, the last shreds of allegiance to any natural-force-gods or clan-gods. It was the prophets whose inspired vision led the people to understand that Yahweh must indeed be not only a national God but the God of the whole world; for Yahweh had founded their nation in a miraculous escape and had many times since brought them back from capture and exile by foreign powers (chiefly the Babylonian Exile from 587 to 536 B.C.). If He were not the God of the whole world, He could not have had such power over history. Therefore, the gods of other nations could not really be gods at all but were lifeless images in gold and silver and wood and bronze: lifeless images of a power that does not exist, that just plain *is not*—in contrast to Yahweh, "He Who Is."

So powerfully did the Jewish people learn this lesson from the prophets that, by the time of Jesus, theirs was the only nation in the whole Roman Empire that did not bow to Roman gods, or worship the emperor as god, or even allow the emperor's picture to be minted on the coins they used or the Roman eagle to stand in their temple. This was the strength of their reaction against anything that faintly resembled worship of any power but the Only One Who Is.

Since the first century of the modern era, the Jewish people have continued to exist, although they were scattered throughout the world as the result of the destruction of the Temple and of Jerusalem in A.D. 70 by Roman armies retaliating for an attempted rebellion. In recent times the nation of Israel has been reestablished as a homeland for those who choose to live there and as a focal point of Jewish identity for those who remain in other parts of the world.

From the highlights of Jewish religious history sketched above, we can extract some key themes in the Jewish understanding of God and people who did not exist with such force anywhere else in the world and would not exist in the wider world today if it were not for the presence of Judaism and its offspring, Christianity.

The God of Jewish Faith

As we have said, the concept of God as Jewish people perceive Him developed over many centuries. As told in the Jewish Bible, God identified Himself to Moses as "Yahweh." This name is hard to translate. It may suggest God's Mysterious Beyondness if translated *"He Is Who He Is."* It is also sometimes translated "He Who Is" or "He Who Causes To Be." In any case, so greatly did the Jewish people respect this name that eventually in Old Testament history it was forbidden to pronounce it. Whenever a public Scripture reader at synagogue services came upon this name, he would pronounce simply "The Name" or, at a later period, would substitute the Hebrew word *Adonai* which means "The Lord." This later practice is still continued in Jewish synagogues today.

But the Jewish people believe that God not only revealed His name in the Bible, He also revealed His nature. According to Jewish belief, God is One, Personal, Saving, Faithful, and Above All.

1. God is one

Not much needs to be said here in explanation of this point, since it is the fundamental principle of the evolution of the Habiru tribes into the People of God.

As the oneness of God grew in Jewish understanding, they showed more and more reaction against the beliefs of their polytheistic neighbors. They grew up in a world where natural forces were considered to have personalities: There was a sun god, a wind god, a moon god, storm gods, and so on. As belief in one God grew, the Jews had to reinterpret the symbols of the cultures surrounding them. Every one of the rival gods had to be "dethroned." The wind, instead of being a separate god, came to be thought of as "the Breath of Yahweh." The storms were "the anger of Yahweh." The sun and moon (the chief gods in other belief-systems) were dethroned so low that in the Creation Poem of Genesis, chapter 1, they are created by Yahweh only on the fourth day, three days after He had already created light! The various winged-lion and winged-bull gods of Babylon became mere messengers of Yahweh. (From the Greek word *angelos* meaning "messenger," we get our English word "angel.") The Ark of the Covenant was covered with an empty throne in the shape of two winged bulls spreading their wings as a seat for the Unpicturable One. In these and many other ways, the Jews expressed their growing awareness that Yahweh is God—not just "a god."

2. God is personal

In contrast to some aspects of primitive religion and ancient religions, where the power(s)-over-the-universe can be natural forces or animal spirits, and in contrast to some Eastern religions where God is an impersonal, aloof, "eternal essence," Jewish insight takes a definite stand that reality is ultimately personal. People are not an accident floating on a sea of blind fate; they are partners with God in a Covenant, in a two-way relationship of faithfulness. People are not alone in life; their entire lives are spent in the presence of One Who Cares.

3. God is saving

Jewish people's conviction that God cares is based on what they experienced throughout their entire history. In their miraculous escape from Egyptian slavery they learned that the power over the universe was on their side; theirs was a *Saving God.* Their entire history, in fact, was experienced as a *Salvation History.* They interpreted their temporary declines as a nation as God's punishment for their unfaithfulness to Him and their unconcern for their fellow Jews. They saw in their deliverance from oppression the faithfulness of God saving them, calling them to a new possibility for greatness when they would repent of their past mistakes. They learned that God takes people seriously; what they do is important to Him.

4. God is faithful

When they found God rescuing them time after time from the punishment that infidelity after infidelity had brought them to, an immensely inspiring truth about God hit home to them: God would not divorce Himself from His people, even though they were giving Him sufficient grounds to do so.[3] God keeps His Covenant even when people do not. As Jeremiah said: "Have you not noticed what these people are saying: 'The LORD has rejected the two tribes which he had chosen?'. . . Thus says the LORD: 'When I have no covenant with the day

3. The rather constant depiction in the Old Testament of Hebrew infidelity illustrates the fidelity of God. It was not meant to show the Hebrews as constantly unfaithful—they were not.

The Jews Define Themselves

by Rabbi Marc Tannenbaum

What are some of these basic components of Judaism?

The most important fact that needs to be understood is: Judaism is NOT just another one of the world's great religions.

Judaism constitutes a Divine "breakthrough" in the consciousness of mankind. The Exodus from Egypt was a turning point in human history which decisively altered our conceptions of God, man, and society. The Lord God of Abraham, Isaac, and Jacob intervened in the events of history and brought about a mighty redemption of the children of Israel from slavery.

Their liberation was two-fold: They were liberated from the spiritual bondage of idolatry and paganism in Egypt. They were also liberated physically from persecution and oppression. From that moment of the Exodus and thereafter, the God of Israel was experienced as a redeeming God who identified Himself with His suffering slave people.

So transforming was the power of that experience of God as liberator, that the children of Israel and their Jewish descendants have reenacted the Exodus event each year for 3,500 years by means of the Passover seder service.

Jewish families, in unbroken continuity with the biblical past, recall the Exodus not simply as a memoriam of a past event, but as a living encounter with the Divine Presence in their midst, which commits them to struggle against idolatry, injustice, and oppression in every generation.

The Exodus, however, was not an end in itself, but was rather a prelude to Mount Sinai where God, out of His boundless grace and love, entered into a Covenant with Israel.

Before Sinai, the Israelites were slaves, "untouchables" in Egypt's caste system, without any human dignity, disposable work-commodities whom Pharaoh could dispose of with the flick of his royal finger. At Sinai, upon entering into the "B'rit" (the Covenant) with the Lord of Israel and accepting to become the bearers of the Ten Commandments among the human family, these brick-making slaves were transfigured into a state of holiness.

The entire people were to become "a kingdom of priests and a holy nation." Each human life, no matter what his or her former status or indignity, became irreversibly the bearer of the Divine image.

To the believer, nothing could thereafter change that appreciation of the infinite preciousness of human life—individual or corporate.

Sinai stamped upon Israel its indelible character as a "messianic people." The Covenant obligated them to carry out a task of redemption in society. Israel was to create a "model society" that did justice, loved mercy, and walked humbly with God.

And that is where the "land of Israel" comes into the picture. Just as God freely elected the People of Israel for a Divinely-appointed task, so God also elected through His Covenant with Abraham to choose the Land of Israel as the site for building the messianic society.

"Now the Lord said unto Abram," the Bible records in Genesis 12:4 through

13:15, "for all the land which thou seest, to thee will I give it, and to thy seed for ever."

From that time forward, across nearly 4,000 years, the Promised Land—Israel—became the center of orientation of the Jewish people, the scene of their biblical origins and the setting for the Messianic future. Only with that historic background in mind can one make sense of the powerful hold that Israel continues to exert on Jews everywhere today.

There is another central theme in Judaism: God's election of the Jewish people is permanent and is subject neither to cancellation nor replacement. As proclaimed in Deuteronomy 7 (and Psalm 89 and elsewhere in the Bible and in post-biblical rabbinic Judaism), "Know that the Lord thy God, he is God, the faithful God, which keepeth the covenant and mercy with them that love him and keep his commandments to a thousand generations."

That certain knowledge of the constancy and faithfulness of God who keeps His promises with His people "for a thousand generations" is the ultimate key to understanding how the Jewish people have endured anti-Semitic pogroms, inquisitions, discriminations, ghettos, yellow badges of shame, even Auschwitz, and have prevailed to this day.

Source: © 1975 NC News Service. This article was part of "Know Your Faith," an adult religious education program through diocesan press.

Bas Mitzva at conservative Temple ETZ CHAIM, Thousand Oaks, California

and night, and have given no laws to heaven and earth, then too, will I reject the descendants of Jacob and of my servant David . . .' '' (Jeremiah 33:24–26).

In Jewish eyes, it is God who calls and people who answer or refuse to respond, but God does not take away His constant call. God calls every person into being, and each person answers "yes" or "no" to what God calls him or her to be. If someone answers "yes," he or she cooperates in a personal creation and becomes the kind of person he or she is capable of becoming. If someone answers "no," he or she chooses a personal defeat and by rights deserves to become less than capability would allow. God will not force one to become the best possible self, but He will never abandon a person: the possibility of becoming one's best self is always present, not because one deserves it, but because God has promised it.

5. God is above all

In contrast to primitive and early religions—and to some features of superstition in any age—the Jews believe that God is not a being or spirit who can be controlled by magic, commanded by ritual, converted by prayer, or computerized by human theories. It is people who must be sensitive to the will of God. God is not an extension of people, some kind of superman. He is *Absolutely Other.* People can extend their control over nature, but they can have no control over God. They can express their dependence upon God through ritual, but they must recognize that God is never dependent upon them. They can pray to God for help to know and fulfill His plan, but they dare not pretend that God will substitute their plans for His. They can grope after that mystery called God, but they can never wrap Him up in a final formula that would protect people from mysteries.[4]

The Place of People in Jewish Faith

The Jewish understanding of God—so radically different from the ideas of gods among their contemporaries—led the Jews to conceive of people's place in the world and their ultimate relationship with God and other people in equally radical ways. The Jews differed from those among whom they lived in the following areas.

1. The dignity of people

Perhaps in no other way did the Jewish people differ from their neighbors so radically as in their understanding of the place of people in the created world. In contrast to other groups who believed that people were the slaves or playthings of the gods, or helpless in the vast scheme of things, the Jews saw people as fundamentally good because God made them that way (Genesis 1:24–31 & 2:7–24). They saw them as God's partners in making the world a suitable place to live.

Because of their own experiences, also, as slaves who were freed to become a people, the Israelites came to see in every unfortunate person a son of God. Though they were not yet enlightened enough to do away with slavery entirely,[5] the

---

4. What makes the Jewish insights concerning God all the more remarkable is that they lived in the midst of cultures much more successful in material terms than their own whose gods apparently took care of them.

5. Social evolution, like all evolution, is slow. We must recall, for example, that the leadership of Moses for the freedom of his people occurred about 1285 B.C., but the Emancipation Proclamation in the United States was not made until A.D.1863—over 3,000 years later. Even now, more than 100 years later, not all Americans are truly free, though they are legally free. Will people 3,000 years from now look upon Americans also as socially primitive?

Jewish laws regulating slavery were more humane than those of their pagan neighbors. Furthermore, every person was considered God's friend, not God's slave as in Babylonian and other religions; therefore, all practices such as mutilating the body in religious rites were forbidden. Forbidden also was human sacrifice, including the burning of babies, a practice common in neighboring countries. The dignity of women was protected in family laws, and the rights of children were protected.

2. True morality

For the Jewish people, being a good person meant a great deal more than merely conforming to a social code. It meant even more than obeying society's laws in order to be fair to one's fellow humans. It included these things but went much deeper. It penetrated to the ultimate motive for these things: faithfulness to God. Every Jewish person's very existence was founded upon the Covenant with Yahweh. The ultimate dignity of a person is that God and he or she are partners in a lifelong conversation and a lifelong friendship. God had chosen His people and they had accepted Him, and both sides had sworn to be faithful.

The binding on of a leather box containing scriptural passages worn by Jewish men for morning weekday prayers.

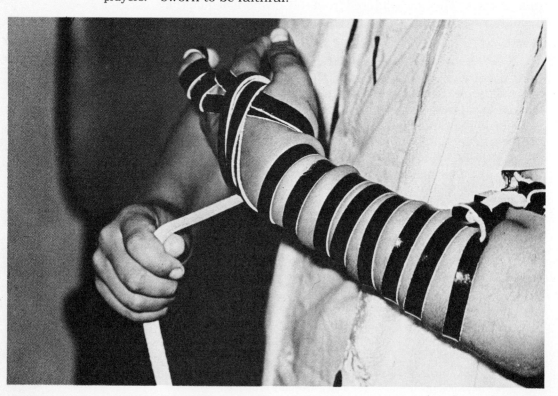

The World's Living Religions

The social code which guided each Jew to be fair to his fellow Jew was seen as God's plan for creating the People which was His chosen family. Thus, observance of the Torah was more than a new social convention or necessity or convenience. It was the way God wanted the Israelites to live. Hence, devout Israelites observed the Torah because this was their way of being *faithful* to God, Who was faithful to them. They observed the law with joy because the law was God's will for them.

The ultimate core of morality for the Jewish people was much deeper than mere external conformity to laws. The core of morality was as deep as the deepest heart of man—his capacity for personal fidelity to another person. Respect for the Person of God made the Jewish people extra sensitive to the person of their neighbor. Under the leadership of the prophets, the Israelites came to understand over the centuries that their original Covenant to Yahweh in the desert implied an obligation to become better and better motivated, not only fair to their fellow Jews but positively loving in their regard. The Jewish people developed a legal system designed to protect the poor, to promote justice, to extend God's benign influence from one person to another. When rulers or people fell away from these ideals, prophets rose up to warn them to change their ways lest they be destroyed; for God had intended them to be His People, a shining example of humanity for the enlightenment of the world—"the light of the nations."

3. Sin

Every religion has within it some form of explanation for the mysterious sense of guilt which every person experiences. What is evil, and how did it come into the world? What makes people commit sin, and how can people overcome the evil in themselves?

a. The nature of sin. Many pagan religions show in their myths an attempt to shrug off the problem, to put the blame for evil on something outside people. In effect they say, "Well, people are just that way—that's the way the gods made them." In the Babylonian myth of Marduk, for example, people were made from the blood of the corpse of a bad god—to imply that sin is "in people's blood"; evil was present in the very making of the universe.

The Jewish people, however, tell a different story. Since they felt that the heart of humankind, the essence of humanity, lies in a capacity for personal faithfulness, they interpreted sin as personal unfaithfulness: breaking the Covenant with Yahweh.

In the book of Genesis, chapters 2 and 3, a parable about the first man and woman is told. Yahweh creates a human statue out of clay[6] "and breathes the breath of life into him; from the man's rib he fashions a woman."[7] There is no evil built into them; however, faced with temptation (in the form of a serpent), the man and woman freely decide to break God's law.

b. Redemption from sin. In a world where people are created evil in their nature, there can be no redemption from sin; the best that can be hoped is to "buy off" the gods through magic or human sacrifices.

In the world as the Jewish people saw it, where God created everything good and wants to fashion His People as a community in His own image and likeness, God is always trying to "buy back" *(re-deem)* His people from their freely committed sins and the consequences of their sins. *God is faithful to the Covenant, even when people are not.*

The prophets helped the Israelites to understand that, just as God has rescued His people from Egyptian slavery in the beginning, so He was always ready to rescue them from any slavery or punishment or consequences that their sins had brought upon them if they would allow Him to rescue them from sin itself. Returning to the Law of God was always for them a response to the call of God to do so; the initiative was always God's, the response was people's.

4. Destiny

The Jewish people brought a unique notion of people's destiny into the world. For them, history was forward-looking. If contemporary societies (whether Jews, Christians, Communists, or secular humanists) have any notion of progress in the world, if hope for a better world in the future is something we can never completely lose, it is because we have

---

6. The Book of Genesis does not represent peoples as connected with the evolutionary process, simply because the ancient authors did not know anything about evolution. In the primitive scientific view, every species had always been the way it was from the beginning; each species was a direct creation of the gods (or for the Hebrews, a direct creation of Yahweh). Modern science has not established whether or not the human race actually descended from a single pair, or from a large community, or even from several communities or pairs which evolved separately in different parts of the world from different subhuman species. The Bible does not settle this scientific question, for the Adam and Eve story is a parable based upon primitive scientific assumptions.

7. In this feature of the parable we see the enlightened Jewish notion of the dignity of women—she is equal to man, not inferior to him. In a world where women were often treated with disrespect as inferior creatures, the Jewish myth portrays her as created, not from an inferior substance, but from the very substance of man.

inherited this concept from the Jews. All other religions before and alongside the Jewish religion looked back to the past as the "Golden Age"; the gods had created the world in the past and now everything was settled. Many of those religions (and many Eastern religions even today) conceive of history as an eternal cycle continually repeating itself. Only the Jewish God Yahweh is continually creating. He is creating His People, the People of God.

Beginning with their escape from Egypt, continuing with their conquest of the Promised Land and their constant rescue from enemy capture and re-creation after exile, the Jewish people came to depend upon Yahweh to be continually at work, re-creating the Covenant People.

The prophets taught them to long for the day when sin would be conquered, when people would love each other, when God would bring His community to such great perfection that it would be the light of the world and finally all nations would "beat their swords into plowshares" (Isaiah 2:4) and live in peace and harmony. This "Golden Age" is today called the *Messianic Age*[8] because at its center would be a kingly ruler of such perfection that he would be an ideal person to rule an ideal people.

Today's Jewish people still long for the Messianic Age, although they interpret it divergently. Orthodox and Conservative Jews believe the Messiah will come to inaugurate the Kingdom of God at the end of time. Reform Jews believe that no one person, but all people, will be God's anointed community at the end of time. All religious Jews believe that, in the end, all people will accept God's name. Their *Aleuu* prayer reads:

We, therefore, hope in you, O Lord our God, that we shall soon see the triumph of your might, that idolatry shall be removed from the earth, and false gods shall be utterly destroyed. Then will the world be a true kingdom of God, when all mankind will invoke Your name and all the earth's wicked will return to You. Then all the inhabitants of the world will surely know that to You every knee must bend, every tongue must pledge loyalty. Before You, O Lord, let them bow in worship; let them give honor to Your glory. May they all accept the rule of Your kingdom. May you reign over them soon through all time. Sovereignty is Yours in glory, now and forever. So is it written in Your Torah: The Lord shall reign for ever and ever. Such

8. From the Hebrew word *Messiah*, meaning "anointed one" (because Jewish kings were anointed with oil during the coronation ceremony). In Jewish tradition, the Messiah will be a human being who comes to reinstate Jewish political sovereignty by throwing over the yoke of oppressors.

is the assurance uttered by the prophet: "The Lord shall be King over all the earth; that day the Lord shall be One and His name one."[9]

Arising out of this belief in a *future* Golden Age is the Jewish notion of the resurrection of the dead. All early religions believed in some kind of "soul-land" where departed spirits go. But since there is for them no future Golden Age on earth, there is no particular reason for the dead to return. However, the Jewish insight that God is continually at work perfecting His creation through His people made them uncomfortable with the notion that the departed dead are forever removed from this world. If God takes this world so seriously that He is continually resurrecting His chosen community throughout history, then does He not take this world seriously enough to resurrect each individual member of the community at the end of history? *Such was the unconscious principle that brought the hope for bodily resurrection into Jewish consciousness*[10] *during the centuries immediately preceding the Common Era.*[11]

Jewish Expressions of Their Relationship to God

All religions have some form of ritual called *worship*, whereby people stand before the face of reality itself and act out what it means to be human and what kind of relationship they have with their reality.

If people think reality is a group of natural forces who "have it in for them" because they are an evil creation made from the corpse of bad gods, then people try to "buy off" the forces, for example, by sacrificing human babies or the most perfectly formed young man or young woman.

On the other hand, if people think reality is the creation of One Loving Person who is creating a people of loving concern in His image and likeness, then people open themselves to the creative activity of God.

Because the Jews experienced God as a person, their primary symbol for relating to Him was not a "natural"

9. Excerpt from the *Weekday Prayer Book,* © 1961 by The Rabbinical Assembly of America. Reprinted by permission.

10. Today Orthodox and Conservative Jews still believe in the resurrection of the body; Reform Jews do not, but they do believe in immortality.

11. The Jewish people refer to B.C. and A.D. as "Before the Common Era" and the "Common Era." For this they use the initials: B.C.E. and C.E.

Mount Carmel

symbol such as a bear or the sun, but a "personal" symbol—the Word. Where other gods created the hard way (through winning a battle), Yahweh created just by giving the *Word:* "Let there be light . . . Let the land and water separate themselves . . . ." (See Genesis 1.)

When God created His Chosen People, He did so by His *Word* of Torah. When God wished to re-create His people after each of their fallings-away, He spoke His *word* to them through the prophets. And the fundamental relationship, the Covenant, was itself a *word* of promise between God and His people.

Thus it is that, although the Jewish people had many forms of worshipful expression (including the sacrifice of animals), the one they put most emphasis on, the one that increased in importance while others evolved out of existence, and the heritage that they have passed to the rest of the world, involved *worship through word.*

Their special worship services, when each Jewish person turns his attention directly to Yahweh, were (and are now) conducted principally in their synagogues.[12] Jewish synagogue services are based on the principle that prayer is not a monologue: a person talking to God. It is a dialogue: God talking to people and people responding. There is a rhythm,

12. The Jewish people had only one temple—in Jerusalem—where God "resided." All other Jewish worship services were held in special buildings or places where the people could gather for worship and instruction. The word *synagogue* comes from the Greek word for "gathering of people."

and an alternating, between reading the Word of God (excerpts from the Bible) and responding to that Word in prayers, sacred hymns, preaching and explanation, and exhortation. For the Jewish people, worship is not a passive watching; it is an active correspondence with God.

Because worship is a dialogue for the Jewish people, God has to speak to them. They believe He does so through His Word, the Bible. *It is because of this usage that the Bible came to be considered God's Word.* Its core is the books of the Torah, the first five books of the Hebrew Bible.

Beginning at the time of Moses, the people were reminded that they had been saved through the mighty acts of God. They responded with prayers and hymns of thanksgiving. After the time of Moses, these same exploits were read to the people in ritual services, and they responded with promises of fidelity to God, just as their ancestors had done. As centuries rolled on, other collections of books were added to the original. Some contained history, some contained collections of songs and hymns that came down from their forbears. Some were created to fit special services, and some books contained the preaching of the prophets.

These were not all considered one collection of equal value until the Babylonian Captivity (587–536 B.C.), when the Jewish population was defeated and deported to Babylon.[13] There, in the absence of temple worship, it was only the Torah and the traditions surrounding it that kept the people together. Synagogue services had their roots in the Sabbath meetings of this time when these various writings, as well as the Torah, were read and explained to the people as God's half of the dialogue and they responded with their sacred hymns. The various books (actually in scroll form) which were most commonly used in this way became standard and were gradually considered as much God's Word as the Torah was. Thus, it became possible to conceive of them as one collection, and to codify them into the Hebrew Scriptures.

It is impossible to measure the influence of the Jewish religion upon the Western world. From its beginnings in polytheistic times, through its evolution toward unity, to its dedicated loyalty today to the One God who has chosen this People to be His light to the world, the Jewish religion is a remarkable monument to people's ability to respond to the call of that mysterious One behind all of reality and, in responding, to be transformed.

13. Some material was added to this collection probably in the second century of the Common Era. Among these are Ecclesiastes and the Song of Songs.

The World's Living Religions

Jewish Scriptures as an Expression of the Jewish Relationship with God

As we mentioned earlier, once a religion began to take some kind of form and its stories of the origin of the world and of the gods became a part of the folklore of a people, a body of such materials (stories, poetry, song, and myth) became standard and formed a kind of sacred lore associated with religious ceremonies. At first these stories were handed down from generation to generation by word of mouth. Later, when writing became a part of the culture of a people, this body of material was codified and written down and became known as a people's scripture, or sacred writing.

The Jewish Scriptures have such a history. Their stories of the origin of the world and of their ancestors were part of the folklore of the Jews long before they became a part of their sacred writing. They took on a more or less codified and standard form, as we said above, about 550 B.C. when many of the Jewish leaders were in exile in Babylonia. At that time, the sacred literature was divided into three parts: The Law, The Prophets, and The Writings.

The Law consists of the five "books of Moses": Genesis, Exodus, Leviticus, Numbers, and Deuteronomy. These books, called, the Torah, are the principal, or most important, part of the Hebrew Scriptures, or the Bible.

Genesis contains the story of creation (Adam, Eve, Noah, the Flood, and so forth) and the stories of the Jewish patriarchs, the famous ancestors of the Jewish people (Abraham, Isaac, Jacob, and others). Exodus is the story of the escape from slavery in Egypt and of the Covenant made with Yahweh (and contains the Ten Commandments). Leviticus is a book about the worship of the Jews and about their priesthood. Numbers is a book about the experiences of the Jews in the desert. It contains a listing of the people who made the escape from Egypt. Deuteronomy contains a second accounting of the Law proclaimed on Mt. Sinai and an explanation of the Law.

The Prophets, as the name indicates, contains the activities and the words of the prophets. It is divided into two parts: the "former" prophets (often referred to as the Judges and the Kings of Israel, Saul, David, and Solomon) and the "latter" prophets (the ones who passed judgment on Israel and reminded them of their promises to God, such as Isaiah, Jeremiah, Ezekiel, and so forth). The Writings contain all the other material of the Jewish Scriptures, like the Psalms, the Proverbs, the Chronicles, Job, and the Festival Scrolls.

In all, the Jewish Bible contains twenty-four books, all of which were (and are) referred to as "the books of the law," "the holy books," or simply, "the books." They not only occupy a special and sacred place in Jewish history and worship, expressing the relationship of the Jewish people with their God. They also form the first part of the Christian Bible (called "the Old Testament") and are considered to be among the great pieces of writing in world literature.

Most Jews believe that their Bible is inspired. That is, they believe that God inspired the writers to write what He wanted them to write so that His people would know His will. Most Jews consider the Bible as God's book—a book sent by God through His holy men containing a message for His people.

If the Exodus and the Sinai Covenant "made" the Jewish people a religious nation, the Bible has kept them so. It has played a major role in making the Jewish people what they are, and has been a major force in shaping the culture of Western civilization.

The Talmud

One cannot speak of the Jewish Scriptures and/or the Law without speaking of the Talmud and the Mishnah, or as it is sometimes called, the Mishna-Talmud.[14]

The Talmud is a collection of Jewish law and traditions consisting of the *Mishnah* and the *Gemara.* The Mishnah is a collection of oral laws handed down by word of mouth made by a Rabbi Judah ha-Nisi around A.D. 200. The Gemara is a collection of commentaries on the Mishnah. There are two principle editions of the Talmud. The first is the Palestine edition put together by the rabbinical schools in Palestine about A.D. 400. The second, larger and more definitive, was put together by the rabbinical schools in Babylon about A.D. 500.

The Talmud is generally described as an interpretation of the Pentateuch and a divinely revealed guide of morals and conduct. It developed as a collection of materials used to settle ticklish problems concerning the obligations imposed on Jews by the Law.

The Talmud, then, is a compilation of Jewish doctrine and discipline based and built on the Law. It is considered as having equal value and authority in Jewish life with the Law and is subject to the same discussion and interpretation. Although the Torah is, as we said, often used to refer to the Law, or the first five books of the Jewish Bible, it is widely used to mean the whole body of Jewish law contained in the Pentateuch and the Talmud.

Jewish Feasts and Celebrations as an Expression of the Jewish Relationship with God

The nature of Jewish religious awareness and their religious philosophy and spirit are best understood through their religious services, feasts, and celebrations. The general nature of Jewish synagogue services is described on page 93;

---

14. *Talmud* comes from the Aramaic word meaning "teaching." *Mishnah* is an Aramaic word meaning "oral teaching." Aramaic was the common language of the Jews both before and after the time of Jesus.

A Jewish mother praying for her family at the beginning of Sabbath

some of their major feasts and important religious observances are described below.[15]

The Jewish Sabbath

The Jewish people have been referred to as the "people of the Sabbath." The makers of the Talmud considered the observance of the Sabbath as the very foundation of the Jewish faith. For six days a man labors and does all that he has to do; the seventh he keeps holy. On that day he remembers why he works, he recollects who he is, and he concentrates upon the Creator who made him and all that is, in order that he may be made holy. Thus made new, refreshed, and strengthened, he returns to the duties of the week.

It has been said that "More than Israel has kept the Sabbath, it is the Sabbath that has kept Israel," and this statement is hardly an

15. Reprinted from Lee A. Belford, *Introduction to Judaism* (New York: Association Press, 1961), pp. 85–87 and 104–114. Used by permission.

The World's Living Religions

exaggeration, because the Sabbath has received so much emphasis through the centuries that all other days find their meaning in this one day. The poets personified the Sabbath and referred to it as a "lovely bride," "charming princess," and "gracious queen." By tradition the home is especially tidied and everyone bathed and dressed in his finest clothes to welcome "her."

The Sabbath officially starts at sundown on Friday and ends at sundown on Saturday. Normally, the mother lights two candles shortly before the beginning of the Sabbath, concluding with the blessing: "Blessed art Thou, O Lord, our God, King of the universe, who has sanctified us with His commandments, and commanded us to kindle the Sabbath light." She then usually adds another prayer for the members of her household.

When the father—with or without his family—returns from the synagogue, the evening meal is ready to begin. The father blesses the wine, the two loaves of twisted white bread called "hallah" which are invariably a part of the meal, and the children. There is a meal after the synagogue service on Saturday morning and an important meal to bring the Sabbath to a close. At the latter there is not only a benediction of the wine but a blessing of spices kept in a special box for the occasion. Often a special twisted candle is lit at the conclusion of the Sabbath, as a farewell to the "princess" until the next week.

The outsider frequently thinks of Sabbath observance as a grim experience, but its four notes are holiness, joy, honor, and rest. Thirty-nine types of work are forbidden in the Bible, but the amplification of these is legion. An Orthodox Jew does not carry money, a fountain pen or pencil, nor any other reminders of his daily pursuits. He avoids all contact with tools, fuel, or matches. He is limited in the distance he walks and is forbidden to travel unless he is on a long sea voyage. However, all the regulations pertaining to the Sabbath must be disregarded if a human life is at stake.

Rosh Hashana

Rosh Hashana ushers in the new year with the blowing of the shophar, a ram's horn, just as it did in biblical times. It also begins a ten-day period of penitence, which is concluded with Yom Kippur, the Day of Atonement. Rosh Hashana is also called the Day of Memorial or the Day of Judgment because, figuratively, the books of heaven are opened, and the deeds of every person are inscribed by the recording angels and signed by the soul of the individual. After the synagogue service on the first night it is customary to extend the greeting, "May a good year be inscribed for you."

The penitential season is for the reaffirmation of faith, for self-examination, and for prayers for forgiveness. The theme is echoed in the words of Hosea, "Return, O Israel, to the Lord Thy God." Not only is a person to repent his sins with the resolve not to commit the same sins again, but he must make amends wherever possible. The Rabbis say that, although the Lord forgives man his sins against heaven if he is truly penitent, sins against one's fellow men can be atoned for only by actual steps to repair the damage. Therefore every effort must be made to compensate those upon whom injuries have been inflicted, to apologize for slander, and to right all other wrongs in whatever way possible.

Yom Kippur

Yom Kippur is the climax of the solemn season, the holiest day of the year. Beginning at sundown, as is customary with all observances, there is a period of solemn fast, prayer, and meditation. Some men even spend the night in the synagogue in order that their prayers may not be interrupted. Traditional Jews do not wear leather shoes on this day, and no food or drink is taken for the entire period.

The most essential element is confession, repeated often, where all present ask for pardon for their sins and pray for God's mercy, not on the assumption that they deserve it, but out of faith that God, in his compassion, is far more eager to forgive than to punish. As part of the biblical justification, there is the following

A rabbi blowing a note on the Shofar, the ram's horn, during the Rosh Hashonah

The World's Living Religions

verse: ". . . you shall afflict yourselves, and shall do no work, either the native or the stranger who sojourns among you; for on this day shall atonement be made for you, to cleanse you; from all your sins you shall be clean before the Lord" (Leviticus 16:29–30). In the most ancient part of the service the congregation prays that God may hasten the time when all the people of the earth will be brothers and wickedness will pass away like smoke in the sky.

As a part of the Yom Kippur service, the Kol Nidre is chanted to a haunting melody. The hymn, which is really a prayer asking for absolution from oaths of a religious nature made either hastily or unwillingly, is Talmudic in origin and is related to the legal formula by which oaths might be abrogated under jurisdiction of the court. It received particular importance in medieval times, when some Jews renounced their faith and became titular Christians or Muslims under duress. As a part of the service, there is a memorial for the departed, with the petition that their good examples may be followed. The service is concluded with the blowing of the shophar once again.

The selection of a palm branch for the ceremonies of the "Feast of Tabernacles"

Sukkoth

Sukkoth is a harvest festival similar to the American Thanksgiving and is called the "Festival of Ingathering," but its most popular name is the "Feast of Booths" or "Tabernacles," commemorating the wilderness wanderings when the Israelites followed Moses to the promised land, a time when no more substantial dwellings than booths can be built.

Sukkoth is a very joyful holiday, which begins five days after Yom Kippur and lasts for nine days. A little hut or booth is built with an open roof of branches or leaves, within which the family eats its meals and spends as much time as possible. In New York, booths are frequently built on the flat roofs of apartment buildings, but in many instances the family is forced to settle for a community booth built in or alongside a synagogue.

Fall fruits and vegetables, flowers, and branches, are used to decorate the booths to symbolize the season. As a part of the synagogue ceremony, a palm branch is held in one hand, along with sprigs of myrtle and willow, while a citron, a type of lime, is held in the other, in response to the biblical injunction, "And you shall take on the first day the fruit of goodly trees, branches of palm trees, and boughs of leafy trees, and willows of the brook; and you shall rejoice before the Lord your God seven days" (Leviticus 23:40). These symbols are waved in all directions to show that God, who gives the fruits of nature, is found on every side.

The eighth day of the thanksgiving season is marked by a minor festival, during which prayers are said for rain and good crops in the coming year—and although it might be raining torrents at the

time, the prayers for rain are said nevertheless, because the reference is especially to the Holy Land, where rain is always important.

This holiday is a reminder that God is the Lord of nature and the Lord of history. Ethically, it suggests that the accumulation of physical possessions is no substitute for a faith in God who provides for men according to their need.

Hanukkah

Hanukkah, the "Feast of Dedication," like many other festivals, emphasizes the achievement of freedom. Antiochus Epiphanes desecrated the Temple in 168 B.C. by erecting pagan idols there and ordering the Jews to bow down and worship them, a sacrilege that led to the Maccabean revolt and religious independence. At the first opportunity the Temple was cleansed so that services could be resumed. Pure olive oil was needed for the kindling of the lamp that was to burn continuously, but only one vial was found and it contained enough oil for just one day. But miraculously the oil lasted for eight days, until fresh oil could be prepared by the priests.

Hanukkah is celebrated each December, occasionally coinciding with Christmas. On the first day of Hanukkah one candle is lit, and another added each day for the full eight days. The concern with lighting the candles in order until the full candelabra is glowing has lead to the occasion's being called also the "Feast of Lights." The emphases of the season are religious freedom and loyalty.

Hanukkah is another holiday in which the children rejoice, and games have been played on this occasion for centuries. Even gambling is permitted, although the prizes are traditionally petty, since gambling for money or high stakes is frowned upon. The dreydel, a four-sided top with Hebrew letters on each side, is used for a traditional game of chance. The letters stand for the Hebrew words which mean a "great miracle happened there."

Purim

Purim, the "Feast of Lots," tells the story of the defeat of a tyrant as it commemorates the familiar biblical story of Esther. Haman, who was powerful in the court of the Persian king, plotted to obliterate the Jews, and he cast lots to determine the most favorable time for the executions—which gives the festival its name. Esther, famous for her beauty, had gained the affection of the king. Through her cousin, Mordecai, she heard of Haman's plot; with great daring she went to see the king and had the tables turned, so that Haman was hanged on the high gallows he had erected for another purpose.

Like Hanukkah, this feast is not required by the Bible. It is a particularly gay time for children. The Book of Esther is read in the

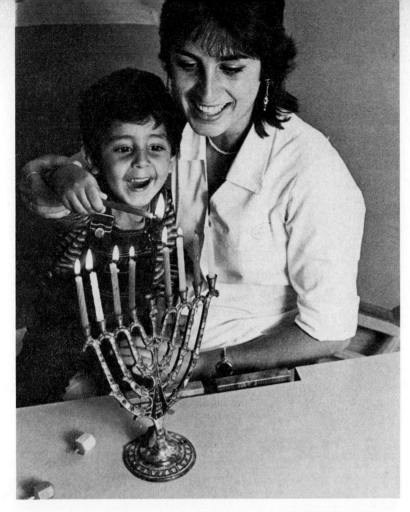

synagogue, and whenever Haman's name is mentioned the children are encouraged to hiss, stamp their feet, clap, or use noisemakers to blot out his name. It is a time for carnivals, masquerade parties, dances, and other forms of entertainment. Non-Jewish friends look forward to invitations to participate in the festivities. It is also a time for the exchange of gifts and, as is the case with so many of the festivals, a time to give charity to those in need. The gift of charity has its roots in the biblical tax of one-half shekel which was levied against all Jewish men for the maintenance of the Temple. Now that it can no longer be given to the Temple, it is given to some other worthy cause.

Purim comes in February or March. It might be noted that just before Purim there is a fast to commemorate Esther's three-day fast prior to her appearance before the king. Then, as is usual with Jewish holidays, certain foods are associated with the day itself, the chief one in this instance being the "hamantashen," a delicious three-cornered pastry filled with jam or poppy seeds.

Pesah

Pesah, or Passover, comes in the spring and is of particular
interest to Christians because of its association with the Last
Supper. It has its roots in a spring agricultural festival, but it also
points back to the escape from Egypt. Each family of the Israelites
killed a male lamb without blemish and put some of the blood on the
doorposts and lintel so that when the last of the plagues, the death
of the firstborn, afflicted the Egyptians, the houses of the Israelites
would be passed over (Exodus 12:5–13).

The Israelites left Egypt in such a hurry that they could not
wait for the bread to rise, so they baked wafers of unleavened
bread, or *matzoth,* to carry with them. Originally the *matzoth* were
round, shaped like a wheel, from which the Christians adapted the
conventional communion wafers of unleavened bread; but later,
Jews began to make *matzoth* in squares. This is the only kind of
bread that may be eaten throughout Passover, because no foods
made with yeast, baking powder, or baking soda may be eaten at
all. In Orthodox homes special dishes and utensils are used
throughout the Passover season to avoid possible contamination
from food that has been "leavened."

Passover begins with a special dinner called a Seder, which
means order. The order is found in the Haggadah, a word which
means "telling," from the biblical injunction: "And you shall tell your
son on that day, 'It is because of what the Lord did for me when I

The World's Living Religions

came out of Egypt' '' (Exodus 13:8). Near the beginning of the service, the youngest son asks four questions of his father, the first being "Why is this night different from all other nights?" The father then relates the story of the hasty departure from Egypt.

The food includes *matzoth;* unseasoned horseradish, which represents the bitterness of Egyptian slavery; a dish of chopped apples mixed with nuts, cinnamon, and wine, representing the mortar with which Jews were forced to make bricks in Egypt; a shankbone of lamb, as a reminder of the paschal, or Passover, lamb which was offered as a sacrifice in the Temple; a roasted egg, symbolic of the freewill offering that accompanied the sacrifice of the paschal lamb; vegetables such as parsley or radish, to suggest life, hope, and redemption; and salt water (in which to dip the vegetables), symbolic of the tears so often shed.

At the Seder each individual partakes of four cups of wine, two before the meal—which is served halfway through the reading of the Haggadah—and two after the meal. They symbolize the four different phrases in which the redemption of Israel is announced in the Book of Exodus.

A special goblet of wine is poured for the prophet Elijah who, according to traditional beliefs, will foretell the coming of the Messiah. During the service the cup is raised, indicating that Elijah is welcome, and the door is opened for a few minutes as a further symbol of the welcome extended to him.

As may have been inferred, the Passover Seder is primarily a family service; but it is also a time of great hospitality, and frequently Gentile friends are invited to participate.

Shavuoth

Shavuoth, or the "Feast of Weeks," is better known to non-Jews as Pentecost, the Greek word which indicates that it comes on the fiftieth day after Passover. Originally it was a spring harvest celebration, when offerings of the new grain and fruit crops were made in Temple ceremonies; but it gained added significance as the birthday of the Jewish religion, for it is believed that on this date Moses received the Ten Commandments on Mount Sinai. Although the Eastern Orthodox churches still set their date for Easter according to the date of the Jewish Passover, the western Christian and Jewish calendars no longer coincide, and the Christian Pentecost is counted from the day of Easter according to the western church calendar.

Shavuoth is now observed in Reform Judaism as a day for holding confirmation ceremonies, when boys and girls renew the promises of their forefathers to obey the Ten Commandments and other teachings of the Jewish religion. Because of the nature of Reform Judaism, much of the emphasis is upon God's revelation and the importance of making the principles a part of one's life.

Selections from the Hebrew Scriptures

The Lord said to Abram, "Leave your native land, your relatives, and your father's home and go to a country that I am going to show you. I will give you many descendants, and they will become a great nation. I will bless you and make your name famous, so that you will be a blessing.

I will bless those who bless you,
But I will curse those who curse you.
And through you I will bless all
    nations."

When Abram was seventy-five years old, he started out from Haran, as the Lord had told him to do; and Lot went with him. Abram took his wife Sarai . . . and they started out for the land of Canaan. When they arrived in Canaan, Abram traveled through the land until he came to the sacred tree of Moreh, the holy place at Shechem. . . .

The Lord appeared to Abram and said to him, "This is the country that I am going to give to your descendants."

—Genesis 12: 1–7

The Lord said to me, "I chose you before I gave you life, and before you were born I selected you to be a prophet to the nations." I answered, "Sovereign Lord, I don't know how to speak; I am too young." But the Lord said to me, "Do not say that you are too young, but go to the people I send you to, and tell them everything I command you to say. Do not be afraid of them, for I will be with you to protect you. I, the Lord, have spoken!"

. . . The Lord told me to proclaim this message to everyone in Jerusalem.

"I remember how faithful you were when you were young, how you loved me when we were first married; you followed me through the desert, through the land that had not been planted. Israel, you belonged to me alone; you were my sacred possession. I sent suffering and disaster on everyone who hurt you. I, the Lord, have spoken."

—Jeremiah 1:4–8, 2:1–3

A good reputation is better than expensive perfume; and the day you die is better than the day you were born.

Sorrow is better than laughter; it may sadden your face, but it sharpens your understanding.

It is better to have wise people reprimand you than to have stupid people sing your praises.

When a wise man cheats someone, he is acting like a fool. If you take a bride, you ruin your character.

Keep your temper under control; it is foolish to harbor a grudge.

Wisdom does more for a person than ten rulers can do for a city.

—Ecclesiastes 7: 1,3,5,7,9,19

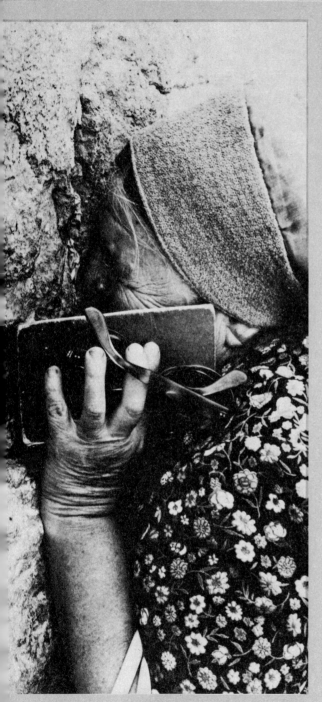

The people of Israel left Rephidim, and on the first day of the third month after they had left Egypt they came to the desert of Sinai. There they set up camp at the foot of Mt. Sinai, and Moses went up the mountain to meet with God. The Lord called to him from the mountain and told him to say to the Israelites, Jacob's descendants: "You saw what I, the Lord, did to the Egyptians and how I carried you as an eagle carries her young on her wings, and brought you here to me. Now, if you will obey me and keep my covenant, you will be my own people. The whole earth is mine, but you will be my chosen people, a people dedicated to me alone, and you will serve me as priests." So Moses went down and called the leaders of the people together and told them everything that the Lord had commanded him. Then all the people answered together, "We will do everything that the Lord has said," and Moses reported this to the Lord.

—Exodus 19: 1–8

Praise the Lord, my soul!
   All my being praise his holy name!
Praise the LORD, my soul,
   and do not forget how kind he is.
He forgives all my sins
   and heals all my diseases.
He keeps me from the grave
   and blesses me with love and mercy.
He fills my life with good things,
    so that I stay young and strong like an
      eagle.

—Psalm 103:1–5

Summary

1. Jewish faith is based on a covenanted relationship with the God of the Jewish people.

2. Judaism was born in the Sinai desert during the flight of the Israelites from slavery in Egypt.

3. The Jewish belief in one God is the cornerstone of all succeeding religious faiths of Western civilization.

4. Jewish religious faith is expressed in Jewish life whose heart and soul is the Law as presented in the Talmud.

5. Jews recall their history and their faith in the celebration of their religious feasts.

For Review

1. The human societies of the world are divided, generally, into three categories. What are these categories and what seems to differentiate them from each other?

2. What are the three principal Western religions? What distinguishes them, generally, from ancient religions?

3. What is the heart of Judaism?

4. Can you describe in general terms the differences between Jewish religious awareness and the religious awareness of the people among whom they lived? To what do you attribute this difference?

5. What is the basic difference between Jewish history recorded in the Bible and the secular history of the time? Is Jewish history "real"? why? why not?

6. How did the Jewish understanding of God arise because of their history? To whom did the Jewish people ascribe their successful escape from Egypt: Moses or God? How does this differ from the history of other peoples of the time?

7. If the acts of God were revealed in Jewish history, what function does the Bible play in revelation?

8. Describe how the understanding of God's nature developed as Judaism evolved.

9. How have the Jewish people influenced the thinking of others concerning the future?

10. Be sure that you can define Western civilization, Eastern civilization, Yahweh, Covenant, Exodus, Genesis, Orthodox, Conservative, Reform (as applied to Judaism), Sabbath, Passover, prophet.

For Discussion

1. Discuss the significance of the Jewish religious experience on people's understanding of God. Has it helped you better understand who God can be for you? In an open forum, exchange ideas about God with your classmates.

2. Discuss how the Jewish Scriptures can be God's Word to people. Do you think they are? why? why not?

3. Viktor Frankl, world-renowned psychiatrist and an inmate of the infamous Nazi concentration camps for Jews, has written: "After all, man is that being who has invented the gas chambers of Auschwitz; however, he is also that being who has entered those gas chambers upright, with the Lord's Prayer or the *Shema Yisrael* on his lips." What does this tell you about people's religious sense and the Jewish faith in God?

For Research

1. Prepare a chronological chart of the development of the Jewish religion.

2. Prepare a report on the geography, agriculture, and climate of Palestine.

3. Prepare a report on The Star of David and the Menorah.

Words You Should Know

If there are any words given below that you are not familiar with, look them up in the Word List at the back of the book.

Adonai	inspired	polytheism
angel	Messianic Age	symbol
codify	nuances	synagogue
conservative	orthodox	Talmud
deductive	patriarchs	Torah
inductive		

chapter 5

Christianity

Judaism was conceived in the events associated with the lives of the patriarchs and Moses and the experience of the people in Egypt and the desert. It was born in the covenant made with God on Mt. Sinai. Christianity was conceived in the appearance of Jesus and was born when certain followers of his said they experienced the Divine Presence at Pentecost, fifty days after they said they experienced him alive after his death by crucifixion.

Christianity can only be understood in terms of that Pentecost experience—as this experience is told by those involved in it. This extraordinary experience is reported by Luke, a physician, the chronicler of the first days of the followers of Jesus. In his Acts of the Apostles he wrote:

When the day of Pentecost[1] came it found them [the disciples] gathered in one place. Suddenly, from up in the sky there came a noise like a strong, driving wind which was heard all through the house where they were seated. Tongues as of fire appeared, which parted and came to rest on each of them. All were filled with the Holy Spirit. . . .

Staying in Jerusalem at the time were devout Jews from every nation under heaven. These heard the sound, and assembled in a large crowd. They were much confused because each one heard these men speaking his own language. The whole occurrence astonished them. They asked in utter amazement, "Are not all of these men who are speaking Galileans? How is it that each of us hears them in his native tongue?" . . . They were dumbfounded, and could make nothing at all of what had happened. "What does this mean?" they asked of one another, while a few remarked with a sneer, "They have had too much new wine!"

Peter stood up with the Eleven, raised his voice, and addressed them: "You who are Jews, indeed all of you staying in Jerusalem! Listen to what I have to say. You must realize that these men are not drunk, as you seem to think. It is only nine in the

1. The Jewish festival of *Shavuoth*, commemorating the giving of the Ten Commandments by God to Moses. (See page 105.)

Opposite page—View of the Old City Jerusalem from Dominus Flauus Church on the Mount of Olives

morning! No, it is what Joel the prophet spoke of: *'It shall come to pass in the last days, says God, that I will pour out a portion of my spirit on all mankind. Your sons and daughters shall prophesy, your young men shall see visions and your old men shall dream dreams. Yes, even on my servants and handmaids I will pour out a portion of my spirit. . . .*

"Men of Israel, listen to me. Jesus the Nazorean was a man whom God sent to you with miracles, wonders, and signs as his credentials. These God worked through him in our midst, as you well know. He was delivered up by the set purpose and plan of God; you even made use of pagans to crucify and kill him. God freed him from death's bitter pangs, however, and raised him up again, for it was impossible that death should keep its hold on him. . . . This is the Jesus God has raised up, and we are his witnesses. Exalted at God's right hand, he first received the promised Holy Spirit from the Father, then poured this Spirit out on us. This is what you now see and hear. . . . Therefore let the whole house of Israel know beyond any doubt that God has made both Lord and Messiah this Jesus whom you crucified."

When they heard this, they were deeply shaken. They asked Peter and the other apostles, "What are we to do, brothers?" Peter answered: "You must reform and be baptized, each one of you, in the name of Jesus Christ, that your sins may be forgiven; then you will receive the gift of the Holy Spirit. It was to you and your children that the promise was made, and to all those still far off whom the Lord our God calls.

—Acts of the Apostles 2:1–39

This account reveals four things about the origins of Christianity and tells what a Christian is:

1. **The followers of Jesus experienced him alive after he had been put to death.** This they described as his resurrection. (See the Gospel according to Matthew 28, the Gospel according to Mark 16, the Gospel according to Luke 24, and the Gospel according to John 21.)

2. **The experience of Pentecost began to make clear to the followers of Jesus who he really was.** This they spoke about and explained. The record is contained in what is known as the New Testament section of the Christian Bible.

3. **A Christian is a person who believes what the apostles said about Jesus, is baptized in his name, and follows the way of life prescribed by Jesus.**[2]

4. **Christianity did not begin as a religion separate from Judaism.** It began as a plea to the Jewish people among

God's Self-Revelation as Christians See It

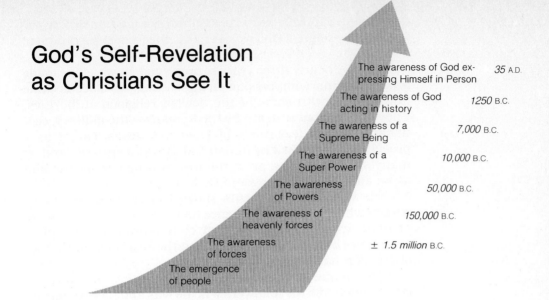

The awareness of God expressing Himself in Person	35 A.D.
The awareness of God acting in history	1250 B.C.
The awareness of a Supreme Being	7,000 B.C.
The awareness of a Super Power	10,000 B.C.
The awareness of Powers	50,000 B.C.
The awareness of heavenly forces	150,000 B.C.
The awareness of forces	± 1.5 million B.C.
The emergence of people	

whom Jesus had lived to accept him as the promised Jewish Messiah.[3]

Today, there are over 1,432,686,519 Christians living in every quarter of the world.[4] About 219 million live in North America; 348 million in South America; and 415 million in Europe. There are 128 million in Asia; 203 million in Africa; and 20 million in Oceania (Australia, New Zealand, and the islands of the South Pacific).

Who Is Jesus for Christians?

If the Jewish breakthrough in people's religious awareness was so remarkable, so, too, was the emergence of Christianity. Briefly, its story is this:

One day a Jewish man from Galilee by the name of Jesus appeared at the Jordan River where a Jewish prophet known as John the Baptizer was preaching repentance and a return to the pure observance of the Jewish Convenant with God.

2. There are many kinds of Christians (Protestant, Catholic, Orthodox, for example) who interpret the way of life Jesus prescribed in different ways—ways they think help them best live the life they believe Jesus commanded.

3. The circumstances which caused the separation of Judaism and Christianity are too complex to be discussed in this survey.

4. According to David Barrett, author of *World Christian Encyclopedia*, Christianity is the first truly universal religion. It is found in every country and among all people including many nearly inaccessible tribes.

After being baptized, Jesus began his own mission of preaching that the reign of God was at hand (the Gospel according to Mark 1:15).

During nearly three years of preaching, in which he made an extraordinary impression on all who met him, Jesus came into conflict with some of the Jewish religious authorities. They had him put to death by the Romans—the military, economic, and political rulers of Palestine. Jesus' career as a preacher was marked by unusual ability as a speaker, and by many signs that led a great number of people to accept him as an authentic messenger of God.

He was, as later events showed, a very extraordinary person who had untold influence on people's lives, the course of history, the development of civilization, and people's awareness of the nature of God and the relationship that all of creation has with God.

As unique as the person and career of Jesus was, the event which told his followers who he was and how unique he

The Son of God

Jesus was born in Bethlehem, a small town southwest of Jerusalem, about five B.C. His parents took him to Egypt for a short period to escape a threat to his life posed by Herod, the Rome-appointed king. After returning from Egypt, Jesus and his parents settled in Nazareth, a town in Galilee, a Jewish province in the northern part of Palestine.

Jesus grew up in Nazareth and worked as a carpenter when he came of age until he was about thirty years old. At that time, he moved from Nazareth to Capernaum, a town on the northern shore of the Sea of Galilee, and became an itinerant preacher.

For nearly three years he preached what came to be known as "the good news" throughout Palestine. He preached about God's love for people and about how people should live together in loving concern for each other. He attracted many followers by his words and actions and because of the many good works he performed for people.

He ran afoul of certain powerful religious leaders among the Jews, was tried in the Jewish court as one who subverted the people, was tried in the Roman court as an enemy of Caesar, and condemned to death by crucifixion. After having been scourged by the Roman guards and crowned with thorns, he was forced to carry a cross to Golgatha, a hill of execution outside the city of Jerusalem.

He was nailed to the cross and exhibited to curious onlookers between two thieves who, like him, were crucified. After three hours on the cross, Jesus died. After a Roman guard ran a spear through his heart to insure his death, he was taken down from the cross by his friends, anointed with burial oils and herbs and buried in someone else's tomb near Golgatha. He was, perhaps, thirty-three years old.

really was, was his resurrection from the dead. His followers said they saw him alive, talked with him, ate with him, and met with him on several occasions after he had been buried. When they became convinced of who they believed him to be, they preached about him, not simply as the Messiah (a human person sent by God to lead the Jewish people to their days of glory), but as the Son of God—God himself, expressing himself as a human person.

This is what Christian faith is all about: Christians believe that Jesus is the Son of God who became a man, lived in a particular place during a particular historical time, was put to death, rose from the grave to a new life, and lives now as the Lord of the universe and the Lord of history.

As Christians see it, God's self-revelation in Jesus is the logical climax to people's search for an answer to the mystery of life. For them, God revealed Himself gradually as the chart on page 113 illustrates.

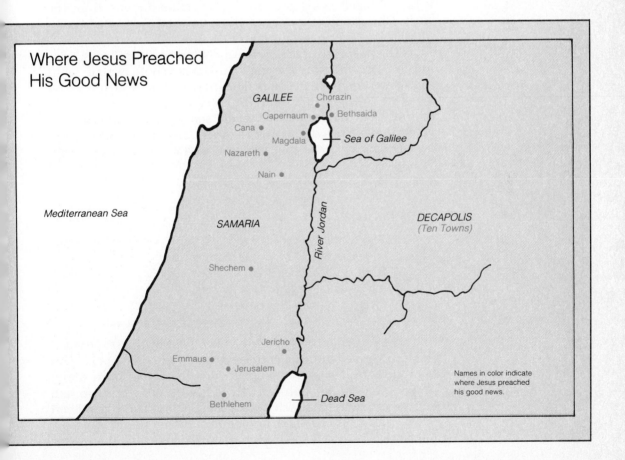

Where Jesus Preached His Good News

GALILEE
Chorazin
Capernaum • • Bethsaida
Cana •
Magdala •
Nazareth •
Nain •

Sea of Galilee

Mediterranean Sea

SAMARIA

River Jordan

DECAPOLIS
(Ten Towns)

Shechem •

Jericho •
Emmaus • • Jerusalem

Bethlehem •
Dead Sea

Names in color indicate where Jesus preached his good news.

This acceptance of Jesus as the Son of God enables Christians to develop answers to four main questions about life: (a) What is the nature of God? (b) What is the meaning of human existence? (c) What is the meaning of death? and (d) How does a person live a meaningful life? The Christian answer for each of these gives Christians a security, a faith, and a hope that is distinctly Christian.

Who—or What—Is God for Christians?

The roots of Christian faith are firmly planted in the soil of the Jewish heritage from which it sprang. (Jesus was a Jew; his trusted apostles were Jews; his first followers were Jews.) God is identified as not just any god, but as the Almighty Creator of the universe—in other words, Yahweh. And yet, although the Christian belief is thoroughly Jewish in its roots, it is organized along principles that came directly from the early Christians' experience of Jesus and from their community life after his resurrection.

The basic structure of the Christian belief in God is Trinitarian. The only way the early Christians could explain what they experienced in Jesus and heard from him was to say that *The One God is so personal He is really three Persons.* They did not say this because it "made sense"; they said this because they believed that was the way Jesus' disciples remembered experiencing and learning of God when they were with Jesus.

I know men and I tell you that Jesus Christ is no mere man. Between him and every other person in the world there is no possible term of comparison. Alexander, Caesar, Charlemagne, and I have founded empires. But on what did we rest the creation of our genius? Upon force. Jesus Christ founded his empire on love; and at this hour millions of men would die for him.

—Napoleon Bonaparte

The external facts of Jesus' life do not by themselves adequately convey the impact this extraordinary man made upon his followers. He was a prophet; but there had been many prophets, including John the Baptist, and none of them had started a new religion. He was a martyr; but there had been many reformers crucified, and none of them had galvanized a following who could feel his living presence among them after

his death. Yet, such was the power of this man that, after his death his disciples were so enthusiastic about what he started that when they started telling everyone about it, they were accused of being drunk.

The apostles believed that the same God they had known since childhood had raised Jesus from the dead, made him Lord of the universe, and sent his own breath of life into them. This is what they preached. From that time on, it was impossible for those who believed in Jesus to think of God in terms other than what the apostles had preached. For them, Jesus and the Holy Spirit of God were part of their awareness of God.

But why did early Christians think of God as three persons? And why, if they accepted the idea of three persons, did

Nazareth

they not think there were three Gods? The reason lies in the Jewish heritage about God and in the people's experience of Jesus while he lived among them.

Contrary to the concepts of God and His actions held by their contemporaries, the Jewish people did not picture God as having to "do" anything to achieve His goals. He did not have to fight any wars, horse trade with other gods, perform acts of magic or trickery. The Jewish God (Yahweh) was not an enemy of the people, a benevolent despot, or an indifferent spirit living in a world all His own. He was Almighty, Personal, Loving, and Faithful.

For the Jews, God created by giving a command, gave life by breathing the breath of life into living things, and sustained them in existence through His will. They pictured God as acting in the universe through His spirit and through His word.

After the Resurrection and Pentecost experiences, the apostles recalled that Jesus used these two ideas to refer to himself and his work. He claimed to have the spirit of God, and he spoke with authority about how people should live. They remembered how, for example, on one occasion:

He came to Nazareth where he had been reared, and, entering the synagogue on the sabbath as he was in the habit of doing, he stood up to do the reading. When the book of the prophet Isaiah

The World's Living Religions

was handed to him, he unrolled the scroll and found the passage where it was written: "The spirit of the Lord is upon me; therefore he has anointed me. He has sent me to bring glad tidings to the poor, to proclaim liberty to captives, recovery of sight to the blind and release to prisoners, to announce a year of favor from the Lord." Rolling up the scroll, he gave it back to the assistant and sat down. All in the synagogue had their eyes fixed on him. Then he began by saying to them, "Today this Scripture passage is fulfilled in your hearing."

—Luke 4:16–21

As Jesus went around doing good, and preaching the Good News (as his followers called it), people sensed in him a uniqueness and authority that was more than that of a prophet. He seemed to have the spirit of God and to speak of God in a totally new way. One of his witnesses, the apostle John, said:

It was winter, and the time came for the feast of Dedication in Jerusalem. Jesus was walking in the temple area, in Solomon's Portico, when the Jews [that is, some of the leaders of the Jews] gathered around him and said, "How long are you going to keep us in suspense? If you really are the Messiah, tell us so in plain words." Jesus answered: "I did tell you, but you do not believe. The works I do in my Father's name give witness in my favor, but you refuse to believe because you are not my sheep. My sheep hear my voice. I know them, and they follow me. I give them eternal life, and they shall never perish. No one will snatch them out of my hand. My Father is greater than all, in what he has given me, and there is no snatching out of his hand. The Father and I are one."

When some of the Jews again reached for rocks to stone him, Jesus protested to them, "Many good deeds have I shown you from the Father. For which of these do you stone me?" "It is not for any 'good deed' that we are stoning you," the Jews retorted, "but for blaspheming. You who are only a man are making yourself God."

Jesus answered: "Is it not written in your law, 'I have said, You are gods'? If it calls those men gods to whom God's word was addressed—and Scripture cannot lose its force—do you claim that I blasphemed when, as he whom the Father consecrated and sent into the world, I said, 'I am God's Son'? If I do not perform my Father's works, put no faith in me. But if I do perform them, even though you put no faith in me, put faith in these works, so as to realize what it means that the Father is in me and I in him."

—John 10:22–38

Time and again, his followers remembered, Jesus spoke in God's name on his own authority. (See, for example, the Gospel according to Matthew 5–7, where Jesus uses phrases like: "You have heard . . . What I say to you . . ."; or expressions like, "Do this," "Do not do so and so," "Ask," "Seek," and so on.) They recalled that when he performed some miracle, it was always done by him in his Father's name.

So, reflecting upon this uniquely authoritative person, who treated God's Spirit and God's Word as his own (and whose life of good works backed him up), early Christians could come to only one conclusion: *Jesus was the Word of God!*

They believed that just as God had spoken His word in creation and in their Scriptures, so did He speak to them in the person of Jesus. For them, Jesus as the Word of God was God Himself. This is how one of the early Christian documents put it:

> In the beginning was the Word; the Word was in God's presence, and the Word was God. He was present to God in the beginning. Through him all things came into being, and apart from him nothing came to be. . . . The Word became flesh and made his dwelling among us, and we have seen his glory: the glory of an only Son coming from the Father, . . . No one has ever seen God. It is God the only Son, ever at the Father's side, who has revealed him.
>
> —John 1:1–18

But, if the Word of God (Jesus) was really a Divine Person, Jesus' first followers naturally asked themselves about God's Spirit. Remembering what Jesus had said, the first Christians recalled that Jesus not only possessed God's Spirit, *he also had it to give!* Before his resurrection Jesus had said,

> "I will ask the Father and he will give you another Paraclete— to be with you always: the Spirit of truth, . . . the Paraclete, the Holy Spirit whom the Father will send in my name, will instruct you in everything, . . .
>
> —John 14:16, 26

The first followers of Jesus experienced the fulfillment of this promise at Pentecost, as we pointed out at the beginning of this chapter.

They realized then that Jesus and the Father are One, yet he was distinct enough from the Father to ask Him to send His Spirit—he and the Father are one and the same God but two separate Persons. And when he promised them Another

The God of Christians

Too often, people think of God
    as a common name that has become part of everyday language;
    as a vague "being" who is supposed to have magical powers;
    as the creative force behind the universe and its evolution;
    as an idea that can be demonstrated in order to comfort the minds of men;
But this alone is not the God of Christians.

Too often, and for too many people, the "act of faith"
    is summed up in this manner: There is "something" greater than we,
    something inapproachable because it is so distant, unknowable because it
    is mysterious; something we must contend with and bear; something we
    must try to bend to our own will; something whose good will we must
    cultivate.
This is in no way the faith of Christians.

Too often men speak of "being religious" or of "having
  religion." They refer to a complex
    of badly assimilated religious information,
    of badly observed moral laws,
    of rituals, often idolatrous in themselves, performed distractedly,
    of social concepts which are as ultraconservative for
        some as they are revolutionary for others.
This is by no means the religion of Christians.

The God of Christians is not just
    a god-object
    a god-idea,
    a god of morality,
    a god of social order.

The God of Christians is
    a person
    a person who is called Jesus Christ;
    a person who, historically, once lived among men.

The God of Christians is not merely
    "something" greater than we, *but someone among us.*

Source: Michel Quoist, *"I've Met Jesus Christ,"* translated by J. F. Bernard, translation, pp. 82–83. Copyright © 1973 by Doubleday & Company, Inc. Reprinted by permission of the publisher.

One like himself, Another whom they experienced as God's Spirit, they could only realize that God's Spirit, like God's Word, is one and the same God but a *third* Person of God.

What the early Christians learned and experienced was that the ancient Jewish poetry had instinctively been alive to something that they now realize is more than poetry but is Reality. God's Word and His Spirit are Himself.

This belief in the Trinity (Tri-unity) of God has never been adequately explained by Christians, for they believe it is beyond anyone's power to explain completely. They believe that the early Christians discovered it, not by understanding, but from what they saw and heard when with Jesus. They believed that they met God's Word personally in Jesus, and they felt God's Spirit personally at Pentecost as he promised. Their community life was developed on the basis of their relationship to this Trinitarian God.

The World's Living Religions

The Christian View of Human Existence

Steeped as they were in their Jewish heritage that people are created in God's image, the first Christians came to believe that because of Jesus, people are not only made on God's image, they are also destined to share God's life. They remembered that Jesus had said:

"Anyone who loves me will be true to my word, and my Father will love him; we will come to him and make our dwelling place with him."

—John 14:23

In other words, because of Jesus, Christians believe that the world is saved from an existence outside of God, and that, because people share in God's own life, they possess a unique dignity and ought to be regarded with the respect that belongs to things that are sacred—that are God's. They believe that because people do share God's life, they are created for more than simply an existence in this world. They believe they are destined to live with God forever. This view brought a whole new meaning to human existence for Christians.

Christians believe this because of what Jesus had said:

"Do not let your hearts be troubled. Trust in God still, and trust in me. There are many rooms in my Father's house; if there were not, I should have told you. I am going now to prepare a place for you, and after I have gone and prepared you a place, I shall return to take you with me; so that where I am you may be too. You know the way to the place where I am going."

Thomas said, "Lord, we do not know where you are going, so how can we know the way?"

Jesus said: "I am the Way, the Truth and the Life. No one can come to the Father except through me. If you know me, you know my Father too. From this moment you know him and have seen him."

Philip said, "Lord, let us see the Father and then we shall be satisfied."

"Have I been with you all this time, Philip," said Jesus to him "and you still do not know me? "To have seen me is to have seen the Father, so how can you say, 'Let us see the Father'? Do you not believe that I am in the Father and the Father is in me? The words I say to you I do not speak as from myself: it is the Father, living in me, who is doing this work. You must believe me when I say that I am in the Father and the Father is in me; believe it on the evidence of this work, if for no other reason. I tell you most solemnly, whoever believes in me will perform the same works as I do myself, he will perform even greater works, because I am going to the Father. Whatever you ask for in my name I will do, so that the Father may be glorified in the Son. If you ask for anything in my name, I will do it.

If you love me you will keep my commandments. I shall ask the Father, and he will give you another Advocate to be with you for ever, that Spirit of truth whom the world can never receive since it neither sees nor knows him; but you know him, because he is with you, he is in you.

I will not leave you orphans; I will come back to you. In a short time the world will no longer see me; but you will see me, because I live and you will live. On that day you will understand that I am in my Father and you in me and I in you.''

—John14:1–20

For Christians, people belong to God. They have been created by Him, claimed for Him by His Son, Jesus, and formed into His People by the action of the Holy Spirit. For Christians, people are not foolish mistakes of a blind force, playthings of the gods, or even servants of the Utterly Other. They are, by adoption in Christ, God's children. This belief was voiced by Paul in his letter to the Romans. He put it this way:

All who are led by the Spirit of God are sons of God. You did not receive a spirit of slavery leading you back into fear, but a spirit of adoption through which we cry out "Abba!" (that is, "Father"). The Spirit himself gives witness with our spirit that we are children of God. But if we are children, we are heirs as well: heirs of God, heirs with Christ. . . .

—Romans 8:14–17

This view of the meaning of human nature and of human existence created a whole new pattern for living among Christians. For the first Christians who, as we said, were Jews, the pattern for living was not simply the Torah. It was a Person—the man Jesus who had come to live among them. They accepted, and put into practice, his command to love others for the love of God. This, too, gave new meaning to their lives.

They acted not out of selfish gain, not to escape punishment, not to curry the favor of others, but because Jesus, who had given new meaning to their lives, had showed them how to live.

The Meaning of Death for Christians

For all people, death is a great mystery. Since the time of Jesus, Christians believe they have the answer to that mystery. Before Christ, life after death was a hope; since Christ, life after death, for Christians is a surety. Before Jesus, life after death was, at best, ambiguous; since Christ, life after death for Christians is clear.

As the resurrection accounts tell Christians, the experience of Jesus alive after death means three things: (a) The certainty that death is not the end of existence; (b) The whole

How Christians Express Their Faith

I believe in God, the Father almighty, creator of heaven and earth; and in Jesus Christ, His only Son, our Lord: who was conceived by the Holy Spirit, born of the Virgin Mary, suffered under Pontius Pilate, was crucified, died, and was buried. He descended into the land of the dead. The third day He arose from the dead. He ascended into heaven and sits at the right hand of God, the Father almighty; from thence He shall come to judge the living and the dead.

I believe in the Holy Spirit, the holy Catholic Church, the communion of saints, the forgiveness of sins, the resurrection of the body, and life everlasting. Amen.*

*All Christian groups subscribe to the main ideas expressed in this creed which is called "The Apostles Creed."

person lives on through death and experiences a new dimension of existence called, "the risen life"; (c) This new person lives with God and experiences the life of God unencumbered by the limitations of earthly existence—the limitations of time and space, the limitations of sin, and the limitations of the necessities required to sustain life here on earth.

Because of Jesus, Christians believe they can face death with courage and joy. For them, death is the moment of the total person's passing into that eternal dimension of life for which he or she was created. For Christians, death is not the end. It is the means for entering into that mode of existence by which a person can participate in the Divine Life to the fullest degree possible for him or her.

What Is a Meaningful Life for Christians?

The Christian response to the question about how one leads a meaningful life has a two-fold answer given to Christians by Jesus as reported in the Gospels:

A teacher of the Law was there who heard the discussion. He saw that Jesus had given the Sadducees a good answer, so he came to him with a question: "Which commandment is the most important of all?" "This is the most important one," said Jesus. 'Hear, Israel! The Lord our God is the only Lord. You must love the Lord your God with all your heart, and with all your soul, and with all your mind, and with all your strength.' The second most important commandment is this: 'You must love your neighbor as you love yourself.' There is no other commandment more important than these two." The teacher of the Law said to Jesus: "Well done, Teacher! It is true, as you say, that only the Lord is God, and that there is no other god but he. And so man must love God with all his heart, and with all his mind, and with all his strength; and he must love his neighbor as he loves himself. It is more important to obey these two commandments than to offer on the altar animals and other sacrifices to God." Jesus noticed how wise his answer was, and so he told him: "You are not far from the Kingdom of God."
—Mark 12:28–34

For Christians, this response of Jesus (made in different words on different occasions) summarizes the philosophy by which a person should live. It encompasses two things: (1) a

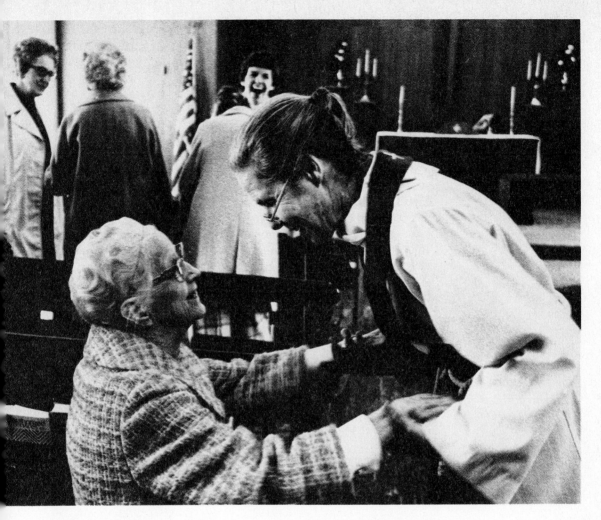

person's relationship with God, and (2) his relationship with people.

Episcopal priest greets member after services.

Like all other religious people, Christians express their belief in action. Believing in the divine dignity of people, Christians express their relationship to God by making it possible, through various acts of love, for less fortunate people to experience a condition of existence that goes beyond the constant search for food, shelter, and clothing. Through their acts of charity, Christians believe that they worship God in every person by doing for that person what God has intended: making life worth living.

Believing also in the divine worth of life, Christians celebrate life in their direct acts of worship of God. Believing that they are united with Christ through baptism, Christians come together to celebrate the Lord's Supper in imitation of Jesus who, giving his body and blood to his apostles under the appearance of bread and wine at the Last Supper (his final Passover or Seder meal), asked his followers to celebrate his presence among them:

> When the hour came, Jesus took his place at the table with the apostles. And he said to them: "I have wanted so much to eat this Passover meal with you before I suffer! For I tell you, I will never eat it until it is given its full meaning in the Kingdom of God." Then Jesus took the cup, gave thanks to God, and said, "Take this and share it among yourselves; for I tell you that from now on I will not drink this wine until the Kingdom of God comes." Then he took the bread, gave thanks to God, broke it, and gave it to them, saying, "This is my body which is given for you. Do this in memory of me." In the same way he gave them the cup after the supper, saying, "This cup is God's new covenant sealed with my blood, which is poured out for you.

> —Luke 22: 14–20

Baptism of an infant in Montero, Bolivia

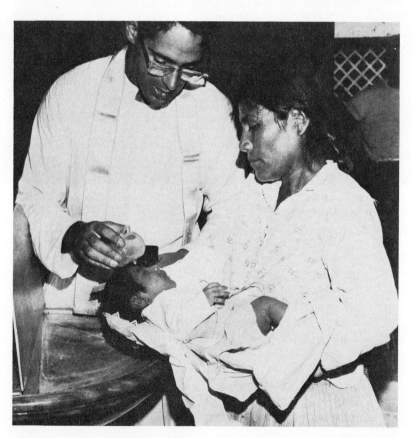

The World's Living Religions

Various Christian groups celebrate other life situations (marriage, coming to maturity, ministry, death, and so on) in their own ways. They call these celebrations "sacraments" because through them they believe their lives are made more holy and their relationship with God is strengthened.

Relationships with People

Taking their cue from Jesus also with regard to their relationships with people, Christians summarize Jesus' message to them in this regard by recalling his words: "This is my commandment: love one another as I have loved you."[5]

It is called a summary of Christ's way to live because no other counsel given by Christ occupies so important a position in his scheme of things. For him, it was to be the distinguishing mark of a Christian's life: "This is how all will know you for my disciples," Jesus said, "your love for one another."[6]

Jesus Christ is the outstanding personality of all time. . . . No other teacher—Jewish, Christian, Buddhist, Mohammedan—is still a teacher whose teaching is such a guidepost for the world we live in. Other teachers may have something basic for an Oriental, an Arab, or an Occidental; but every act and word of Jesus has value for all of us. He became the Light of the World. Why shouldn't I, a Jew, be proud of that?

—Sholem Asch, a Jewish writer

It was so important that Paul, an apostle of Jesus, writing to Roman Christians from Corinth, Greece, about A.D. 57 did not hesitate to say: "The commandments, 'You shall not commit adultery; you shall not murder; you shall not steal; you shall not covet,' and any other commandment there may be are all summed up in this, 'You shall love your neighbor as yourself.' Love never wrongs the neighbor, hence, love is the fulfillment of the law."[7] For Christians, love of neighbor is the starting point of all ethical considerations.

For Christians, love is the key to a meaningful life—love of God and love of neighbor. It opens a person's heart, they believe, to the spiritual and social realities of human existence.

5. John 15:12.
6. John 13:35.
7. The Epistle of Paul to the Romans 13:9–10.

The Priesthood and Ministry in Christianity

All Christian groups have persons who are designated or ordained to be priests or ministers of religion. These persons are specially trained to minister to the religious needs of their people. They preach the gospel, teach, lead in the religious celebrations of their groups, and administer the affairs of their religious group.

Greek Orthodox patriarch

The Christian Scriptures

The Christian scriptures, the codified and standardized sacred writings of the Christian people, are commonly known as the Bible. The Christian Bible has two parts: the Old Testament, which contains the materials of the Hebrew Bible, and the New Testament, which is an authorized collection of some of the writing of those most closely associated with Jesus.

The New Testament has four parts: the Gospels, the epistles, the Acts of the Apostles, and the Book of Revelation. The Gospels contain the traditions about Jesus. The epistles are letters about how to live Christ's way. The Acts of the Apostles gives the early history of the Christian community. The Book of Revelation is the Christian book of prophecy. The Gospels are the most important part of the Christian Bible because they contain what Christians believe are the words and actions of Jesus. They are the norm by which Christians explain and profess their faith.

There are four Gospels, entitled the Gospel according to Matthew, the Gospel according to Mark, the Gospel according to Luke, and the Gospel according to John. These are four versions, or traditions, of the meaning of Jesus.

There are twenty-one epistles, thirteen attributed to Paul and eight by other apostles or close associates of the apostles. The Acts of the Apostles and the Book of Revelation are single books.

Christians believe that their scriptures are inspired by God, and are, for them, revelation. For Christians, they tell what God wants known about Himself, the origin of the world, His plans for people, and how to live.

Christian Feast Days

Adoration of the Magi by Leinweber

Christian feasts, or days of Christian celebration, are recollections of God's saving actions in Christ in the past, and celebrations of His saving actions in Christ in the present. These celebrations, or liturgies, as they are called, are the Churches' official, public worship of God in Christ.

Although various Christian groups celebrate these actions in various ways, and each group has its own special feast days (like World-wide Communion Sunday among many Protestant groups or Ascension Thursday among Catholic groups) all Christian groups celebrate three major feasts: Easter Sunday, Pentecost Sunday, and Christmas Day.

Easter Sunday, the most important feast day for Christians, recalls and celebrates what Christians believe was Jesus' resurrection from the dead. Christians believe that Jesus rose from the dead on the second day after his death by crucifixion. They believe, as we said, that he rose to a new dimension of existence called "the risen dimension." It is, however, more than a celebration of a past event. It is also a celebration of a present reality for Christians: Christ's presence in his Church and the resurrection of all people to a new life in God.

Pentecost Sunday recalls and celebrates what Christians believe took place some fifty days after Jesus' crucifixion. They believe that on that day the Holy Spirit came to the Apostles to enlighten them about Jesus. This feast is not, however, simply a celebration of a past event. It is also the celebration of a present reality for Christians: the action of the Holy Spirit in the continuing creation of the world, and his action in the life of each Christian.

Christmas Day, December twenty-fifth, celebrates the birth of Jesus. Although it recalls and celebrates a specific event in history, it also celebrates what is for Christians a reality: the presence of God in the world and the presence of Christ in his community of believers.

In addition to these yearly feasts, Christian groups come together for worship each Sunday. For them, Sunday is "the Lord's day." It is a day set aside each week specifically for worshipping God as a community. They do this through special liturgies, rest, and recreation. Sunday replaced the Jewish Sabbath because Christians believe that Jesus rose from the dead on Sunday and to remind Christians that they are called to a new life in Christ through their baptism.

Selections from Christian Scriptures

"Make certain you do not perform your religious duties in public so that people will see what you do. If you do these things publicly, you will not have any reward from your Father in heaven.

"So when you give something to a needy person, do not make a big show of it, as the hypocrites do in the houses of worship and on the streets. They do it so people will praise them. I assure you, they have already been paid in full. But when you help a needy person, do it in such a way that even your closest friend will not know about it. Then it will be a private matter. And your Father, who sees what you do in private, will reward you."
—Matthew 6:1–4

"I tell you, my friends, do not be afraid of those who kill the body but cannot afterward do anything worse. I will show you whom to fear; fear God, who, after killing, has the authority to throw into hell. Believe me, he is the one you must fear!

"Aren't five sparrows sold for two pennies? Yet not one sparrow is forgotten by God. Even the hairs of your head have all been counted. So do not be afraid; you are worth much more than many sparrows!"
—Luke 12:4–7

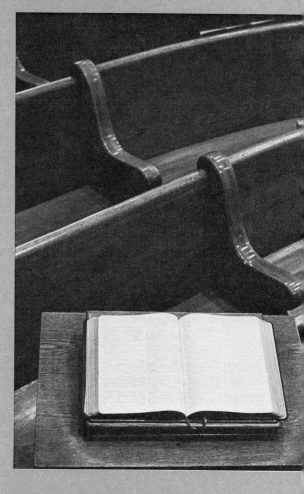

"Do not store up riches for yourselves here upon earth, where moths and rust destroy, and robbers break in and steal. Instead, store up riches for yourselves in heaven, where moths and rust cannot destroy, and robbers cannot break in and steal. For your heart will always be where your riches are."
—Matthew 6:19–21

"Do not judge others, and God will not judge you; do not condemn others, and God will not condemn you; forgive others, and God will forgive you. Give to others, and God will give to you. Indeed, you will receive a full measure, a generous helping, poured into your hands—all that you can hold. The measure you use for others is the one that God will use for you."
—Luke 6:37, 38

"Why do you look at the speck in your brother's eye, but pay no attention to the log in your own eye? How can you say to your brother, 'Please, brother, let me take that speck out of your eye,' yet cannot even see the log in your own eye? You hypocrite! First take the log out of your own eye, and then you will be able to see clearly to take the speck out of your brother's eye."

—Luke 6:41, 42

Jesus answered, "I am telling you the truth: you are looking for me because you ate the bread and had all you wanted, not because you understood my miracles. Do not work for food that spoils; instead, work for the food that lasts for eternal life. This is the food which the Son of Man will give you, because God, the Father, has put his mark of approval on him."

—John 6:26, 27

"You have heard that it was said, 'An eye for an eye, and a tooth for a tooth.' But now I tell you: do not take revenge on someone who wrongs you. If someone slaps you on the right cheek, let him slap your left cheek too. And if someone takes you to court to sue you for your shirt, let him have your coat as well. And if one of the occupation troops forces you to carry his pack one mile, carry it two miles. When someone asks you for something, give it to him; when someone wants to borrow something, lend it to him."

—Matthew 5:38–42

"A good person brings good out of the treasure of good things in his heart; a bad person brings bad out of his treasure of bad things. For the mouth speaks what the heart is full of."

—Luke 6:45

"A healthy tree does not bear bad fruit, nor does a poor tree bear good fruit. Every tree is known by the fruit it bears; you do not pick figs from thorn bushes or gather grapes from bramble bushes."

—Luke 6:43, 44

"But when you pray, go to your room, close the door, and pray to your Father, who is unseen. And your Father, who sees what you do in private, will reward you. When you pray, do not use a lot of meaningless words, as the pagans do, who think that God will hear them because their prayers are long. Do not be like them. Your Father already knows what you need before you ask him. This, then, is how you should pray:
'Our Father in heaven:
May your holy name be honored; may your Kingdom come; may your will be done on earth as it is in heaven.
Give us today the food we need.
Forgive us the wrongs we have done, as we forgive the wrongs that others have done to us.
Do not bring us to hard testing, but keep us safe from the Evil One.' "

—Matthew 6:6–13

"Also, the Kingdom of heaven is like this. A man is looking for fine pearls, and when he finds one that is unusually fine, he goes and sells everything he has, and buys that pearl."

—Matthew 13:45

Summary

1. Christians are those who believe that Jesus is the Son of God who became a human being.

2. Christians believe that Jesus is the final step in God's revelation of Himself to people.

3. Christians believe that God has revealed Himself as Triune.

4. Christians believe that all people are called to share God's life forever in a risen dimension of existence.

5. Christians believe that human morality can be summed up in a single phrase: love your neighbor as much as you love yourself.

For Review

1. What is the central belief of Christians?

2. Why is the Pentecost experience important in Christianity? Would there have been a Christian answer to the mystery of life without it? Why? Why not?

3. What is the chief source for the world's understanding of Jesus? Explain in some detail.

4. In what way is the Christian concept of God different from other ideas of God? What motivated the Christians to conceive of God in this manner?

5. When Christians say the roots of Christianity are found in Judaism, what do they mean?

6. According to Christian belief, what is the key to meaningful relationships with people? Do you agree or disagree? Explain your viewpoint.

7. What does the resurrection of Jesus tell Christians about their own destiny?

8. What does Christian worship essentially celebrate? What are the principle feast days of Christians? What do they celebrate?

9. Prepare a summary of the life of Jesus.

10. Be sure that you can define Pentecost, risen dimension of existence, apostle, gospel, epistle, the Acts of the Apostles, the Book of Revelation, New Testament.

For Discussion

1. Some people reject Christianity because of the way some Christians live. Discuss whether or not this seems to be a valid reason for rejecting Christianity.

2. Some of the major beliefs of Christians, like the Trinity, Jesus' resurrection, the divinity of Jesus, and life after death seem hard to believe. Discuss whether or not they are unreasonable.

3. Discuss whether or not people would accept Jesus or one of his apostles today.

For Research

1. Prepare a report on the essential differences between Roman Catholic, Protestant, and Orthodox Christians.

2. Prepare a report on the role of Paul in the spread of Christianity.

3. Read Matthew 5–7 and prepare a report on its contents.

4. Read the First Epistle to the Thessalonians in the New Testament. Be prepared to say why it is an epistle and what its various parts are about. Where was Thessalonia?

5. Read chapters 27 and 28 of the Acts of the Apostles in the New Testament. Be prepared to say what they are about.

6. Prepare a report on the art and architecture of early and medieval Christianity. If possible, illustrate your report.

7. Prepare a report on the priesthood and the ministry in various Christian religious groups.

Words You Should Know

If there are any words given below you are not sure of, look them up in the Word List at the end of the book.

Baptism	galvanize	sacrament
chronicler	Lord's Supper	triune
epistle	Revelation	unencumbered

chapter 6

Islam

From one end of the world to the other, from the malarial jungles of the Philippines and Indonesia, across the vast steppes of central Asia, the desiccated plains of India and Pakistan, the cities and deserts of the Middle East, the oil sheikdoms of the Arabian peninsula, the oases of the Sahara and the swarming souks (marketplaces) of North Africa, and now the cities of Europe and the ghettos of America, the world hears five times a day the great Muslim prayer chanted from the minarets to call the faithful: "**There is no God but Allah, and Muhammad is His Prophet!**"

It echoes among people of all races, Semitic, black, brown, yellow and white. (Only the American Indians lack Muslims.) Blue-eyed Europeans—Yugoslavs and Albanians—as well as dark-eyed Bengalis, almond-eyed Turkoman nomads, swarthy Afghan mountaineers, the blacks of African jungles, all prostrate themselves at the appointed times in submission—Islam—to the Divine Name of Allah. Virtually wherever one goes, one is in or near a world of Muslims—the people who submit—who honor God under the name of Allah, and Muhammad as His messenger and prophet.

But who is this "God" called Allah, and who is His prophet Muhammad?

Allah (Muslims always add "Blessed be His Name" when He is mentioned) is none other than the same supreme God worshipped by Jews and Christians—the Torah's "El" of Elohim, the Lord God Jehovah of Christians. And Muhammad, according to Muslims, is the last of His prophets or messengers in a line that commences with Adam and includes Abraham, Noah, Isaac, Job and Isaiah, King David, and of particular interest to Christians, John the Baptist and Jesus Christ.[1]

Islam is the proper name of a religion of 723 million people which some misname "Mohammedanism." The word Islam comes from the Arabic word *Salam*, meaning peace, or surrender. Hence, "the perfect peace that comes from total surrender to Allah," is Islam.

Opposite page—Two Muslim women descend the steps from the Dome of the Rock, Jerusalem

1. Edward Rice, *Columban Mission*, November 1981, pp. 4, 5.

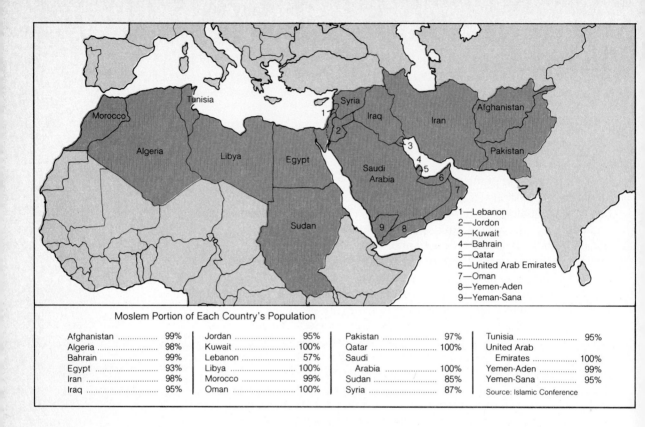

Moslem Portion of Each Country's Population

Afghanistan	99%	Jordan	95%	Pakistan	97%	Tunisia	95%
Algeria	98%	Kuwait	100%	Qatar	100%	United Arab	
Bahrain	99%	Lebanon	57%	Saudi		Emirates	100%
Egypt	93%	Libya	100%	Arabia	100%	Yemen-Aden	99%
Iran	98%	Morocco	99%	Sudan	85%	Yemen-Sana	95%
Iraq	95%	Oman	100%	Syria	87%		

Source: Islamic Conference

Within map:
1—Lebanon
2—Jordon
3—Kuwait
4—Bahrain
5—Qatar
6—United Arab Emirates
7—Oman
8—Yemen-Aden
9—Yemen-Sana

People who profess Islam are called "Moslems," or "Muslims," a term derived from the word Islam. It means an adherent, or believer in Islam. Moslems resent having their religion called Mohammedanism because they consider God, not Mohammed as central to their faith.

Most Moslems live in the Arabic countries and in Northern Africa, although there are twenty-five million in Europe and nearly three million in North America. So powerful a force is Islam that nearly 100 percent of the people in Arabic countries and North Africa profess Islam.

What Is Islam?

Islam is faith in Allah[2] and in his prophet Mohammed, "the last and the greatest of prophets," and observance of the five obligations, or rituals, sometimes referred to as "The Pillars." For Moslems, the phrase "There is no God but Allah and

Mohammed is his prophet" is not simply a slogan or a pious phrase. It is an act of faith.

Brought to life as it was in the hot, barren desert of Saudi Arabia in A.D. 622, Islam was a boon to a people whose ancient religion was dying out and whose lives and fortunes were subject to the fates of the desert *jinns*,[3] of spirits, the marauding of desert Bedouins, the whims of the ruling class, and the exploitation of the merchants.

Centuries of contact with Judaism and the Christians of the Near East, Egypt, and North Africa had readied the people of Arabia for at least a notion of a God. What was unique about Mohammed's preaching was not monotheism, but *the idea of a single God who spoke to his people through his prophet calling them to a new way of life and a new concept of religion*.[4]

Even though some claim that Islam is a curious mixture of Judaism and Christianity, it is incorrect to think of Islam as an amalgam of Judaism and Christianity suited to a desert people. Many things in Judaism and Christianity do converge in Islam—and not by accident—but Islam is as different from Judaism and Christianity as Christianity is different from Judaism.

Moslems believe, as do Jews and Christians, in *the* God. They believe that God spoke to Abraham, that Moses was God's prophet, that Jesus was a great prophet (here departing from the Jewish concept of Jesus), but that he was, like Abraham and Moses (here departing from Christians), *not* God. They believe that Mohammed is the last and the greatest of prophets and that he brought them enlightenment from God's messenger, the Angel Gabriel, in the form of sayings or revelations which have been written into the *Koran* or Islamic bible. They believe that there is a direct line from Abraham to Mohammed through Ishmael, the half brother of Isaac, the son of Abraham, who settled in Palestine and fathered the Jewish people.[5]

They believe that the "great nation" promised to Hagar and her son is the Arabian nation brought to its promise by

2. Allah means *the* God. It combines the Arabic article *al,* meaning "the" with the Arabic word *Illah,* meaning "God."

3. Any one of a class of spirits capable of taking on human forms and of influencing human beings for good or evil.

4. There are two major sects in Islam. The "Sunnis," found principally in the Middle East, Africa, and Indonesia, trace their origins to the elders associated with Mohammed. The "Shi'a," found mostly in Iran, Iraq, Pakistan, and India, trace their origins to Ali, Mohammed's son-in-law.

5. See Genesis 16:1–16 and 21:1–21.

the efforts of Mohammed. And they believe that Jerusalem is a holy city because it was a holy city for their revered prophets. It was the city where Solomon's Temple was built, where Jesus taught and worshipped, and it was the city from which Mohammed sprang to heaven on a horse.[6] It is worthy of note, also, that it was toward Jerusalem that Mohammed turned to pray until the Jews in Medina turned against him. He then directed his prayers toward Mecca which is now the holy city of Islam.

But Islam is not part Judaism and part Christianity. It is a religion with its own beliefs, rituals, and practices.

The Origin of Islam

Mohammed, "The Seal of the Prophets," was born about A.D. 571 in Mecca, an Arab town in western Saudi Arabia, about 800 miles east of Cairo, Egypt. His parents were members of the Quraish, a leading tribe in the city. Because his father had died before Mohammed was born and his mother died when he was six years old, Mohammed was taken care of by his grandfather.

When Mohammed was nine years old, his grandfather died. One of his uncles took him in and Mohammed worked as a shepherd until he was old enough to work in his uncle's caravan business. Eventually, because of his talent and industry, Mohammed was put in charge of all caravans and made many trips into Christian and Jewish cities. It was in these cities that he learned the principles that were to influence his later thinking about God.

Tradition tells us that, in spite of his problems and the chaotic and immoral situations he faced, Mohammed was honest, upright, trustworthy, and faithful to his duties. The names later applied to Mohammed—"The Upright," "The Trustworthy One," "The True"—were earned, it is said, during this period of his life.[7]

When he was twenty-five, he was hired by a wealthy widow, Khadija, to manage her affairs. His uprightness and honesty impressed her, and eventually they were married. Khadija played an important role in his life, for she was the

---

6. A sacred Moslem shrine, the Dome of the Rock, was built on the spot where this supposedly took place. The shrine was built in the seventh century A.D. and remains one of the world's most famous sights.

7. The name, Mohammed, means, in Arabic, "highly praised." It has been borne by more males than any other name.

Arabs, Persians and the West

Islam is a religious culture, not a religion attached to a culture, as Christianity is attached to the West. Westerners always separate the secular and the divine. Muslims never do.

Worship and love of country, religion and law, evangelism and war are not separable in Islam. A Muslim regards with equanimity that the Koran prescribes, in addition to the prayers and religious duties of the believer, the sexual conduct of man and woman and the statesmanship of princes.

If religious and secular unity are the substance of Islam, its essence, its characteristic note, is that of the desert. Its tone, its feel, are those of early Judaism, its absoluteness that of the Pentateuch.

On the blazing wastes of the Ar Rub al Khali, as on the Sinai, the spirit is dessicated until the soul expands to meet the limitless horizon.

Bent on knees before Yahweh and Allah, with the sun blinding your eyes and the elohim singing in your ears, duty is absolute and zealotry an acceptable heroism. Righteousness, an emotion so puzzling to the Buddhist or Hindu, is the gift of the desert. The tone of the Koran is one of continuous exhortation (wrapped in a blanket, Muhammad dictated the book in a trance) which a Westerner finds stupefying and a Muslim uplifting.

In the world's harshest climate, tolerance and compromise are alien. They are the virtues of the mercantile economies and moisture-laden climates of the temperate zone.

It is not for nothing that three of the world's great religions, Judaism, Christianity and Islam, were born within

600 miles of each other. Monotheism, not oil, is the most phenomenal export of the Middle East.

Islam, like Christianity, is syncretic. It alloys the purest worship of one, invisible God with the earthy rites from the ancient paganism of the oasis of Mecca. Thus the otherwise inexplicable practice of throwing pebbles at stone demons at one station of the Hadj and the veneration of a meteorite within the Kabaa.

Islam's austere theology and worship are leavened by innumerable mystic cults. In the West, these are usually known only in their more spectacular manifestations: the dervishes who whirl, eat live coals or swallow snakes while in ecstasy. Far more to Muslims than to Christians, mysticism provides a spring of spirituality and the direct union with God that is difficult to achieve through orthodox practice. Many of these mystic cults have originated, and reached their fullest flower, in Persia, present-day Iran.

Source: Wes Denham, ''Arabs, Persians and the West,'' *Sarasota Herald Tribune,* November 23, 1980.

The Mosque of Omar
(Dome of the Rock)

first to believe his visions of what should be done for the people of Mecca, and, when he was about to give up his mission because of trouble and persecution, she remained steadfast and encouraged him to continue. If there had been no Khadija, undoubtedly, there would be no Islam.

The Messenger of Allah

Mohammed was a compassionate, sensitive man. He was troubled by the inhumanity he saw every day, by the barbarism, drunkenness, murder, stealing, and general lawlessness and immorality which destroyed any claim the common man and woman had for security and peace. He often went off by himself to pray and meditate, seeking a solution to the problems he saw which were destroying his people and his city. For fifteen years, he went, whenever possible, to his "place of solitude," a cave in Mount Hira, three miles from Mecca.

There was a huge barren rock on the outskirts of Mecca known as Mount Hira, torn by cleft and ravine, erupting unshadowed and flowerless from the desert sands. In this rock was a cave which Mohammed, in need of deep solitude, began to frequent. Peering into the mysteries of good and evil, unable to accept the crudeness, superstition, and fratricide that were accepted as normal, 'this great fiery heart, seething, simmering like a great furnace of thought,' was reaching out for God.

The desert *jinn* were irrelevant to this quest, but one deity was not. Named Allah, he was worshipped by the Meccans, not as the only God, but as an impressive one nonetheless. Creator, Supreme Provider, and Determiner of man's destiny, he was capable of inspiring authentic religious feeling and genuine devotion. Through vigils often lasting the entire night, Allah's reality gradually became increasingly evident and impressive for Mohammed. Fearful and wonderful, real as life, real as death, real as the universe he had ordained, Allah, Mohammed became convinced, was far greater than his countrymen had supposed. This God, whose majesty overflowed a desert cave to fill all heaven and earth, was surely not a god nor even the greatest of gods. He was what his name literally claimed: The God, One and only, One without rival. Soon from this mountain cave was to sound the greatest phrase of the Arabic language: the deep, electrifying cry which was to rally a people and explode their power to the limits of the known world:[8] "**La Ilaha Illa Allah!** There is no God but Allah."[9]

Mohammed became so convinced of this truth that he felt a compulsion to preach it in order to free his fellow Meccans from the superstition, idolatry, suffering, and degradation to which they were subject. One night as he was in deep meditation, he felt such an utter compulsion, tradition tells us, that he heard a voice say three times, "Recite." "What shall I recite?" asked Mohammed, in complete terror.

Recite in the name of thy Lord!
Who created man from blood coagulated.
Recite: Thy Lord is Wondrous kind
      Who by the pen has taught mankind
      Things they knew not.[10]

He rushed home and, suffering from the physical manifestation of vision—trembling, sweating, unconsciousness—he related his experience to Khadija, who convinced him that he was not mad, but could be "the prophet."

8. Within 100 years of Mohammed's death the Moslems had penetrated from India to Spain across the whole northern section of Africa.

9. From page 220, in *The Religions of Man*, by Huston Smith (Harper & Row Publishers, Perennial Library edition). Copyright © 1958 by Huston Smith. By permission of Harper & Row, Publishers, Inc.

10. The *Koran* XCVI, 1–4.

The rest of Mohammed's life was spent in uncompromising and unrelenting effort to bring the message of Allah to the people. Mohammed was a basically kind, gentle person; but he could be hard as nails in his devotion to his mission. He bore no illusions about himself ("God has not sent me to work wonders; he has sent me to preach to you." "I never said that Allah's treasures are in my hand, that I knew the hidden things, or that I was an angel. . . . I am only a preacher of God's words.") and suffered the fate of all prophets: persecution, ridicule, humiliation.

The causes for the opposition are not hard to find. It often happens that leaders of established religions, fearing any sort of deviation from the standard line, at first hold prophets in contempt, then try to silence them. Failing this they use the righteousness of religion to instigate persecution. In Mohammed's case they feared, first, that his monotheism would cut into the revenues paid at the shrines in their temples.[11] Second, they resented his vision of humanity which insisted that all people are equal (this threatened the rigid social structures which enabled the upper class to exploit the poor). Third, his moral code, which was stricter than theirs, threatened to upset the licentiousness, murder, illegal traffic, and degradation of women which was an entrenched way of life for some among the upper classes in Mecca.

For his pains, Mohammed and his few followers were literally run out of town. This flight,[12] tragic as it was for those concerned, turned out to be an important event in the history of Islam, for the date of this *hegira* (flight)—A.D. 622—is the Islamic cutoff point in reckoning dates. It also marks the end of Mohammed's period of vision and preaching alone and the beginning of the activity to establish his "religion." It was not thought of either as "his" or a "religion"—it was simply his total effort to bring the message of God to the people by whatever means were available.

The results of his preaching were meager at first. After three years he had less than forty followers, but in ten years he had made such an impression by his zeal, courage, and honesty that he had more than 5,000 followers.

Assuming the leadership of the town to which he had fled, Mohammed proved to be a skillful leader, consummate politician, and fierce warrior—all in the name of Allah, whose

11. In one temple in Mecca there were over 360 shrines—one for every day in the year.

12. To Yathrib, later called Medina, the "City of the Prophet of God," about 270 miles north of Mecca.

The World's Living Religions

humble servant Mohammed continued to be. For ten years Mohammed struggled to establish his message and his way of life. He succeeded, for upon his death in A.D. 632, he had virtually all of Arabia under his control. One hundred years later (when Moslem expansion was halted by their defeat in a decisive battle at Tours, France, by Charles Martel) Moslems controlled virtually all of the civilized world around the Mediterranean and into India.[13]

The Moslem Way of Life

What was it that made Islam so successful? Aside from the fact that the people were ready for political and religious reform, Islam is basically simple. It has no complicated theology or theological system (Why speculate? say the Moslems. It's all God's work.), no list of miraculous events, no elaborate

13. It must be clearly understood that, although Islam originated in Arabia and is often thought of as "Arabian," it is *not* a racial or ethnic term. There are Berber Moslems, Persian Moslems, Philippine Moslems, Indian Moslems, and American Moslems, just as there are German Catholics, Mexican Catholics, Chinese Catholics, or American Jews, Australian Jews, and English Jews.

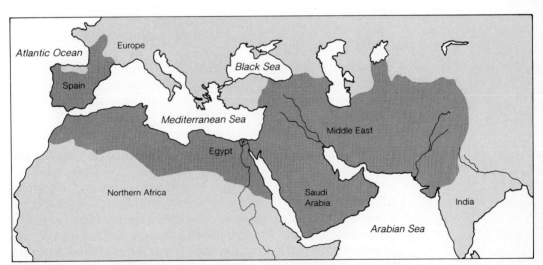

The Spread of Islam in the Eighth and Ninth Centuries

■ Represents Islamic controlled areas in the 8th and 9th centuries

liturgy, and no complicated moral code. It is based on five principles, or pillars as they are called in Western circles, which
are basic to Islamic life.

The five principles, or obligations, imposed by the Koran,
Islam's scripture, give Islam an uncomplicated, universal faith
and practice which has endured, virtually unchanged, for over
1,300 years. The five obligations are:

1. A profession of faith

All Moslems publicly profess acceptance of Allah as the
One God and Mohammed as the messenger of God. They believe that angels are spiritual beings who carry out the will of
Allah, and that the Koran is Allah's infallible and eternal word.
They believe that prophets are the messengers of God, and that
there will be a day of judgment and resurrection at which time
those faithful to the Koran will be rewarded and those who fail
to observe its obligations will be punished.

2. The obligation to pray

The Moslem duty to pray is fulfilled in two ways: private
prayer which can take place any time in any place; and public, or formal prayer, which is obligatory five times during the
day. At dawn, at noon, in the afternoon, at sunset, and after

*Muslim men and women
covered by Chaudar, a
cape to conceal the
female form, walking a
city street in Meshed,
Iran*

The World's Living Religions

dark, the faithful Moslem answers the call to prayer by first ritually purifying himself with pure water (in the desert, sand is used). He then stands erect, facing the principle house of worship in Mecca, and recites the first chapter of the Koran. He then bends forward, rises, kneels, touching his forehead to the floor in adoration of Allah, sits up on his heels, all the while reciting words of prayer and concentrating on Allah. These actions may be repeated during the time alloted for this formal prayer.

If at all possible, a Moslem tries to go to a *mosque*, the Moslem house of prayer and worship, for the noon call to prayer. There he joins other Moslems, first removing his shoes, then getting into a straight line behind a leader who calls the group to prayer. Moslems make a special effort to go to the mosque at noon on Friday, the Moslem Sabbath, at which time the leader, called *Imam*, preaches a sermon.

In towns that are predominantly Moslem and ruled by the *Sharia*, or Koranic law, the call to prayer is made from the minaret, a tower attached to or close by the mosque, by the *muezzin* (moo-ez-in), the Islamic prayer announcer. The minaret and the call to prayer sound are characteristic of Moslem towns.[14]

Moslem call to prayer

3. The giving of alms

Every Moslem has the obligation of giving at least two and one-half percent of his earnings per year to charity. This money is given for the care of the poor and to defray the expenses of worship. Moslems believe that only by giving to the poor, either directly or indirectly, can a person's wealth be "purified," or be pleasing to God.

4. The obligation to fast

The fourth major obligation imposed on every adult Moslem is *Ramadan*, or fasting during the ninth lunar month,[15] called Ramadan. Unless excused, adult Moslems abstain from food, drink, and sexual activity from just before dawn until after sunset every day during the month. When the fast is broken after sunset, special prayers are recited and special passages from the Koran are read.

At the end of the month, Moslems celebrate the "Post-fast Festival," the most important Moslem holiday. The sec-

---

14. Bells are not used because Mohammed suffered a great pain—like the thudding of muffled bells—during his prophetic visions.

15. Ramadan does not come at a fixed time each year. It is the ninth month in the Islamic calendar and may be in winter or summer.

ond most important Moslem festival is the "Festival of Sacrifice" celebrated on the tenth day of the twelfth lunar month. This festival marks the end of the pilgrimage season and is kept in honor of Abraham whose son, Ishmael, went to Mecca, according to Moslem tradition, and became the "father" of all Arabic peoples. This is the Biblical Abraham, one of the many major prophets, like Adam and Noah, whom the Moslems venerate.

5. The pilgrimage to Mecca

Every adult Moslem has an obligation to visit Mecca and to pray at the *Ka'ba*, the rectangular sacred shrine of Islam located in the courtyard of the Great Mosque, built, Moslems believe, by Abraham and Ishmael. Those who are able, make the pilgrimage every year; but the obligation is fulfilled by visiting Mecca once during a person's life. Not all Moslems, of course, for one reason or another, can make the pilgrimage, but hundreds of thousands do, coming on foot, by donkey, horse, camel, cart, bus, car, ship, or airplane. The pilgrimage is considered the highlight of a Moslem's life—"more important than birth or death." It is so important, in fact, that some devout Moslems, after seeing the *Ka'ba*,[16] blind themselves because "there is nothing more to see in this life."

Prayer of the Pilgrim

O God, I ask of Thee a perfect faith, a sincere assurance, a reverent heart, a remembering tongue, a good conduct of commendation, a true repentance, repentance before death, rest at death and forgiveness and mercy after death, clemency at the reckoning, victory in paradise and escape from the fire, by Thy mercy, O Mighty One, O Forgiver, Lord, increase me in knowledge and join me unto the good.

—(Said while making the seven circuits)

The pilgrimage, or *hajj*, as it is called, has several complementary elements. When the pilgrim enters Mecca, he performs the ablutions or cleansings, dresses in white robes and has his head shaved. He then circles the shrine seven times during which he kisses the sacred Black Stone. After that, the pilgrim makes a barefooted ceremonial run between two set

---

16. *Ka'ba* (kah ba) is an Arabic term meaning "cube." The shrine contains the sacred black stone of Moslem veneration.

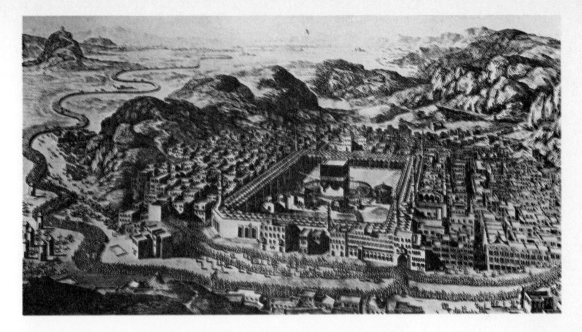

points in memory of the search for water made by Hagar, the mother of Ishmael, the son of Abraham.

View of Mecca and the Kaaba, the most sacred place of Islam, and the chief goal of pilgrimage

Having completed these "preliminaries," on the eighth day, the pilgrim begins the pilgrimage proper. First he listens to a long discourse in the Great Mosque. Then he sets out for Mina and Arafat, two cities five and thirteen miles from Mecca. At Arafat, the pilgrim stands from noon to sundown listening to sermons by Imams. The night is spent in the open. The next day the pilgrim throws seven stones on a large stone heap, symbolizing his rejection of Satan. Following this, the pilgrim sacrifices a sheep or a goat, has his head shaved again, and prepares to leave his consecrated state. He returns to Mecca, visits the Great Mosque again, and bathes in the water of the Holy Well.

Having completed this bathing, the pilgrim relaxes for a day or two, then prepares to return to his home. There he shares his trip and his experiences with his family and friends, and receives a new title. He is called *Hajji*, a term of respect and pious envy. It means, "One who has made the hajj."

Other Things of Importance to Moslems

There are other things of great importance to the faithful Moslem, like the prohibition against alcohol, pork, and gambling, the things Mohammed believed caused the downfall of the people of Mecca.

Many Moslems celebrate various religious feasts and holidays, like *Maulid*, which marks both the birth and death of Mohammed. All Moslems put great store in complete submission to Allah and heartfelt gratitude to Allah for all things He provides. Central to every Moslem's life is unquestioning faith in Allah, the acceptance of Mohammed as the last and the greatest of the prophets, and reverence for the Koran and the observance of its laws. One source put the things that are important to Moslems this way:

> Islam may be described as a religion of centers. God is the center of realities. The Ka'ba is the center of worship. The mosque is the center for the community. And the Prophet Mohammed, who called for recognition of all the preceding missions and who cautioned against his being considered more than human, is the central model and ideal example of righteous conduct.
>
> The divine teachings, laid down by God, are eternal and unchangeable. They are compatible with the needs of all times and all situations. Whether stated specifically or categorically, or in general terms such as the lawfulness of all that is useful and the prohibition of harmful things, they are not subject to human whims. Islam today is the same Islam as when it was born fourteen centuries ago. There is no modern or ancient Islam, no Oriental or Western Islam. Reform movements aim at the return of the faith to its original purity and the removal of the ramifications of cultural traditions misunderstood in some areas to be part of the religion.
>
> Islam is a religion of moderation, catering to spiritual and material needs. Neither should outweigh the other. While it is virtuous and righteous to be generous and charitable, arrogance and extravagance are condemned. A good Muslim observes the law of Islam, including the obligatory and supererogatory rituals, but a Muslim also endeavors to earn a living and to enjoy the lawful pleasures of life.[17]

The Achievements of Mohammed

The assessment of the life and works of any great man must always be made in the light of the times in which he lived, what he was trying to do, the realities of the real situation he faced, and the capacity of the people to absorb and to implement his program. This is especially true of Mohammed. He

17. Miami-Dade Community College, *Student's Guide to the Long Search* (Dubuque: Kendall/Hunt Publishing Company, 1978) p. 212.

was trying to shape and form a society. Measured by their results, his efforts rank with the greatest achievements of civilization. Among the more important achievements of Mohammed, the following seem to stand out:

1. He formed a people formerly divided into classes and ridden with superstition and polytheism into a proud, fierce, monotheistic people among whom all persons, theoretically, are equal.

2. He impregnated his society with an overwhelming awareness of the majesty, power, and transcendence of God.

3. He gave them a list of sayings later codified and standardized to form the Koran or Islamic scriptures as direct revelations from God. No book has so affected the lives and thinking of a single people as the Koran.

4. He improved the status of women from property or chattel to respected members of society. He forbade the killing of baby girls, insisted that women have a right to inheritance, discouraged divorce, forbade licentiousness, encouraged education for women, and limited the practice of polygamy within bounds which were more humane than was the custom in harems of his time.[18]

5. He insisted on absolute racial equality. In his view, and in his preaching, Mohammed saw every person as a creature of God—hence, there is no such thing as the superiority of one race over another. (Moslem wars against Jews and Christians were based on religion, not on race. They were religious enemies bent on corrupting the faithful Moslem.)[19]

6. He successfully challenged the economic inequalities of the Arabian world of his time and based his economic statutes on charity and brotherly love. In a world full of human misery and exploitation of the poor, Mohammed injected the principle that each person is everyone's concern and that social welfare called for serious effort by all.

---

18. By present-day standards in Europe and North America, Mohammed's reforms concerning the status of women do not seem so earthshaking. But in the world in which he lived, his reforms were monumental.

19. We are the One Who revealed the law to Moses. . . . Through the standards of the Torah, Jews have been judged by the prophets. . . . We sent Jesus son of Mary [and] gave him the Gospel. . . . To you we sent the scripture in truth sealing the scripture that came before it. . . . So judge between them by what God has revealed and do not follow their vain desires that diverge from the truth that has come to you . . . and do not follow their ways, lest they seduce you from part of which God has revealed to you. . . . O you who believe, do not take Jews and Christians for friends. . . . God does not guide the wrongdoing people. . . . All they do will be in vain, and they will fall into ruin (*The Koran* 5:47–69).

Noon prayers at the Al-
Hussein mosque, Cairo

7. He insisted on religious toleration. Christians, Jews and Hindus lived in relative peace and harmony under Moslem rule, although they were not given the same degree of rights as members of the official Moslem religion.

The charge that Moslems lived by the sword is only partly true; their record is no better and certainly no worse than any other nation professing to bring "the faith" to "pagans, infidels, and unbelievers." That "Holy Wars" were carried on by corrupt caliphs is unquestionable, but these were wars of conquest, using religion as a means to stir the emotions and bolster the courage of the fighting men.

Viewed as a whole, however, Islam unrolls before us one of the most remarkable panoramas in all history. [It contains] the march of Muslim ideas, the development of a fabulous culture, the rise of literature, science, medicine, art and architecture, the glory of Baghdad and Damascus, the splendor of Spain under the Moors [and] the heartening story of how during the long centuries of Europe's dark ages Moslem philosophers and scientists kept the lamp of learning bright, ready to rekindle the Western mind.[20]

The World's Living Religions

Islam's Scripture: the Koran

Islam cannot rightly be understood apart from the Koran,[21] the sacred writings of Islam. Its 78,000 words are divided into 114 chapters which, Moslems believe, were dictated to Mohammed by the Angel Gabriel during twenty-two years of specific ecstatic, prophetic moments.

Moslems believe that the Koran completes and corrects all previous scriptures (the Torah of the Jews and the Gospels of the Christians), and are the final revelation of God. They believe that all the words in the Koran are the words of God spoken to Mohammed through the Angel Gabriel just as they are written in the Koran; hence, they cannot be changed in any way whatsoever. For Moslems, the words of the Koran are absolute, complete, and infallible. Because they are, they regulate every phase of Islamic law, religion, culture, and politics. They are the sole guide of the true believer's life.

In the tradition of Islam, as well as in the prophetic traditions of Judaism and Christianity, the prophet was known as a prophet solely by virtue of his message and never because of his character. The prophet himself, in the case of Muhammad, was highly revered as a man. But no question existed in the orthodox Muslim mind regarding the priority of things. The prophet's message did not originate with the prophet himself. He only recited what had been spoken in heaven beforehand and conveyed verbatim to him by one of God's angels. Thus to the Muslim the Qur'an had been sent as the spoken word of God, borne into human experience through the lips of Muhammad, the inspired messenger.[22]

The Koran is a collection of Mohammed's recitations made during his moments of ecstasy which were written down by his faithful followers. These sayings, or recitations, were codified and standardized about A.D. 650, about twenty years after Mohammed's death.

In addition to the Koran, Moslems preserve a body of sacred tradition called *Hadith*, a collection of Mohammed's

20. From page 251, in *The Religions of Man*, by Huston Smith (Harper & Row Publishers, Perennial Library edition). Copyright © 1958 by Huston Smith. By permission of Harper & Row, Publishers, Inc.

21. *Koran* (Core ahn) is the English form of the Arabic word *Qur'an*, meaning "book," or "reading."

22. Reprinted from *Religious Literature of the West*, by John R. Whitney and Susan W. Howe, © 1968, 1971, by permission of Augsburg Publishing House.

words, sayings, explanations, and examples designed to help the true believer follow the Koran exactly. "Thus, the Muslim learned from the Qur'an that he must pray. But he learned from the Hadith, the particular form of prayer appropriate for a Muslim as commended by the practice of Mohammed. From the Qur'an, the Muslim learned that he must give alms. But he learned particular procedures for giving alms from the Hadith as it cited custom and advice of the Prophet in this respect. In each case, the Muslim traced the Hadith tradition back to prescriptions and prohibitions laid down by the Prophet, and the practices he followed from former times or initiated himself to be the way of Islam."[23]

Mohammed did not want these "ways, judgments, and actions" written down lest they be confused with the revelations of the Koran. However, after his death, his close followers collected those oral traditions of what Mohammed had said and done concerning the revelations and formed them into a collection of things that would guide the true believer in his observance of the prescriptions in the Koran. A typical story in the Hadith, for example, tells how Mohammed was taken by a mysterious animal to Jerusalem, and carried into heaven where he met Abraham, Moses, and Jesus.[24]

Among the basic doctrines of the Koran are four major themes: (1) Allah is the all-powerful One who created the world in which people live. (2) Allah, who created people for himself, will do with them as he wishes. (3) People, therefore, must perform the tasks Allah has assigned to them. (4) The day of judgment will find people deserving of reward in heaven or punishment in hell.

Interpretations of various sayings in the Koran are made from time to time, but the sayings of Mohammed which reveal the eternal truths (and, of course, reflect the culture, climate and topography of Arabia) are, according to Moslems, sufficient guidance for any person. "What need have we of a savior?" Moslems say. "We have a book that tells us how to live." Moslem life, from the Hegira in A.D. 622 to the present time is a reflection of the saying of the Koran and the five pillars of Islamic life.

Islam is having difficulty adjusting to the insights about the world and people from modern science, psychology, and anthropology. Born into a world that had a static concept of

Washing before prayer at the Dome of the Rock, Jerusalem

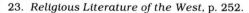

23. *Religious Literature of the West*, p. 252.

24. This incident was supposed to have taken place at "the rock" in Jerusalem, a spot not too far from where the Jewish Temple had stood. It is enclosed under the famous "Dome of the Rock," a sacred Moslem shrine.

The World's Living Religions

Selections from the Koran

Reward for prayers said by people assembled together are twice those said at home.

Our life is transitory, our life is a loan.

When the sun shall be darkened,
When the stars shall be thrown down,
When the mountains shall be set moving,
When pregnant camels shall be
   neglected,
When savage beasts shall be gathered,
When the seas shall be set boiling,
When Hell shall blaze and Heaven be
   brought near,
Then shall a soul know what it has
   produced.
On that day you shall be exposed, not one
   secret of yours concealed.
Then, for him who is given his book in his
   right hand,
he shall be in a lofty Garden,
its clusters close to gather . . .
But for him who is given his book in his
   left hand, he shall say: "Would that I
   had not known my own reckoning!"

Then will it be said: "Take him, and fetter
   him, and then roast him in Hell! . . .
He never believed in God the Almighty;
   therefore today he has not one loyal
   friend.

O you who believe! So that you may understand all that you say, do not approach prayers with a mind befuddled with alcohol, nor in a state of ceremonial impurity . . . without washing your whole body. If you are ill, or on a journey, . . . and you find no water, then take for yourselves clean sand or earth, and rub your faces and hands with it. For God blots out sins and forgives again and again.

Fight for the cause of God against those who fight against you, but commit not the injustice of attacking them first, God loves not such injustice . . . kill them wherever you find them, and eject them from whatever place they eject you. The sacred month [Ramadan] and the sacred precincts have safeguard against reprisals.

Surely this Koran guides to the way that is the straightest and gives good tidings to the believers who do deeds of righteousness. The Lord has decreed that you shall not serve any but Him, and be good to your parents, and give your relatives their rights, and never squander. . . . Approach not fornication; it is surely indecent and evil. Walk not proudly on the earth; you shall never tear it open, . . . nor attain the mountains in height.

Koran class in Bhopal, India

people and the universe ("Man has been launched in life, he must endure.") Islam, under the genius of a man who saw that the real world he knew needed a religion which spoke to people in their terms and not in terms of a past culture, presented a world view much different from that of the present day.

Moslems are discovering that, even though "man has been launched," he can do something besides endure. Devout Moslems, like devout Christians, Hindus, or Jews, are torn between loyalties to the revered past and imperatives of the present and future. In this uneasiness they, like so many others, are forced into the painful task of distinguishing between the essentials of their religion, which should always remain, and the minor details, which are conditioned by time and place and therefore need to be changed to enable them to live in the world as they experience it. They do what they can to express

The World's Living Religions

their pieties—observing those things which can be reasonably observed in a world no longer bound by the desert or the necessities of eking out an existence in a hostile world.

Summary

1. Islam is a religion whose name describes its essence: total surrender to God.

2. Moslems believe that Mohammed is the last and the greatest of a long line of prophets sent by God to reveal His will to people.

3. The five major obligations of Islam are total surrender to God, daily prayer, almsgiving, fasting and self-restraint during Ramadan, and a pilgrimage to Mecca.

4. Mohammed is one of history's most influential religious leaders.

5. Islam's scripture, gathered into a book called the Koran, consists of the sayings Mohammed received, Moslems believe, from the angel Gabriel, God's personal messenger to Mohammed.

For Review

1. What is Islam? Where did it arise? What are some of the probable causes for its emergence?

2. What expression constitutes the Moslem act of faith?

3. Be able to give brief details of Mohammed's life.

4. What are some of the things Islam has in common with Judaism and Christianity?

5. What experience sparked Mohammed's move to change the conditions of life for the people of Mecca?

6. What is the significance of "Hegira," "Medina," and "Mecca" in Islam?

7. What are the five obligations or "Pillars" of Islamic life? Briefly describe each.

8. What is the Koran for Moslems?

9. What are the two sacred shrines of Islam? Explain the significance of each.

10. In what areas of the world is Islam the dominant religion? What were some of the causes for the rapid spread of Islam after Mohammed's death?

11. What did Mohammed accomplish for Arabic society?

For Discussion

1. Discuss the Arab-Israeli conflict in light of what you know about Judaism and Islam.
2. Discuss the impact of modern science on religions rooted in the past. Should the advance of learning have a bad effect on religion? Why? Why not?
3. Do you think it would be good to have a government highly influenced by religious laws? Why? Why not?

For Research

1. Prepare a short report on the Crusades.
2. Prepare a report on Arab contributions to learning in Europe in the Medieval period.
3. Prepare a report on the influence of Islam on the history, art, and architecture of Spain.
4. See if you can find out why Moslems are forbidden alcohol, pork, and gambling.

Words You Should Know

If there are any words in the list which you are not sure of, look them up in the Word List at the end of the book.

Allah	Imam	minaret
eke	instigate	mosque
exploit	Islam	Muslim
fratricide	Koran	polygamy
Hegira	Mecca	

The Living Religions of the Eastern World

"God is Many"

Belief as Religion

When students of religion in the West turn their attention to Eastern civilization, they are entering a world which is largely unfamiliar to them. As we said before, the mind-set of people raised in the cultures of the East is vastly different from the mind-set of people influenced by Western culture.

The Golden Temple, Amritsar, India

The World's Living Religions

People of the East have their own ways of looking at reality, and their own ways of responding to that reality. Among the Eastern peoples, generally, contemplation is valued more highly than action, and actions are done not so much "to get things done" as to be the right kind of person. For Eastern peoples, style is more important than achievement, self-control more important than ostentatious display, and manners more important than results. Politeness, civility, respect, and passivity are hallmarks of Eastern peoples because their ways of looking at the world and at people develop in them a timelessness, a sense of proportion, and a fatality that is foreign to those raised in Western societies.

It is impossible to include all the belief systems of such a vast part of the world, but we will survey two countries and two major beliefs of each. From the land of India, we will survey Hinduism and the reaction against it, Buddhism. And from the land of China, we will survey Confucianism and the reaction against it, Taoism.

Actually, the belief systems examined here are not limited to the lands with which they are originally associated. Buddhism, for example, has spread beyond India and is adhered to by millions of Chinese; on its way through China one branch of Buddhism was filtered through Taoism and reached Japan in the form of Zen Buddhism, which is now one of the major beliefs in Japan.

A general title "Beliefs of the Eastern World" might be given to this section because, in the strict sense of a religion involving the worship of a God, some of the belief systems we shall discuss do not have such worship. Buddha, for example, was somewhat of an agnostic on the question of God and the afterlife. Confucius organized a way of life for this world without directly concerning himself about the next. Taoism cultivates a union with the processes of nature but does not see any necessity for God, for nature is self-sufficient. But, insofar as they are all responses to the mystery of life, they are religions. It is in this sense that the beliefs of the Eastern world are religions. It is in this sense that they are included in this survey of the religions of the world.

Hinduism

Half a world away from the busy metropolitan centers of the Western world, and the great capitals where the economic and political decisions which affect the lives of millions of people are made, live hundreds of millions of people, made up of many racial mixtures and divided into thousands of castes speaking 845 dialects. These are the people of India, the largest country in the subcontinent of Asia.

In spite of this tremendous diversity, these people have corporately had a spiritual impact on the world which would not have been possible without a unity and identity that is hard to define but is unmistakably present.

India is the country which produced the great concept of nonviolence. It has pushed human meditation into the depth of things deeper than almost any other culture. It has produced a remarkable atmosphere of toleration for differences of opinion. At the same time, due perhaps to the qualities that have made it what it is, India is the country where poverty and starvation afflict most of the people, where discrimination is most openly practiced and defended, and where indifference to social needs has created a society of untold misery almost incapable of solving even its most pressing problems. What makes India what it is—with both its strengths and its weaknesses—is Hinduism.

What Is Hinduism?

Hinduism, the basic religion of India, is marked by a fundamental openness of mind; openness above all of the depths of things and openness to the infinite. It is characterized by an instinctive unwillingess to stop at a particular idea or truth and think that it is the limit of knowledge or experience. Its distinguishing characteristic is a constant, restless search beyond the limits of what one already knows.

Hence, for the Hindus, Ultimate Reality is unknowable. No one, they believe—much less any one religion—can claim

Opposite page—
Kataragama Festival, Sri Lanka

163

for itself absolute and final truth. Hindus believe that all religions are partially true insofar as they are attempts to be open to the Ultimate, who may or may not be a Person, a Father, a Creator, a Ruler, a Savior, a Spirit, a Power, or a Force. For them, Ultimate Reality, or Brahman, is the ground of being.[1]

"A real Hindu will not circumscribe what he believes," says Doctor Raymond Panikkar, a Catholic theologian and philosopher whose mother was a Spanish Catholic and whose father was a Hindu Brahmin (the highest caste of Hindu). "He does not belong to 'a religion,' to a sect. He interprets Hinduism in his own way. Where to put the boundaries? Nowhere. There are no boundaries. Neither can one place Hinduism in relation to other religions. In a sense it is all religions."[2]

Hinduism is an insight (or rather, several diverse, or many times even contradictory, insights) into the nature of reality, and the entrance of the entire person into reality by means of insight. "Hinduism," says Lowell Streiker of Temple University, "is a subtly unified mass of wild mythologies, yogic disciplines and dogmatic speculations. The history of Hinduism is the chronicle of continual experimentation with *new forms* to produce *new ideals* to suit *new conditions*."[3]

There are 583 million Hindus in the world living mostly in India. A few live in countries bordering India, and some live in Africa, the Pacific Islands, and in the Americas.

In the United States, Hinduism and its offshoot, Buddhism, have enjoyed a singular popularity for the past few years among certain people, mostly young adults. They have found the experience of religion, the return to deeper realities, and the communing with God which Hinduism encourages, foster a response to their own seeking for answers to the mystery of life.

Hindu deity, Bali, India

The Origin and Growth of Hinduism

Hinduism is a genuine expression of primordial, that is initial, first, or beginning, religious awareness. It does not have a founder and it is the crystallization of the religious instincts of the people of India through the ages. Its beginnings are shrouded in mystery.

1. Brahman, or Brahma, is, for Hindus, the impersonal supreme being and the primal source and ultimate goal of all beings.

2. *Sign Magazine*, June, 1970, page 32.

3. *The Ecumenist*, September/October 1968, reprinted by permission, © 1968 by Paulist Fathers, Inc., 1865 Broadway, New York, N.Y.

Prehistoric Indian people had their nature gods, their forces of power, their spirit gods, their religious rituals, and their ways of coping with the particular forces of nature they experienced. All of these are reflected in Hinduism as we know it today. The land and the climate of India shaped and molded the Indian concept of the gods, and the geography of India played as important a role in the gradual development of what was eventually to become modern Hinduism as another factor.

India[4] is framed on the north by the majestic Himalaya Mountains which prevented invasions from that direction (and

4. The name *India* and the word *Hindu* come from the Sanskrit word *Indus*, the Persian name for the river flowing from Tibet through Kashmir and Pakistan to the Arabian Sea. Sanskrit is an Indo-European language used as the literary and religious language of India since 1200 B.C..

chapter 7 Hinduism   165

Hinduism

Can one rather define Hinduism by its elements? Actually, this will have to be done; but in attempting to find such a unifying definition we run the risk of generalizing to such an extent that we fail to grasp the infinite diversity of forms which constitute Hinduism. . . .

Hinduism is indeed a complex and rich religion. No founder's initiative, no dogma, no reform have imposed restrictions on its domain; on the contrary, the contributions of the centuries have been superimposed without ever wearing out the previous layers of development.

In fact, according to what phenomena one considers, Hinduism can appear either as an extrovert religion of spectacle, abundant mythology and congregational practices or as a religion which is profoundly interiorized. To the first view belong the activities of the sects, the *bhakti* movement, and the worship of the cow, in which some find the concrete symbol of Hinduism; here, too, could be included the principle of nonviolence, at least in its social application. To the view of Hinduism as an interior life belong the paths of spiritual progress, the quest for liberation, the tendency to renunciation, and finally the intensive concentration on problems which in other cultures are more often reserved for theologians or philosophers. Hinduism, which is eminently popular in its practices and external manifestations, is essentially also a religion of the learned: it cannot be understood if the *Vedanta* and the *Samkhya* have not been fully comprehended or if, at the outset, there is no idea of the immense network of

symbolism which underlies and links together all Indian thought.

Finally, Hinduism characterizes society as a whole. The caste system with its various "stages" of existence is part of Hinduism. Life is looked upon as a rite; there is no absolute dividing line between the sacred and the profane. In fact, there is no Hindu term corresponding to what we call "religion." There are "approaches" to the spiritual life; and there is *dharma,* or "maintenance" (in the right path), which is at once norm or law, virtue and meritorious action, the order of things transformed into moral obligation—a principle which governs all manifestations of Indian life.

Source: Louis Renou, editor, *Hinduism* (New York: George Braziller Company, 1962) pages 16–18.

consequently, the religion-shaping forces of China and the Far East), and on the west by the lands which are today Pakistan, Iran, Afghanistan, and Iraq (the Persian territories of 2500 B.C.). Its western boundaries were open to successive invasions, the most significant of which—as far as religious development is concerned—was the Aryan. This is the same wave of northwestern European tribes which swept over Greece, Syria and Mesopotamia, bringing their nature gods, and their gods of war and fire and destruction, of power and force, of fertility and generation. Other invasions, from the Greek under Alexander in 327 B.C. to the European conquest after Vasco de Gama's arrival in A.D. 1498, influenced Indian religion but did not basically change it.

Perhaps the chief characteristic of the Hindu religion is its ability to absorb, to enfold in its religious concepts the religious philosophies, theology, ritual, and ceremony of any other religion. This is not a form of syncretism, but a flexibility, an ability to "see" in other religions an expression of their own. The Indian is, in the main, passive, capable of waiting, believing that the cycle of creation will bring all things back to what they were—so why fight it? This is especially so in religion, for the Hindus, believing that they have only a partial vision of the great Brahman, see in other religions a manifestation of the limitless expressions of Brahman. They see the Hebrew God, the Allah of Islam, and the Trinity of Christianity as nothing more than various manifestations of their own deity, who can manifest Himself as Brahma, the Creator; Vishnu, the Preserver; Shiva, the Destroyer, or as any other particular "god." *Thus, the Hindus see the various major religions as alternate and comparatively equal roads to the same Reality, the prime source of all things and ultimate ground of all being.* Reality, for the Hindus can have many faces and many names and even many gods—still it is One Reality.

If flexibility and adaptability are characteristic of Hinduism, what basically *is* Hinduism, if it is not some shapeless grab-bag of all religions?

Arising as it did from people's basic encounter with their universe and shaped as it was by centuries of speculation, Hinduism presents a complex symphony of miracle and magic, faith in a universal power, a kind of nature worship, a polytheism,[5] a pantheism,[6] and a system of theological-philosophical reflection on the deities that rival the complex theologies of the West.

5. *Polytheism* (pol-y-thee-ism) means belief in many gods.
6. *Pantheism* means that the entire universe is God.

Perhaps the simplest way to describe Hinduism (or rather the religion of India since there are many expressions of Hinduism) is to describe its concept of God, its understanding of self, and a person's path to Brahman (God).

The Hindu Concept of God

Brahman, the Hindus contend, cannot be defined, described, or properly conceived by the human mind because the mind evolved to cope with the problem of survival in this universe. It deals with, or conceives of, only finite objects. Because The Great One is not finite, because he is the Power Beyond, the Unsearchable, the Unknowable, he will never be "known." Perhaps the best "description" of the Hindu idea of God comes in the prayer of Shankara, a great Hindu philosopher: "O Thou before whom all words recoil."

The Hindu concept of God is defined most clearly in their scriptures, especially in that segment known as the Upanishads.[7]

Namaste Hindu greeting, Nepal

The Upanishads center around the doctrine of the identity of *Brahman,* the universal Spirit, and *Atman,* the true Self of each individual. A man's true self is an expression or manifestation of the divine Spirit. In the Chandogya Upanishad, this identity is expressed in the formula which is at the core of all Hindu religious thought: *tat tvam asi* ("that art thou"). When a man, through the fulfillment of all duties, the discipline of all physical functions and the control of all mental faculties, penetrates to the very center or ground of his being, he discovers the one identity of his true Self with the one really existent entity, the all-inclusive, unitary Being.

Of nearly equal importance in the thought of the Upanishadic seers is the *neti, neti* ("neither this nor that") doctrine. The *neti-neti* conception insists, in the words of the Kena Upanishad: "He truly knows Brahman who knows him as beyond knowledge; he who thinks that he knows, knows not." Given any set of alternatives, Brahman is neither, and yet, according to the *tat-tvam-asi* doctrine, *both.* "He is," says the Mandukya Upanishad, "above all distinctions." In the words of the Brihadaranyaka Upanishad, the universal Self "is described as *not this, not that.* It is incomprehensible." Yet, claims the same Upanishad: "He assumed all forms to reveal himself in all forms. He, the Lord, is revealed in all forms. . . ." The divine cannot be poured into a single conceptual mold. Its infinite richness demands a humility on the part of the adherent of any religion, as well as a recognition that his understanding of the truth is but a partial one.[8]

The Hindu Supreme Reality is not, however, a mass of nothing. That God cannot be described does not make nothing of God. Thus, the Hindus, feeling incapable of defining (and thus limiting) God, encourage believers to conceive of God in the way that is best for the individual. For all, God is *Brahman*. For one type of believer, he is Saguna Brahman, the Father—provident, almighty, all-wise, personally concerned about each present moment. For the other type of believer, God is Nirguna Brahman, the goal, an infinite being of infinite consciousness, but aloof, immovable, unconcerned about the infinite world and the present moment. For both, Brahman is the supreme reality, being, or a perfection—the one from whom all things have come and toward which all ultimately return.

Like Christians, Hindus believe that God is at the end of everyone's journey. Their sacred book, the Bhagavad-Gita, *says: "I am the end everyone has to reach. Different people call me by different names and go on different paths, according to their different ways of understanding and illumination. But all paths lead to one goal. Lord Krishna is ever ready, with open arms, to welcome his devotees, no matter by what way they came and what path they followed."[9]*

If God is so conceived, either personally or impersonally, it follows that a person in relation to God will be affected by an individual particular belief. That is why the Hindus have many degrees of relationship to the Supreme Reality and many paths to it.

Hinduism contains a heritage of many gods[10] without seeing in this a contradiction, for it recognizes these many gods as attempts on the part of people to understand a particular aspect of God. One explanation it offers is that the various gods are "faces" of Brahman; but Hinduism does not rely heavily on explanation. Realizing that all explanations are inadequate to Reality, it allows people to approach the One Reality

7. The *Upanishads* (oo-pan-i-shads) are part of Hindu scriptures.

8. *The Ecumenist,* September–October, 1968, p. 177.

9. *Columban Mission,* May 1982, p. 10.

10. It is said that the Hindu "god-list" contains thirty-three million gods. Over and above all, and penetrating all existence, of course, is Brahman. Next in importance are Brahma, the Creator; Vishnu, the Preserver; and Shiva, the Destroyer.

Women bathing along
Ganges, Benares, India

in whatever way or in as many ways as are useful. If a person finds it congenial to come to God through relating to him as many Gods, this is as acceptable as if a person were to admire white light by admiring its rainbow colors refracted through a prism.

The Hindu Concept of Self

The Hindus think of a person not simply as a body or as a unique individual personality, but as *an individual expression of a reservoir of being that never dies, that is an infinite center, a hidden self, or Atman—a kind of World Soul from which all souls come and to which they return. This hidden center-soul is, for Hindus, in reality, Brahman.*

Unfortunately, according to Hinduism, people do not easily realize the hidden greatness of who they are. Instead of identifying themselves with the Total Being which is their innermost soul, they identify themselves with their surface self and the happenings of daily life, and only with difficulty come to realize the full meaning of life.

The World's Living Religions

In an attempt to free people from their surface preoccupations and illusions so that they can attain union with their deepest God-selves (a state called *Nirvana*), Hinduism has developed an elaborate system of explaining people and their paths to God.

According to the Hindu collective understanding, a person has four basic "needs" or "wants": (1) pleasure, (2) worldly success, (3) a desire to be useful or of service, and (4) infinite being. Every person can grow from the first stage to the last, but most people do not manage to do so in one lifetime.

Hence, Hindus believe in reincarnation. Like all beliefs which have their foundations in the past, the Hindu doctrine of reincarnation has evolved to a rather refined or "modern" explanation. It arose from the universal belief that the "soul" must go somewhere, because it does not simply die but has a destiny beyond this tangible life. Unlike the Jewish, Christian, and Moslem belief that a person has but one chance—this life—the Hindus propose that a person has several lives, that everyone is re-born (reincarnated) into a higher or lower form of life according to how well or how poorly a previous life was lived. Belief in reincarnation is not simply belief in being born again as an animal, an insect, or a reptile. It involves a more complicated procedure than fate. It is determined by each person's life and how closely each one approaches the knowledge and final awareness of his or her true self.[11]

Hindus believe that the true self can only be found in a profound search for that inner being, or power, of each person, which is the extension of Brahman and is identical with Brahman. This identity or union with Brahman, arrived at in the state called Nirvana, is the only way to freedom from an endless cycle of reincarnation. Through it, a person, finally breaking through the sheaths of external reality, is no longer bound up with suffering, hatred, emotions, and passions. Such a one is utterly free of the "unreal self" and enters the state of eternal union, or true self.

In order to achieve this unity, each person must be reborn until the "sheaths" that prevent one from getting to the inner self have been shed. To do so a person must lead a "life of perfection"—a constant striving to get rid of the things which interfere with self-perfection. For this reason a true

11. The Hindus, for example, believe that to be born a woman is a punishment for evil actions in a former existence. Hence, for Hindus, salvation does not mean being reborn (in the Christian sense); it means being freed from the endless cycle of reincarnations—achieving Nirvana.

In the beginning there was Existence, One only, without a second. Some say that in the beginning there was non-existence only, and that out of that the universe was born. But how could such a thing be? How could existence be born of non-existence? No, my son, in the beginning there was Existence alone—One only, without a second. He, the One, thought to himself: Let me be many, let me grow forth. Thus, out of himself he projected the universe; and having projected out of himself the universe, he entered into every being. All that is has its self in him alone. Of all things he is the subtle essence. He is the truth. He is the Self. And that, Svetaketu, THAT ART THOU.[12]

moral life—in which a person rejects selfishness, curbs his or her desires, and does "the good"—insures a better condition in the next incarnation. On the other hand, a person who does not lead a moral life is "sheathing" the self, or regressing, and hence may go back to a previous or worse state, say as an insect or snake or rodent or perhaps a magnificent stallion.

Hindus, then, believe that they have lived before and will live again until they reach Nirvana. Their life cycles will perhaps be endless, monotonous rounds of experiences until by self-discipline (hence, the need for yoga, or devotions to lesser deities) they, at some future time (100,000 years? 423,000 years?) enter complete union with the Power, the One Indwelling Deity.

The Hindu Ways to Union with God

A truly religious person, according to Hinduism, is one who seeks to transform his or her nature, to make it into a super nature, a truly complete human being. But because there are basically four kinds of persons[13] (with an infinite variety within the four kinds), there are four ways to attain this supreme reality through four kinds of *yoga*—specific directions

12. *The Upanishads, Breath of the Eternal*, translated by Swami Prabhavananda and Frederick Manchester (a Mentor Book from New American Library, New York). Copyright by Vedanta Society of Southern California, Hollywood, California.

13. Reflective, emotional, active, experimental.

or means to achieve the goal, the union of a person's soul with the deity. It involves physical and mental exercise designed to bring about this integration or union.[14]

The purpose of yoga is to correct the false identification of self with what is apparent and to seek for that which lies underneath the layers in a person's true self. The true practicer of religious yoga is one who is seeking the true self— the "I" who possesses body, mind, and soul but which cannot be equated with any one or all of them.

Depending on the type of person one is, upon his or her particular bent, he or she can achieve this union with the Supreme Reality through knowledge, love, work, or psychological experience.

14. Yoga is not primarily a scheme for physical culture or exercise. It is designed to achieve a spiritual purpose.

Hindu holy man, Nepal

1. Through knowledge

For one who seeks the Supreme Reality through knowledge or contemplation (after physical and mental discipline establish the means for total meditation),[15] the aim is oneness with this reality or the seeking for Atman-Brahman. The sense of identity with the Eternal Spirit is so great that he or she no longer "feels" the finite, the sensible—he or she becomes insensitive to pleasure and pain alike. He has complete control over his body because he "withdraws" from it. For this Yogi,[16] God is an impersonal goal, a depth, a reality to be sought, the ultimate in being. The way to God through knowledge is difficult—it is reserved for the very few.

2. Through love

A far easier way to the Supreme Reality is through love. The practicers of this form of yoga, having a personalist view of God, direct the love that is basic to human feeling toward God. The practitioner of knowledge (Jnana) yoga conceives of God as an impersonal sea of being. The devotee of love (Bhakti) yoga sees God as one to whom love is directed in adoration. Usually this love is expressed to Vishnu. The Hindu Bhakti seeks to love God not by word but by action, and for no other motive than simply God's own self.

The Bhakta distinguishes four kinds of love, hence four ways of looking at God. The first is love of God as protector, provider and benevolent master. The second regards God as friend or intimate companion. The third regards God as a loving Father, and the fourth regards God as one's beloved, one's intimate, one's divine spouse. The ultimate is reached when all things are love because God is loved.

3. Through work

A third way to God—for those inclined to be active—is the way through work. It is known as Karma Yoga.

Hindus realize that everyone must in one way or another be active. But often, people do their work merely for the sake of ego-inflating success. For the Karma Yogi, however, work is performed as an act of devotion—as a service to God, who

---

15. Meditation is an intensification of the mind which is in the fullness of silence. The mind is not still like some tamed, frightened or disciplined animal; it is still as the waters are still many fathoms down. The stillness there is not like that on the surface when the winds die. This stillness has a life and a movement of its own which is related to the outer flow of life, but is untouched by it. Its intensity is not that of some powerful machine which has been put together by cunning, capable hands; it is as simple and natural as love, as lightning, as a full-flowing river. (To paraphrase J. Krishnamurti)

16. Practicer of yoga.

gives the energy for working and thus is working "through" the person. Considering work a part of the eternal purpose, the Karmi does each act as if it were the only thing and the last thing he or she has to do. Distracting desires are discarded and a calm is achieved that stems from concern with the eternal as opposite to the turmoil that stems from personal anxieties. Thus, work is a liberating thing, freeing him from the sense of frustration and limitation which others experience in work.

4. Through psychological experience

The fourth path to God—or the reintegration of self into the deity—is the way of psychological experiment or examination. Such an experiment or examination, however, does not refer to a doctor-patient relationship. It refers to a self-examination and perfection that uses life's personal experiences to delve into one's deeper self to discover the inner Being which can only be reached when the external layers of concern are stripped away. Within each person's being, Hindus believe, is this inner Being, or Being Itself, which is hidden because of the distractions and necessities of the world.

Boys in Kataragama procession, Sri Lanka

Hindus view a person as a "layered" being. What we see and feel affects our outer layer, but by successive yoga practices, a person can "peel away" the layers and thereby enter completely into self, where nothing distracts and nothing draws one from the Utter Reality. A person in this stage has reached the Ultimate; he or she is "back" into the Being from which all things come.

In this Raja Yoga, yoga is practiced to its most intense degree to discipline the body and the mind in such a way that nothing distracts it—not joy or sorrow, pleasure or pain, happiness or irritation. The Raji work long hours to secure such control (the classic yoga position for example, is crossed legs, foot resting on thigh, spinal cord absolutely erect, hands palm up on the lap, one atop the other, eyes half-opened) that he or she can virtually stop breathing. The Raji seeks such absolute control over the body and mind that concentration will lead to complete absorption in God. Unlike Jnana Yoga (knowledge), which presents meditations designed to *convince* the thinker that there is a Universal Being deeper than himself and his world, Raja Yoga presents the deeper *experience* of the "real" self to arrive at a perfect union with this God.

In these four methods of yoga, the Hindus encourage each individual to conceptualize God and to worship as his or her idea dictates. They believe that because no *one* thing can represent God, neither can many things. Hindus are not exclu-

sivists, insisting on one form rather than another. Neither are they indifferent, for Hindus are a God-conscious people. They just respect every person's right to conceive of the Inconceivable in his or her own way.

The Stages of Life According to Hindu Belief

In Hindu belief, a normal, harmonious life consists of four stages. The first is that of a learner. Under the direction of a *guru*, or spiritual director, a true Hindu opens himself or herself to life in such a way that no matter what status or caste he or she seeks to learn to live that life to its utmost.[17]

The second stage is that of marriage or the prime of life, where one should engage himself totally in his family, his vocation, and his community life. If life has been lived properly, the third stage will not be a downhill or a cessation of activity stage. It will be devoted to a mature self-understanding. ". . . business, family, secular life, like the beauties and hopes of youth and the success of maturity, have now been left behind;

17. Everything in Hinduism is predicated on one's being a male. A woman is a woman because in "his" former life "he" did evil deeds of such a nature as to make him be reborn as a female—starting over, as it were. Hindu women, of course, live exemplary lives in order to be born again as a male.

eternity remains. And so it is to that—not to tasks and worries of life, already gone, which come and pass like a dream—that the mind is turned."[18]

The fourth and most exclusive of the Hindu's stages is the last, the state of *Sannyism*.[19] It is the stage arrived at after the prolonged spiritual examination of stage three in which a person neither loves nor hates, seeks or desires, goes forth or resists. He simply is at rest in the Holy Power with all his faculties. In this stage, he prepares himself for his passage to the unknown—that which lies beyond this earthly life.

What lies beyond depends upon *karma,* the chain that binds action and the fruits of action. A life well lived brings rewards in the next incarnation. Being born of low degree, to suffering poverty, and discrimination, supposedly is due to sins committed in previous lives. Hindu folklore abounds in legends about the workings of karma. In one group of morality tales, for example, a foolish man is reborn as a monkey, a cunning one as a jackal, a greedy one as a crow. A tribal myth of Orissa tells of a woman burning with jealousy who is reborn as a chili plant, destined to burn all its life. Conversely, an animal may rise to human status, in stages or all at once if it has done the right deeds, particularly to a person of high caste.

Yet there is another aspect of karma, easier to understand. Within a single lifetime, what one does today shapes his tomorrow; we reap what we sow. For Hinduism, karma makes clear the logic of morality.[20]

This aspect of Hindu belief explains some of the things which characterize India in the minds of Western visitors—things like sacred cows, holy men, starving people, and the caste system. Among these, none is so hard to understand or accept, especially from people who seem to be enlightened and tolerant, as the caste system. It can be explained, perhaps, by saying that the same view of people which permits such diversity in religious thought and expression, also permits the caste system to flourish. It can also be explained in part by the fact that, for Hindus, there are different paths to the Universal One, different life patterns appropriate to various stages in a person's life, and different positions or stations in life in

18. Heinrich Zimmer, *Philosophies of India* (New York: Pantheon Books, 1951).

19. Most Hindus are content to remain in stage two.

20. Dr. Amiya Chakravarty from *Great Religions of the World,* © National Geographic Society 1971, 1978.

the social order because of the way a person lived in his or her former life.

The caste system began some 2,000 years before Christ, probably resulting from a combination of invasion, ethnic and religious differences, health and fertility requirements, and religious taboo. No one knows for sure. But, in India, the normal differences in any society—of intellectual and spiritual leaders, of administrators and politicians, of manufacturers (producers), and of laborers—became fixed and rigid. In the course of time, a fifth group emerged called "untouchables." These social outcasts became the dregs of Indian society.

So rigid did the caste system become in India that marriage outside of the particular caste or level was forbidden, and rising from one level to another impossible. In addition, privileges of caste created burdens for lower levels, making the lowest a veritable hell to be in.

A proliferation of castes within castes[21] spawned a society whose main characteristics are undeserved privilege, exclusiveness, rigidity, and heartless cruelty to lower castes. The lowest castes—the untouchables—are not slaves in the strictest sense; but they are victims of a system which is perhaps as heartless as any system of slavery devised.

One of the reasons the caste system can remain so vital a part of Indian society today lies in the Hindu concept of people's nature and destiny. To the Hindu, the important thing is not the external; it is internal union with God. If a person reaches this union well enough in the present state, he or she will be reincarnated into a higher caste in the next life until perfect Nirvana is reached. If one does not, he or she deserves his fate.

It is not possible to categorize or dogmatize about Hinduism. It is a religion which can, perhaps, be best described as the search for human awareness, the search for the real self, whether this be by practices of primitive worship, the devotions of later insights, or the sophistication of the ultimate yogi. *Accepting the idea of the eternal cycle, the Hindu by one way or another seeks incorporation into the principle, the unknowable Brahman.*

This is the heart of Hinduism. There may be a multitude of lesser gods, but there is one ultimate Brahman; all others are but "faces" of the true. They may be true in their own right, but they are, nonetheless, distinct from and inferior to the Alone. Hence, the Hindu can tolerate all kinds of temples and gods and devotions and practices. Whether his devotion

21. Over 3,000 subcastes are still prevalent in India.

or sacrifice is directed to Krishna or Shiva, or Kali or Parvati or Surya (the sun god, symbolized by the rays of the sun in Hindu devotional images) or the multi-armed images in Hindu temples, the true Hindu hopes for peace and encompassment in the Brahman cradle—or final rest.

Hindu Scriptures

The Hindu scriptures, or body of sacred writing, are a collection of sacred hymns, stories, legends, commentaries, ritual directives, myths, directives for sacrifice, liturgy, mag-

When he casts from him
Vanity, violence,
Pride, lust, anger
And all his possessions,
Totally free
From the sense of ego
And tranquil of heart:
That man is ready
For oneness with Brahman.
And he who dwells
United with Brahman,
Calm in mind,
Not grieving, not craving,
Regarding all men
With equal acceptance:
He loves me most dearly.
To love is to know me,
My innermost nature,
The truth that I am:
Through this knowledge he enters
At once to my Being.

All that he does
Is offered before me
In utter surrender:
My grace is upon him,
He finds the eternal,
The place unchanging.
                    —The Bhagavad-Gita

Source: *Bhagavad-Gita* (New York: The New American Library, 1954) p. 128.

ical spells and charms, philosophy, and theological speculation.

The Hindu scriptures, like the scriptures of other religions, had their origin in oral tradition dating back many centuries before they were codified and standardized in written form sometime between 1500 and 800 B.C. Unlike the scriptures of the religions of the West, however, Hindu scriptures are not selective. They are, literally, collections of the religious wisdom of the Hindus over the centuries.

The Hindu scriptures are divided into two main parts, the *Vedas* and the *Upanishads*. The Vedas are four collections of religious material containing prayers, ritual, liturgy, hymns, and spells and charms of a popular nature. They are, basically, Hindu prayer books. The Upanishads are a collection of philosophical commentaries dealing mostly with Indian deities. While the Vedas deal with nature worship and polytheism, the Upanishads deal with the nature of Brahman.

Hindus believe their scriptures, called *shruti* (from the Sanskrit word meaning "that which is heard") are divinely revealed to seers in each world cycle. They are given the utmost reverence because they contain, Hindus believe, the "divine words" leading to knowledge of Brahman. The Vedas, Hindus believe, contain such divinely revealed material. The *smriti* (that which is remembered), on the other hand, are not divinely revealed—they are the remembered sayings, teachings, stories, epics, and commentaries of the respected gurus of Hinduism. They are, however, an important and respected part of the Hindu sacred writing because they are "infallible guides to right conduct."

Siva and Parvati Enthroned (Courtesy of Museum of Fine Arts, Boston)

In addition to these two basic collections of sacred writings, the Hindu scriptures include the *Vedanta*, a collection of speculative religious thought developed over centuries of interpretation of the Upanishads, and two religious epics, the *Mahabharata* and the *Ramayana*, two sacred myths containing sacred history for Hindus. These, too, are highly regarded, serving as the base for the teachings of the gurus and the inspiration for the moral life of Hindus.

Hindu Ritual and Custom

Worship

Hindu worship is basically individualistic, though at times groups of Hindus seem to be praying together because they are in the same place at the same time.

The World's Living Religions

The Hindu's day begins with washing or bathing. If possible, the Hindu bathes in a river, reciting certain prayers, washing his mouth, and paying homage to the life-giving sun. Offerings may be made during the day, either at a household shrine or in shrines or temples dedicated to certain gods and goddesses. Each caste or subcaste has its own special rites and prayers, and there are certain agricultural observances which resemble the ancient harvest rites of Christian Ember Days.

Rivers play a central role in Hindu worship. If one does not live near a river, the Hindu worships in a pond, a lake, a stream, a fountain—wherever there is water. But the ideal is flowing water, and all rivers are sacred—as well they might be in a land where the temperature commonly runs from a hundred to a hundred and twenty degrees and there are long periods of drought.

Hindu temples are usually staffed by one or several priests. They perform the sacred ceremonies alone, without a congregation. There is no such thing as communal worship nor a "Sunday," though there are certain holy days during the year on which people are more likely to perform their sacred duties. Generally speaking, a Hindu will worship wherever and whenever the spirit comes over him or her. The passing Westerner may turn his head in embarrassment, but a Hindu at prayer will often attract a crowd eager to observe the fervor with which he or she prays.

Sacraments

There is a sacramental system in Hinduism called the *samskaras*, which include a kind of baptism, an initiation rite (confirmation), a marriage ceremony, and a death rite. There are anywhere from ten to forty *samskaras*, depending on one's definition of the term.

One of the most beautiful and elaborate *samskaras* is that of marriage, which takes different forms among different castes. In a typical Hindu marriage ceremony, a young couple sits in the street (where they will remain for five days), while people from their village sit around them, having a party and making ribald remarks about the coming consummation. The young couple are, hopefully, deep in prayer. Normally a bride and groom do not see each other before the ceremony.

Marriages are invariably arranged by the parents. The ceremony itself takes place before a fire, into which certain foods are symbolically cast. Vows are exchanged, and the respective families pledge mutual love and aid. At the end of the

Selections from Hindu Scriptures

The Upanishads

The Upanishads probe underlying truths of human existence. The selections below deal with the related concepts of karma and transmigration. Every action holds its inevitable result; traveling through many bodies, a soul reaps in one life what it has sown in the past:

According as one acts, according as one conducts himself, so does he become. The doer of good becomes good. The doer of evil becomes evil. One becomes virtuous by virtuous action, bad by bad action.

But people say: "A person is made not of acts, but of desires only." In reply to this I say: As is his desire, such is his resolve; as is his resolve, such the action he performs; what action he performs, that he procures for himself. On this point there is this verse:

Where one's mind is attached—
the inner self goes thereto with action,
being attached to it alone.
Obtaining the end of his action,
Whatever he does in this world,
He comes again from that world [the realm of the dead]
To this world of action.

—So the man who desires.

Now the man who does not desire—He who is without desire, who is freed from desire, whose desire is satisfied, whose desire is the Soul—his breaths do not depart. Being very Brahman, he goes to Brahman.

Song of Creation

Who verily knows and who can declare it,
When it was born and when comes this creation?
The Gods are later than this world's production.
Who knows, then, whence it first came into being?
He, the first of this creation whether he formed it all or did not form it,
Whose eye controls this world in highest heaven,
He verily knows it, or perhaps he knows not.

Kali, goddess who destroys evil. Temple painting in Poona, India

To Visnu

I will declare the mighty deeds of Visnu, of
   him who measured out the earthly
   regions,
Who propped the highest place of
   congregation, thrice setting down his
   footstep, widely striding.
For this his mighty deed is Visnu lauded,
   like some wild beast, dread, prowling,
   mountain roaming;
He within whose three wide-extended
   paces all living creatures have their
   habitation.

*The Bhagavad-Gita is part of Hindu
sacred writing in the form of a dialogue
between the hero, Arjun, and his
charioteer, the human form of the god
Krishna.*

Give me your whole heart,
Love and adore me,
Worship me always,
Bow to me only,
And you shall find me:
This is my promise
Who love you dearly.

Lay down all duties
In me, your refuge.
Fear no longer,
For I will save you
From sin and from bondage.

My face is equal
To all creation,
Loving no one
Nor hating any.

Nevertheless,
My devotees dwell
Within me always:
I also show forth
And am seen within them.

Though a man be soiled
With the sins of a lifetime,
Let him but love me,
Rightly resolved,
In utter devotion:

I see no sinner,
That man is holy.
Holiness soon
Shall refashion his nature
To peace eternal;
Of this be certain:
The man that loves me,
He shall not perish.

Source: *Bhagavad-Gita* (New York: The New American Library, 1954) p. 129.

Indore cows and temple, India

ceremony, the wife leads her husband to a spot where they can see the North Star. She says: "You are steady. May I be as steady in my husband's family." The husband says: "The sky is firm, the earth is firm, and this wife is firm in her husband's family." The wife: "I pay homage to you." The husband: "May you be long-lived." He adds: "I bind your heart and mine with the knot of truth. May your heart be mine. May my heart be yours."

There are equally beautiful ceremonies for other *samskaras*, such as on the day when a child is presumed to be conceived, during pregnancy, at birth, on his name day (which would correspond to baptism), when he takes his first hard food, at the first cutting of his hair, and especially at the time when he receives the sacred thread which denotes his full acceptance into the Hindu community.

Sacred Cows

Most Westerners find Hindu reverence for the cow completely incomprehensible. But for the Hindu, sacred cows symbolize the entire subhuman world. Cow protection is an expression of people's affinity to all that lives. The cow is referred to as God Matha and is treated with the same respect one would give his own mother. The cow is thus a symbol of divine motherhood, of life, of the entire animal world, of fecundity, and of abundance. Every cow is considered to be a descendant of Kamadhenu, a heavenly cow with the face of a beautiful woman.

There are more than two hundred million cows in India—one for every three people. As one Hindu put it: "We reverence cows. You eat them: the arms and legs, ribs, tail, liver, stomach, testicles, brains, all the other inner organs, the blood, everything except the eyes. What you don't eat, you wear (the skin). And what's left over you use as soap for washing and for fertilizer to make your vegetables grow. You call it practical efficiency. We call it cannibalism. Would you eat your mother?"[22]

Summary

1. Hinduism is open to all forms of belief and all ways of worshipping. It is basically a meditative faith.

2. Hindus can accept all forms of gods believing that each is an expression of the Ultimate, their Brahman.

3. Hindu life and morality are directed toward final absorption into Brahman.

4. Hindus believe in reincarnation because they believe a person must rid himself of the "selves" that keep him from being incorporated into Brahman.

5. Hindus practice yoga in order to be incorporated into Brahman.

22. Reprinted from *Sign Magazine*, June 1970, p. 33.

For Review

1. Why is Hinduism a near perfect example of the developing religious awareness of people?
2. What is the chief characteristic of Hinduism? Explain.
3. What is God for Hindus? Why do Hindus have so many gods?
4. What is yoga? What are the different kinds of yoga and why are there different kinds?
5. Explain the Hindu concept of self.
6. What is reincarnation? Explain. Why do Hindus believe in reincarnation? What do they mean by "the eternal cycle of life"?
7. Explain the Hindu concept of the stages of a person's life. What is the highest stage of life according to Hindu belief?
8. What is the caste system? How is it possible for the Indian culture to accept the caste system?
9. What are the Hindu scriptures? Explain their main divisions.

For Discussion

1. Discuss the possibility of reincarnation. Do you know any people who believe in reincarnation?
2. Discuss why Hindus seem to be unconcerned about the situation in life in which they find themselves.
3. Discuss the probable causes for the great poverty in India and suggest some solutions. Why does it seem that the great majority of Indians do not accept Western ways to increase food production?
4. Discuss the dharma/karma relationship and whether or not you think it is essentially true.
5. Given the Hindu conception of women, discuss why women in India are faithful Hindus, why Hinduism is accepted by some North American girls, and the impact of Women's Liberation on Hinduism.

For Research

1. Prepare some research on the Ganges River in Hindu life and worship.
2. Look up information on the economic conditions in present-day India.
3. Prepare some research on the Dalai Lama of Tibet.
4. Who was Mohandas Gandhi?
5. Look up information on the interest in Hinduism in the United States.
6. Prepare a report on the caste system in India.
7. Find out what you can about the Hindu "holy men" or fakirs.

Words You Should Know

If there are any words given below that you are not sure of, look them up in the Word List at the back of the book.

Atman	guru	reincarnation
Bhagavad-Gita	karma	Shiva
Brahma	mantra	swami
Brahman	Nirvana	Upanishads
Brahmin	pantheism	Vedas
caste	Krishna	Vishnu
categorize	proliferation	yoga

chapter 8

Buddhism

Closely associated with, but distinct from Hinduism is Buddhism (boodism). Like Christianity and Islam, Buddhism arose in a particular time in a particular place—in India, in the fifth century before Christ. It was the result of the spiritual insights of Siddhartha Gautama who lived from 563 to 486 B.C.

Gautama, or, as he became known, Buddha (meaning The Awakened or Enlightened One), was one of the most remarkable men who ever lived. Although he was raised in the Hindu tradition and enjoyed the benefits of being the son of the chief of the Sakya clan (he had money, servants, prize horses, beautiful women, and exquisite places to live at his command), he broke with Hindu tradition, rejecting the caste system, the concepts of many gods, the need for many rebirths to attain perfect peace, and unquestioning submission to fate. He started out in search of peace and salvation for himself; yet wound up bringing it to millions of others. From his own enlightenment and his preaching to others has come one of the world's great living religions.

There are about 280 million Buddhists in the world today, living mostly in Asia—in Burma, Ceylon, Vietnam, Thailand, Korea, Japan, China, and Mongolia. In North America, there are about 100,000 Buddhists, and, perhaps, another 100,000 "pseudo-Buddhists" who have adopted certain Buddhist practices but who are not true Buddhists.

It is interesting to note that although Buddhism arose in India, it is not widely accepted in India, despite the Hindu acceptance of all forms of religion. The reason for this is that Buddhism is not just another religion to the Hindus. It is a direct assault on the customs, institutions, culture, and religion of India.

Perhaps the best way to describe Buddhism is to say that it "is a faith, a body of philosophy and wisdom, and a group of practices meant to relieve humankind of material, spiritual, and psychological suffering and to resolve the inevitable contradictions of life."

Opposite page—Great Buddha, Kamzkura, Japan

189

Buddhism's concern is not with God or the *why* of life but with *how* humans shall exist in this universe and give value to every breath drawn.[1]

The Origin of Buddhism

Having gone through the first two stages of Hindu life,[2] and seeing that the promised peace of Jnana Yoga came only to the relative few who mastered it and that misery and discrimination were the lot of the many, Gautama went in search of the secret to peace and happiness. For seven years after his twenty-ninth birthday (leaving his wife and child in good care, as Hindu belief demanded), he studied, meditated, fasted, and worked to achieve "the perfect peace." He did not find it. Finally, abandoning the ritualistic practices of yoga and extreme asceticism,[3] Gautama set himself to meditation on the causes for evil and the means to happiness.

As legend tells it, Gautama seated himself under a fig tree in the forest and meditated on the meaning of life and the means to happiness and peace. After long hours of serious thought he suddenly became enlightened.[4] He grasped what he called the Four Sacred Truths of the way to enlightenment. Leaving his meditation spot, he went to tell his companions of his discovery. Convinced of its truth, he spent the rest of his life preaching his way of enlightenment. It is from his experience of being suddenly enlightened that Gautama received the name "the Buddha"—"the enlightened one."

The "Way" of Buddha

What distinguishes Buddhism from Hinduism, from which it sprang? For one thing, it was founded by a man; it was not the result of an accumulation of centuries of prehistoric religious growth. For another, it rejected the wheel of birth idea in favor of going to the very heart of every person's search for Nirvana. It rejected the idea of several deities as outside helpers in people's search for happiness and urged them to

1. Miami-Dade Community College, *Students' Guide to the Long Search* (Dubuque: Kendall/Hunt Publishing Company, 1978) p. 84.

2. See page 176.

3. An ascetic is one who dedicates his or her life to the pursuit of contemplative ideals and practices extreme self-denial for religious reasons.

4. This particular fig tree, called "pipal," is now known as the "Bo" tree, from "bodhi" meaning enlightenment.

The World's Living Religions

Southeast Asia

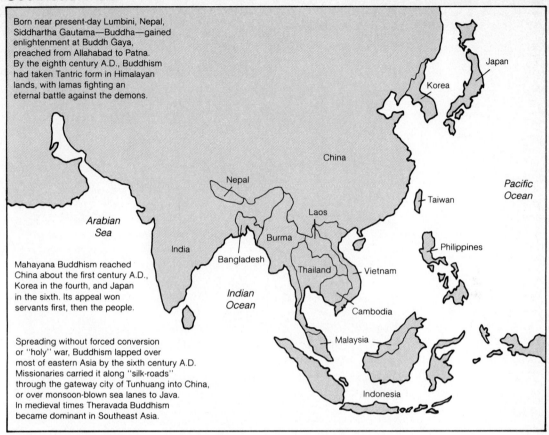

Born near present-day Lumbini, Nepal, Siddhartha Gautama—Buddha—gained enlightenment at Buddh Gaya, preached from Allahabad to Patna. By the eighth century A.D., Buddhism had taken Tantric form in Himalayan lands, with lamas fighting an eternal battle against the demons.

Mahayana Buddhism reached China about the first century A.D., Korea in the fourth, and Japan in the sixth. Its appeal won servants first, then the people.

Spreading without forced conversion or "holy" war, Buddhism lapped over most of eastern Asia by the sixth century A.D. Missionaries carried it along "silk-roads" through the gateway city of Tunhuang into China, or over monsoon-blown sea lanes to Java. In medieval times Theravada Buddhism became dominant in Southeast Asia.

search for the causes of unhappiness within themselves and thereby to rid themselves of unhappiness. It rejected the complexities of Hinduism for the simplicity of search for self.

Buddha had tried the many "true" ways of Hinduism. He found that they did not lead *him* to better awareness of his goal or bring them any closer to it. He found that his path lay not in conformity to the set practices of yoga or in abandoning himself to the fates as prescribed by the cherishing or unfriendly gods, but in himself. He came to realize that happiness lay within each person and his or her capacities, and not in the various and uncertain revelations of many gods.

The Four Sacred or Noble Truths that Buddha discovered were:

1. All things in the world entail sorrow and suffering;
2. The cause of suffering is craving the pleasures of life;

Young Theravada monks
with begging bowls,
Pagan, Burma

3. The end of suffering will come only when the craving for pleasure is ended;

4. The end of craving will come if a person follows the Eightfold Path to perfection.

Buddha preached that every person has the capacity and the ability to resist those desires and drives which cause a person to impose his or her desires on others and thus cause suffering. He preached that a person should resist and eventually destroy in himself or herself that which causes unhappiness. This is done by accepting the first three truths and following the eight steps in the path to the destruction of desires.[5]

5. They are called "steps" because one follows the other. There are no short cuts; there is no skipping. Each one must be mastered in turn.

The World's Living Religions

Buddha's eight steps to the destruction of desires which cause unhappiness are:

1. Right views

A person must accept the key elements of the Buddhist philosophy and accept the Four Truths and the principles that life is not permanent, self must not be a factor in living, and suffering comes from desires.

2. Right resolve

A person must resolve not to think greedily, lustfully, badly, or selfishly, or seek for other ways to happiness.

3. Right speech

A person must not lie nor speak uselessly and never speak badly about others.

4. Right conduct

A person must not kill, steal, abuse others physically or sexually.

5. Right livelihood

A person must not injure another in any way while pursuing a livelihood. He or she must never seek more than is necessary for life or seek those things which will become encumbrances.

6. Right effort

A person must always do the right thing. He or she must avoid evil thoughts about persons and things. He or she must always seek to do things in the best way.

7. Right mindfulness

Through meditation, a person must arrive at a state of consciousness that lifts him or her above the desires of the body, enables him or her to see things in their proper perspective, and gives one control over self in all things.

8. Right concentration

A person must work for the highest form of meditation, contemplation, which enables one to do away with even the minutest cravings and selfish desires, and lifts one to the mystical stage called Nirvana.

Buddha's "way" was not easy (Nirvana was not just for the asking). It required long hours of meditation, strong self-discipline, great dedication, and the refusal to look backward to selfish pleasure.

For the dedicated Buddhist the key to attaining Nirvana, or perfect happiness, lies in following the eight steps successively: each one prepares for the one that follows. For exam-

Tantric Buddhist, Lahdahki

ple, if a person does not have right views on what brings happiness, he or she cannot have the right purpose in achieving it. If one does not have a right purpose (if, for example, he or she has selfish motives), he or she will not have right speech, will not have right conduct, and so on.

Buddhism stresses long hours of thought and prayer to achieve right understanding, and strong self-discipline to rid one's self of avarice, ambition, ill will, malicious talk, lust, and hurt to any living thing. (This is the reason for Buddhist non-violent doctrines.) It asks people to avoid anything which might interfere with a person's direction toward Nirvana.

When a Buddhist has himself or herself under such moral control, extending even to avoiding intoxicating beverages which "cloud the mind," he or she is then ready to move up to steps seven and eight and search out the real goal: absolute denial of self, of status (this is why Buddhists reject castes), of the need to be reborn to find a better life, for he or she now possesses all by possessing nothing which could hinder movement toward self-annihilation and the consequent entering of Nirvana even while still alive.

Having found his own path to personal contentment and the means to rid people of suffering, Buddha set about winning others to his way of thinking. He was a powerful, persuasive speaker who combined knowledge with example. In a short time, he had several disciples who followed his direction. They formed themselves into a "brotherhood" of monks who renounced all things in favor of Buddha's way, and, following his lead, went out to persuade others to search for peace through the Four Noble Truths. These original Buddhist monks became the means for the spread of Buddha's ideas and for the continuity of Buddhism.[6] They are still—after 2,500 years—the secret of Buddhism. Buddhist monks keep Buddha's ideas alive, his way of life viable, and his memory one of the treasured heritages of the Eastern world. Among many Buddhists, Buddha is not simply a good man and a great religious prophet; he is a divine person. He is a god.

Kinds of Buddhism

There have been many offshoots of the original Buddhism, but all have been based on a vigorous simplification of many things inherent in the Hinduism of Buddha's day. Buddhism contains no authority, no ritual, no hidebound tradition, no philosophic niceties to interfere with a person's real

experience, no abandonment to fatalism, no supernatural, preternatural, or superstitious practices.[7]

The principle kinds of Buddhism are Theravada Buddhism, Mahayana Buddhism, Tantric Buddhism, and Zen Buddhism.

In Southeast Asia and in India—where it was born—Buddhism developed along three main lines.

One, Theravada Buddhism, calls itself the Way of the Elders. . . . It prevails today in Ceylon, Burma, Thailand, Cambodia, and Laos. Theravadins stress the sangha (the brotherhood of monks) as the means of following the dhamma (the essential quality or character of Buddhism); a monk who succeeds in reaching Nirvana becomes an arhat, or saint. At the same time Theravada Buddhism gives the layman a positive role in supporting the sangha, winning merit to better his own karma.

[The second] division of Buddhism [is] known as Mahayana, the Great Vehicle, because it offers a broader means of gaining the ultimate goal—a goal open both to the pious monk and to any layman. Further, the goal could be not only nirvana but also a godly existence of self-sacrifice and compassion. The ideal saint became not the arhat, but the *bodhisattva*—he who at the threshold of nirvana postpones his own entry to help others to salvation. . . .

6. In India and Southeast Asia particularly, Buddhism became essentially a religion for monks. Although nonmonks follow Buddha's way, its perfect expression is found in a monastic way of life.

7. However, many of these things have crept back into various forms of Buddhism.

Mahayana Buddhism, once centered in China, now predominates in Korea, Japan and part of Viet Nam. . . .

[A] third branch of Buddhism, Tantric sprouted around the sixth century A.D. and finds its chief expression in Himalayan lands. It interlaced Mahayana Buddhism with Tantric cults of India that invoked deities by magic and rituals. And it expanded the pantheon with an array of new divinities—personifications of Buddha's thoughts and acts, female counterparts of deities, even demons.

Each division of Buddhism musters claims that it represents the original or true form. Actually, each developed by stressing specific elements within the early faith. And as Buddhism spread, it articulated its insights in words and symbols that differed from country to country. In Southeast Asia it learned to speak the language of kingship. In Tibet it learned to speak with shamans. In China it picked up the language of the family. But its essence remains the message of Siddhartha Gautama: "Seek in the impersonal for the eternal man, and having sought him out, look inward—thou art Buddha."[8]

The fourth, and in many ways the most widely known form of Buddhism is Zen Buddhism. It is a development or refinement of Mahayana Buddhism begun in China in the sixth century A.D. (and in Japan in the twelfth century A.D.). It emphasizes enlightenment for the student by the most direct means: accepting formal studies and observances only when they form part of the means. Studies and ritual practices, no matter how worthy or important for someone else, are only a means to an end; they are never an end in themselves.

Zen Buddhism is not a new religion, in the sense that Christianity is different from Judaism or the ancient Egyptian was different from the Babylonian search for an answer to the mystery of life. It is a refinement of Buddhism.

All great religious movements tend to shed the complexities, the extravagances, the rigid philosophical, theological, and moral aspects of institutionalized religion. These religious movements are a reaction to entrenched interests. People, feeling a need for simplification and meaning *for their lives*, eagerly receive the insights and compelling magnitude of a unique person who can bring them the message they know in their innermost being is correct and relevant. So it was with Christ, Buddha, Mohammed, St. Francis of Assisi, and Luther. Thus it was with the origin of Zen.

Theravada Buddhist woman holding prayer sticks, Thailand

8. Dr. Joseph Kitagawa from *Great Religions of the World*, © National Geographic Society 1971, 1978.

The World's Living Religions

The Core of Buddhism

—*excerpts from an interview with Kenneth Grabner, by John Reedy*

Buddhism, especially Zen, doesn't want to discuss the things like "cores"; it sees that approach as destroying the whole thing.

However, with that reservation, the nearest I could come would be: The core meaning of Buddhism is to discover, encounter being—analogously, we would say God. (However, the Buddhist doesn't use the word God.)

This means, especially for Zen, that the more conscious you are of the reality of things, the more you discover, in Western terms, God in them.

If you look at a thing, you don't have to say anything about it. You don't have to decide whether it is ugly or beautiful. That judgment is something *you* do to it. It's a form of egoism by which you use the thing and reduce it to the meaning it has for you.

But if you simply look at it, are present to it, avoid doing things to it, you can come to experience its being, the reality of it, in a way that represents a different kind of knowledge than being able to define or categorize it.

Rod McKuen seems to do this sort of thing when he writes and sings of the sea. For him, the sea is obviously something much more than H_2O with a saline content. It's almost a person who is immediately present to him.

The Buddhist would say that he perceives being in the sea. While this being is not seen as a personal God, its perception is the source of great joy, the source of salvation. . . .

This is put in a sort of crude expression: The Buddha is to be found even in the bushes which surround the privy. Being, if we are open to it, is found in everything we do or encounter. Don't look down on or withdraw from any part of your life. . . .

Look at the phenomenon of pessimistic existentialism. Since World War II, beginning with Camus' *The Stranger*, a constant theme of literature and drama has been the young person who feels alienated from everyone and everything. He feels he's not really in contact with anyone. No one really knows him; he really doesn't know anyone. How can he be loved when he is alone?

The Buddhist who has been able to open his consciousness to reality doesn't experience this kind of alienation. Not only because that consciousness includes the reality of the people whom he encounters, but also because he somehow establishes a relationship, a bond with the reality he experiences in all of life and nature.

Source: *AD Correspondence,* Vol. 2: 9, May 1, 1971, Notre Dame, Indiana.

Buddhism had tended to become formalistic, just as had the yoga exercises of Hinduism. The answer to the search for self was found in the ritual rather than in person. The eightfold path had become a sophisticated form of magic—as long as the action was done, the result was assured. Zen Buddhism was a reaction to this defect which had crept into Buddhism.

Zen Buddhism attempts, by meditation under the guidance of a master teacher, to arrive at the moment of truth— the Satori, or enlightenment (achieved in a flash)—about life. Zen Buddhism teaches that truth does not lie in any particular revelation, wise sayings, person, or particular way. It lies in existence itself. Consequently the Zen Buddhist seeks through serious contemplation on seemingly nonsensical statements (Q. What is the most excellent thing in Zen? A. I sit alone on the great mountain.) to arrive at his own understanding of his life. The Zen Buddhists believe that by concerted effort (the founder of Zen, a Buddhist monk named Bodhidharma [about A.D. 600], contemplated a blank wall for nine years) a person will finally arrive at his or her own enlightenment through a sudden intuition which will shed once and for all the complexities and strivings that keep people in turmoil.

Zen Buddhism is a version of Buddhism stripped of the accumulated traditions and rituals of centuries. Its hallmark is contemplation, which produces an inscrutability, a calmness, an assurance, and a grace that enables a person to face the problems of life because, having become enlightened, he or she no longer worries about life but is seeking the depth of his or her own being where real truth and beauty lie.

As the Zen Buddhists say: "One should not think about life; one should live it." "One should not worry about life or death, heavens or hell or gods or magic or rites or sacrifices. One should seek the exaltation of *Samadhi* (deep contemplation) to arrive at Nirvana." Zen attempts not to take a person to some "pure land" but through the "gateless gate" of the person himself or herself into the awareness of his or her own person.

Buddhist Scriptures

The Buddhists share with the Hindus the Vedic sources. In addition to these ancient texts, they also have what is known as the Pali Canon, a collection of revered writings, or scriptures, recorded from oral traditions and codified and standardized in the first century A.D. These scriptures contain

Buddhist monk with
classic palm umbrella, Sri
Lanka

sermons, rules, and essays on philosophy and psychology.
They are used not only to train Buddhist monks, but also for
meditation by experienced monks, and for pious reading of the
layman who is a believer in the Buddha's way. These scriptures are also called The Tripitaka, or The Three Baskets of
Wisdom, because they are divided into three parts. Other materials have been added to the Tripitaka over the years, but
these later additions do not merit the same reverence as the
originals.

Selections from Buddhist Scriptures

Never in this world is hate
   Appeased by hatred;
It is only appeased by love—
   This is an eternal law.

Victory breeds hatred
   For the defeated lie down in sorrow.
Above victory or defeat
   The calm man dwells in peace.
         —from the remembered
           sayings of Buddha

"No brahmin is such by birth; no outcast is such by birth. An outcast is such by his deeds; a brahmin, is such by his deeds."

           —Buddha

Library of Buddhist scriptures, Wat Phra Singh, Thailand

The World's Living Religions

"Venerable Nagasena," asked the King "why are men not all alike, but some short-lived and some long, some sickly and some healthy, some ugly and some handsome, some weak and some strong, some poor and some rich, some base and some noble. . . ?"

"Why, your Majesty," replied the Elder, "are not all plants alike, but some astringent, some salty, some pungent, some sour, some sweet?"

"I suppose, your Reverence, because they come from different seeds."

"And so it is with men! They are not alike because of different karmas. As the Lord said . . . 'Beings each have their own karma. They are . . . born through karma, they become members of tribes and families through karma, each is ruled by karma, it is karma that divides them into high and low.' "

"Very good, your Reverence!"
—Questions of King Menander

[A bodhisattva] looks on all beings as though victims going to the slaughter. . . . He is filled with great distress at what he sees, for many bear the burden of past deeds which will be punished in purgatory, others will have unfortunate rebirths which will divide them from the Buddha. . . . So he pours out his love and compassion upon all those beings . . . thinking, "I shall become the savior of all beings, and set them free from their sufferings."
—early Mahayana scripture

Living in the world yet not forming attachments to the dust of the world is the way of a true Zen student.
—Zen Buddhism

Those among the living beings, who have come into contact with former Buddhas, and have learned the Law and practiced charity,
Or have held on to discipline and endured forbearance and humiliation,
Or have made serious efforts at concentration and understanding,
Or have cultivated various kinds of blessing and wisdom—
All such beings as these have already achieved Buddhahood. . . .
Men who possess a tender heart.
. . . Those who have offered relics.
Or have built hundreds of millions of pagodas. . . .
Those who have had pictures of the Buddha embroidered, expressing the great splendor which he achieved from a hundred merits and blessings, whether embroidered by himself or by others, have all achieved Buddhahood.
Even boys at play who have painted Buddha figures with straws, wooden sticks, brushes, or finger nails—
All people such as these by gradual accumulation of merits and with an adequate sense of compassion, have already achieved Buddhahood.
—The Lotus Sutra

Summary

1. Buddhism developed out of Gautama's dissatisfaction with traditional Hinduism in his native India.

2. Buddhism stresses that happiness is found in control of self, not in some magical practices or some unknown future.

3. Dedicated Buddhists accept The Four Truths and the Eight Paths to enlightenment.

4. The distinguishing characteristic of Buddhists is extreme self-control.

For Review

1. In what essential ways does Buddhism differ from Hinduism?

2. Who was Buddha? How did he get the name Buddha?

3. What are Buddha's basic principles of life?

4. Do you think that Buddha's view of the reasons for unhappiness in life are correct? Partially correct? Wrong? Give reasons for your answer.

5. What do you think is the chief characteristic of Buddhism?

6. Why is Buddhism essentially a religion for monks?

7. Do nonmonks have any role in Buddhism? Explain.

8. What are the principle expressions of Buddhism? Explain.

9. What is contemplation? Do you think it ought to be part of a person's religious life regardless of his religion? Why? Why not?

10. What seem to be the three essentials of Buddha's "way"? What are the goals of these essentials? What is "Nirvana"?

11. Discuss Buddha's "eight steps," giving examples.

12. Would you classify Buddhism as a religion? why? why not?

13. How do you account for the popularity of Hinduism and Buddhism among certain people raised in Western cultures?

For Discussion

1. Discuss whether Buddhism is a practical form of religion, or way of life, for the average person.

2. Given the basic principles of Buddhism, discuss whether Buddhism as a way of life for the elite only, and, if it is, why it has so many adherents.

3. Discuss why Buddhism and Hinduism are largely confined to the subcontinent of Asia and the Orient.

4. Discuss the similarities between Mohammed and Buddha.

For Research

1. Find out what you can about the life of a Buddhist monk.

2. Prepare a report on the effect of communism on Buddhism in China, Vietnam, and Cambodia.

3. Prepare a report on Buddhism in North America.

4. Prepare a report on Zoroastrianism.

5. Make at least two more readings in Buddhist scriptures; then report on the content and what you think about them.

Words You Should Know

If there are any words given below that you are not sure of, look them up in the Word List at the end of the book.

alienation   preternatural
asceticism   viable

chapter 9

The Religions of China and Japan

In spite of the interest in Oriental cultures, manifested by Chinese/Japanese themes in formal gardens, architecture, and decorating, the heritage and culture of China, and to a lesser extent, Japan, have remained a mystery to most non-Orientals. Interest in and concern about China and Japan have waxed and waned through the centuries since Marco Polo "opened" the East to Western eyes in the fourteenth century A.D.

Since World War II, which ended in 1945, Japan has become rather well-known, but China, due chiefly to the communist takeover in 1949, has remained virtually unknown. Both, however, are still lands of mystery to most Westerners because the heritage and culture of China and Japan are so "foreign" to Western ways and patterns of thought. Chinese and Japanese ways, however, can be partially understood if a person studies the origin of the culture and heritage of each, and the philosophy of life which has shaped their responses to the mystery of life.

The Oriental Response to Mystery

China has been civilized for over 6,000 years. For at least 5,000 years it has been governed by a succession of dynasties, or ruling families or groups, that developed a highly sophisticated system of agriculture, economics, and engineering geared to the preservation and development of the Chinese people.

Japan, according to legend, was organized into an empire by a certain Jimmu, a lineal descendent of the sun goddess, about 660 B.C. Between the sixth and eighth centuries A.D., Japan came under the strong cultural influence of the Chinese. It was during this time that Chinese Buddhism was introduced.

Jidai Festival, Kyoto, Japan

China and Japan, like other lands, have a religious heritage whose origins go back to prehistoric times that have left a legacy of myths, legend, a multiplicity of gods, rituals, and tendencies to the practice of magic. Like other lands, China and Japan have gone through periods of reorganization and reinterpretation of these multiple religious fragments.

The great religions of the West, and to some extent Hinduism (India being midway between West and Far East), have tended to find their principle of organization in the concept of God. The Chinese and Japanese religions, however, have tended to organize their response to the mystery of life around the principle of organizing one's life to achieve happiness. Judaism, Christianity, and Islam stress God and His plan for the world. Eastern religions stress people and their ability to fit into the world. They are not so much concerned about "God" as about "The Way Life Is."

The two principal responses to the mystery of life in China and Japan, Confucianism and Taoism (dowism), combine with Buddhism, and in Japan with Shintoism, to give China and Japan their moral and spiritual base. In the sense that they are, like Hinduism and Buddhism, answers to the mystery of life for the Chinese and Japanese people (but do not deal directly with a god-concept) they are religions. They are treated as such in this survey of world religions.

It is difficult to tell how many people in China are still practicing Confucianism, Taoism, and Buddhism because the Chinese communist government has tried systematically to suppress religious practice in mainland China.[1] In spite of such persecution, however, religion has remained alive in China. Recent reliable figures for the four main streams of religious responses in mainland China show that there are about 300 million Confucianists, fifty-one million Taoists, 100 million Buddhists, 10 million Moslems and, perhaps 2 million Christians. In the Republic of China (Taiwan), there are about 400,000 Christians and 40,000 Moslems. The rest—about fifteen million—are Buddhist/Taoist. In a population of 116 million in Japan, there are about sixty million Shintoists, the same number of Buddhists, a million Christians and a few Moslems.

As we said, the four principal responses to the mystery of life in China and Japan are Confucianism, Taoism, Shintoism, and Buddhism. Of the four, Confucianism and Taoism

1. Since the death of Mao Tse-tung, China's revolutionary leader, the Chinese communist government has relaxed the harsh measures aimed at wiping out all religion. It has done so in order to gain trade concessions from Western nations.

are unique to China and offer a new aspect to the responses to the mystery of life people have found most useful.

O-Torii, famous gate to the shrine on Miyasima Island near Hiroshima

The Oriental Philosophy of Life

Before a person can look at Confucianism and Taoism separately, he or she must become acquainted with the fundamental Chinese life-outlook which underlies both. For the Chinese mind, *all of life has a pattern: the eternal interplay between* **yang** *and* **yin.** "Yang" is a general term referring to any active or positive principle. "Yin" is a general term referring to any receptive or negative principle. The interplay between activity-receptivity is what produces everything we know. Neither can exist without the other. Just as male is not complete without female, or water has no form without a container, or a sound cannot be distinguished unless there is sufficient silence for it to be heard in, so nothing in life can exist without its corresponding opposite.

"Big" has no meaning except by comparison with something "small," "bright" has no meaning except by comparison with something "dark," a man cannot be a "husband" without a "wife," and "life" itself cannot be appreciated without a proper appreciation for "death."[2] Life constantly brings the various opposites together in creative combination: rain

2. Hence, the importance of ancestor worship, or constant remembrance of the dead, in traditional Chinese daily life.

and shine, good and evil, light and darkness, war and peace, life and death. The eternal pattern swirls endlessly on, a continuing interplay of yang and yin.[3]

The Chinese have kept this understanding before them from time immemorial by the traditional symbolic drawing. It shows the two opposites, yang and yin, eternally pursuing each other in a harmonious way. There is opposition, but not conflict; there is order-in-tension; there is balance, but not stalemate.

This drawing symbolizes the way life should be lived. No one can hope for all pleasure and no pain, or all life and no death, or all happiness and no waiting, or all agreement and no disagreement. The art of living is to combine the yang and yin of one's own life into a harmonious balance. One can never stop in life and think he or she "has it made." There are always new factors entering life, requiring new adjustments.

If "harmonious interplay between yang and yin" is the goal of one's life (in other words, if life has no goal outside itself, but is a continually ongoing process), then the question is how to achieve it? How does the individual person—and how does society as a whole—unite all the opposites of life in a harmonious rather than jagged way?

Traditional Chinese culture produced two major answers to this question—**Confucianism** and **Taoism.** Indeed, these two systematic answers complement each other; neither alone seems to have been able to hold Chinese culture together, but the two seem to have balanced each other. The interplay between these two "religions" or "ways of life" seems to be another example of yang and yin in Chinese life. Confucianism stresses tradition, Taoism stresses spontaneity. Confucianism stresses being rational, Taoism stresses being intuitive. Because these emphases are not opposed but complementary, many Chinese persons have chosen to be both Confucianists and Taoists at the same time.

Peking Lama Temple
Yong He Gong, China

In recent decades, of course, China has become rather Westernized—especially since the Communist party took power. It is not yet clear to outsiders how greatly traditional Chinese culture is being transformed by Marxist philosophy. All we know in a general way is that Marxism is being expressed in distinctively Chinese ways. The teachings of Confucius are still taught in many Chinese schools, but are given a Marxist interpretation.

3. This is the philosophy behind Chinese medicine as exemplified in acupuncture.

Confucianism

Confucianism gets its name from Confucius (the anglicized pronunciation of *Kung-Fu-tzu,* which means "Kung the Teacher"), who was born around 551 B.C. Very little is known about his early homelife, except that he was not well-to-do. His father died before Confucius was three, and he grew up with his mother, who lived in poverty. As he grew up, he earned a living by doing manual labor and, thereby, came to know the life of the common people.

At the age of fifteen he began to take studies seriously, and he delved into the Chinese traditions and classics of his time. He became a civil servant in various low-level government positions but gave this up in his early twenties to become a tutor, in which work he found his place. His reputation as an honest and wise man grew, and he seems to have entered politics off and on, but he was always too honest to get far in the political world. He never quit trying, however, for he believed that thoughtful men should not retire from the world but should try to put their good ideas into social action. He died in 479 B.C. at the age of seventy-three,[4] after having spent the last few years of his life teaching and editing the classic traditional literature known in his day.

It is through his teaching and editing that his influence grew. His many disciples continued to spread his teachings, until centuries later Kung-Fu-tzu was a household word and his many sayings had become proverbs.

Confucius lived in a time when China was being torn apart by constant civil wars. Mass slaughters of 60,000, and even on one occasion 400,000, have been recorded as having taken place in those times. The traditions which had held people together were breaking up as individual clans led by powerful warlords claimed the right to establish their own rule.

Conflict was in the air one breathed, and Confucius feared that all of China could become one vast riot area. He saw the need to restore order; and he realized that order on a large scale could not be maintained unless it existed first in the family, then between one family and another, and so on.

Confucious' Way to Civil Order

Confucius did not try to establish new principles for restoring civil peace. Rather, utilizing the Chinese respect for

---

4. It is worth noting that Confucius was active in China at the same time Buddha was active in India and Israelite scholars were editing the Jewish scriptures in exile in Babylon.

tradition, he took the best of the Chinese traditions and edited them into a systematic whole. He then urged that this treatment of the traditions be taught to the people.

Wherever Confucius' disciples gained influence, they undertook the indoctrination of local societies. "Moral ideas were driven into the people by every possible means," says Chiang Monlin, an authority on Chinese history, ". . . in temples, theatres, homes, toys, proverbs, schools, history, and stories—until they became habits in daily life."[5]

The main outlines of Confucius' teaching can be summarized in five principal terms:

1. Jen (humaneness)

This was the virtue of virtues, the foundation of all that would follow. It means basically a respect for one's own dignity as a human person and a corresponding respect for other persons. It means loving another as you love yourself.

2. Chun-tzu (being the ideal person)

This means taking the abstract quality of *Jen* and putting it into habitual action. It means more than etiquette and politeness. It means having the right attitude so much a part

5. Chiang Monlin, *Tides from the West* (New Haven: Yale University Press, 1947), p. 9.

of oneself that it flows out into action no matter what the circumstances.

3. Li (the right pattern)

This has two related meanings: first, doing things the right way; and second, using the correct ritual when doing them. In our own culture we have similar features to which these can be compared. For example, "doing things the right way" means not being too informal in impersonal situations. For instance, when taking an employment test in a room with hundreds of other applicants, one does not show the instructor one's baby pictures.

"Using the correct ritual" means completing all the required formalities such as putting one's last name first, first name last, etc. on the form.

In order to reconstruct society, Confucius stated five general categories of "doing things the right way." He described them in detail and then encouraged appropriate rituals for expressing them:

    a. Using the right name for the right thing.
    b. Choosing the mean between two extremes.
    c. Living the five basic relations correctly:
- The father-son relationship,
- The older brother-younger brother relationship,
- The husband-wife relationship,
- The older friend-younger friend relationship,
- The ruler-subject relationship.

    d. Devotion to the family.
    e. Respect for age.[6]

4. Te (government by moral power)

In his many sayings on this point, Confucius taught that the only way to establish a stable government which people would respect in the long run was to base it, not on military might, but on the power of good example and the obviously sincere intent to serve the welfare of the people. While a tyrannical government can repress the people into outward submission for a time, it is really building up hidden resentment which will one day work against it. The governments that last and are effective are those which win the spontaneous consent of the people.

---

6. Living the five basic relationships correctly, devotion to the family, and respect for the aged (including ancestor "worship") are hallmarks of the Chinese character.

5. Wen (cultivation of the peaceful arts)

Confucius encouraged people to admire musicians, artists, poets, and teachers more than soldiers. If people's ideals are directed toward the good and beautiful things of life, they will not be easily inclined to war, which destroys these things.

Confucius, in laying out in a rational step-by-step order the best of Chinese tradition and exhorting that it be systematically taught to all the people, emphasized the correct way to live in this life. He was a pious man who believed in a heavenly world where spirits went after they died, but he did not focus upon the heavenly side of things. His focus was on this world. He took religious piety for granted but did not explicitly delve into the supernatural side of things.

Three hundred years after his death, Confucianism became the state religion of China. In 130 B.C. it became also the basic training for government officials, maintaining the influence of this power even up to the twentieth century.

Taoism

Taoism derives its name from the Chinese word *Tao* (pronounced "Dow") which means "path" or "way." As used in this belief system, it means roughly "The Way Life Is."

Taoism arose as a counterbalance to the heavily national and traditional emphasis of Confucius' approach to life. Confucius, in effect, had laid out detailed blueprints about The Way Life Ought to Be; many people felt that equal weight should be given to The Way Life Is.

According to tradition, Taoism was born about 500 B.C., when an old man named *Lao Tzu* (meaning "The Grand Old Teacher") was riding a water buffalo into Tibet to become a hermit. He was stopped by a border guard who asked him to put his wisdom into a book so it would not be forever lost. This he did, in the book *Tao te Ching* ("The Way and Its Power"). Then he disappeared across the border and was never heard from again.

Many Taoist legends tell anecdotes of Lao Tzu meeting with Confucius and their having debates. Most scholars, however, think that Lao Tzu is a legendary figure and agree that the beginnings of Taoism cannot be traced with certainty any farther back than about two centuries after Confucius' time, when his teachings were officially established enough to merit a widespread reaction.

Taoism has since split into three branches: (1) a popular superstition leaning heavily upon magic and sorcery; (2) an esoteric form of mysticism which never became popular,[7] and (3) a philosophy of intuitive respect for the "Natural Way Things Have of Working Themselves Out." In this form, it has greatly influenced Chinese art, culture, thinking, and religion. It is this form that we will consider.

The basic principle of Taoism is *wu wei* (translated roughly as "let go" or "let it happen"). Taoists believe that there is in everything a natural tendency to act harmoniously with the rest of the universe. Rain and shine, night and day, pleasure and pain—all things tend to balance out—unless people put artificial obstacles in the way.

Sometimes human plans are short-sighted; human beings attempt to gain a momentary advantage over nature by working "against the grain" of things. When they do this, they upset the balance of nature and their plans collapse. For example, a man who is in a hurry may run too fast for his physical condition; his momentary burst of speed is compensated for by an exhaustion that overtakes him before he can finish his journey, and he winds up arriving later than if he had paced himself at a comfortable speed, letting his body carry him and set its own pace rather than attempting to force his body by sheer willpower. Or a busy housewife may work herself into a nervous breakdown if she anxiously rushes from job to job instead of letting the work carry her along. Or a sculptor may cause his statue to break if he chisels into the stone arbitrarily rather than by studying the grain of the material and carving in accord with it.

Izanagi and Izanami
(Courtesy Museum of Fine Arts, Boston)

In other words, the principle of *wu wei* does not mean human beings should be inactive do-nothings. It means they should act in such harmony with the nature of what they are dealing with that it almost seems the work is doing itself. Thus, there is no need for an excessive number of blueprint directions from the outside in order to do something; the true directions come from the inner nature of what is to be done.

Taoism, rightly understood, applies not only to the fine arts but to every aspect of the art of living. In politics, for example, the *Tao Te Ching* says,

A leader is best
When people barely know that he exists.
. . . Of a good leader, who talks little,
When his work is done, his aim fulfilled,
They will all say, "We did this ourselves."

7. *Esoteric* means meant for only the select few who have special knowledge. It means not common or ordinary, not simple.

Peking Lama Temple,
China

Here again, the human being (in this case the ruler) who lives according to *Tao*—who lets *The Way It Is* be his principle of action rather than imposing his own principles upon it—is active, but he acts "with the grain" of his people. He helps them fulfill their plans; he does not arbitrarily dictate his own plans to them.

The art of "letting go" or "letting it happen" is not an easy one to learn. By over-concentrating on external rules a person can become self-conscious and defeat his or her own purpose—like a baseball batter who works himself into a slump by concentrating excessively on his swing and forgetting about the ball. The way out of his slump is the principle of *wu wei*—he should be absorbed in *what* he is doing, not worrying about *how* he is doing. He should allow himself to see the motion of the ball; he should swing comfortably and naturally.

Actually, "natural hanging-looseness" can be carried to lazy extremes just as much as "rational calculation of one's moves" can lead to the opposite extreme of self-consciousness.

While Confucianism lends itself to the second extreme, Taoism can be oversimplified to the first. That is why Confucianism and Taoism together operate as a yang-yin pair to keep the Chinese mentality in balance. Each needs the principles of the other within itself in order not to go to extremes.

Because they trust the inner "Isness" of things, Taoists see no reason for a God above nature, a Lord to direct it and give it an "Oughtness" from the outside. For them, such a God would be contrary to *The Way It Is.* In some popular forms of Taoism there may be many gods, but these are not the God-Above-All in the Western sense.

Hence, many Taoists find the God of Judaism, Christianity, and Islam unintelligible. Not only does He seem to be a Super-Confucianist making people's decisions for them, but He seems to be a rival to the harmonious order of nature itself.

Furthermore, God (as the Western mind conceives Him) seems to be all yang and no yin: all good and no evil; all activity and no receptivity. In the Western understanding of the struggle between God and the devil (who, strangely, is not pure evil but is represented as having been made good in his nature but having made himself evil in his own will), Western religions foresee the ultimate triumph of God. But the Oriental mind cannot conceive of an end to the eternal conflict, with yang winning out over yin; that would destroy the harmony of the whole universe. It would be contrary to *The Way It Is.*

Perhaps it is the yang-yin philosophy that pervades Eastern thought that leads Westerners to consider the Chinese and Japanese people "inscrutable." It is perhaps also the reason that Eastern people consider Westerners naive. In any case, people of both East and West are basically religious. Both have their own answers to the mystery of life.

The Chinese Religious Sense

In spite of the fact that Confucianism and Taoism seem to be primarily "secularist" religions and deal fundamentally with how to live a happy or meaningful life, most of the Chinese people who are not Moslem or Christian are not pure secularists. They do have beliefs and practices which are distinctly

Religion in China

Although China achieved unity and political centralization more than 2,000 years ago, a nation which expanded and grew so vast over the centuries inevitably embraces a wide variety of subcultures and local religious sects. Specifically, this means that the practical expressions of religion vary from place to place. The unified culture of the educated upper class must be distinguished from the popular practices of the masses, for whom religion serves as a relief from the monotony of daily toil and gives meaning to the drudgery of life.

The popular aspects of China's native, localistic religion may seem a far cry from the sophisticated philosophic reasoning and speculation conveyed by most textbooks on Chinese thought and religion. The average Chinese has only a vague conception of the foundations of his religious observances, and generally grasps only the rituals and popular notions. The purpose of many of these rituals is to manipulate the gods and

spirits by placating, threatening, or even driving them away. Religious observances on a national level also involve such practical objectives. Therefore, the distance between the rites performed by the emperor and the rituals of the villagers was not so great as might be imagined. If such ceremony is divorced from the rest of the complex of Chinese beliefs, it may appear to be superstition. But if we look at the matter from a Chinese point of view, one which admits and demands complementarity, we gain a better understanding of how religion can serve simultaneously as a source of family harmony, political order, poetic and artistic expression, simple festival-type amusement, hygiene, group therapy, and insurance against the unknown.

Christianity, Islam, and Marxism, which made their ways from the West to China, all demand exclusive control of the mind and spirit. Western positivistic science has also weakened the Chinese bias toward balance. Consequently, since

religious in the strictest sense. They do have their gods (literally hundreds of them), their forms of worship, their temples, their shrines, their hymns and stories, their belief in an afterlife, and practices Western people might call magic (but the Chinese would call liturgy, if they had that term).

This particular religious aspect of Chinese life is a mixture of Confucianism, Taoism, Buddhism, and primitive religion. It is characterized by deep reverence, ancestor worship, formal religious ceremonies, ritual practices to particular gods, and religious festivals, the chief of which is the celebration of the Chinese New Year. They also have a scripture made up of stories and legends preserved from ancient oral traditions and the wise sayings of Confucius, Lao Tzu, the Buddhist masters, and unnamed commentaries on Chinese life and worship.

the arrival of these newer religions and faiths, China has undergone torments of doubt and self-questioning. Old beliefs have been shattered, even while old practices and forms of behavior persist. The rise of Chinese nationalism in the late 19th and 20th centuries has offered some replacement for the old sense of cultural security. For this reason Chinese communism, despite its secular Marxist-Leninist basis, offers a new vehicle for expression of ancient beliefs. It has enjoyed remarkable acceptance. It offers programs of social justice which were implicit in the idealistic writings of some Confucianists and other early religious philosophers. It offers a sense of accord with nature, as advocated by the Taoists. It offers political order and stability, as advocated by the legalists. And it has a vision of an ultimate Paradise, though on earth and not—as Buddhists would have it—in the void. Modern Chinese communism accepts and encourages traditional medical and hygienic practices.

It offers a sizable, varied and well-developed body of classical literature. Vigorous attempts have been made to downgrade Confucius, yet Mao Tse-tung was elevated to the position of the great Teacher, pointing the Way. Just a cult of Confucius eventually established itself complete with temples, relics, and a priesthood, so today a cult of the late Mao is developing.* Whether or not this quasireligious tendency progresses further or is inhibited, it may be seen as the latest expression of the long search of the Chinese people for social order and meaning within a harmonious universe.

Source: Miami-Dade Community College, *Students' Guide to the Long Search* (Dubuque: Kendall/Hunt Publishing Company, 1978), pp. 106–7.

*Since this article was written, there has been a shift in the official communist position on Mao Tse-tung. He no longer holds a position of pre-eminence. In fact, many things he was revered for during his life and shortly thereafter, have been repudiated by the current Chinese leadership.

The Religions of Japan

Japan, a tiny island off the coast of China and only a few miles from Korea, has nearly 116 million people packed into 142,800 square miles of land, four-fifths of which is mountains or hills. Its most famous city, Tokyo, is the second most populated city in the world (Shanghai, China, is first) with nearly ten million people. Japan is the most densely populated country in the world with over 748 people per square mile—compared to the United States which has fifty-seven people per square mile.

Japan is a country of contrasts. It is highly developed technologically, yet its culture is extremely traditional. It is a land of almost unbearable pollution in its large urban centers, yet it has some of the most beautiful parks, sacred shrines, formal gardens, temples, and monasteries in the world. Its people are clean, polite, and industrious, yet it tolerates cruelty, harshness, and female discrimination. The Japanese are home loving, family-oriented people, yet they are among the most travelled in the world. Women in Japan are totally subservient to the men, yet they have complete control over the way money is used in the family. The highly educated, scientific-minded people still send messages to the nature gods in the form of small pieces of paper tied to trees "just in case."

"Fortunes" outside shrine, Kyoto, Japan

The World's Living Religions

The Japanese people can only be understood in terms of their culture, which is deeply religious, expressing an inter-relatedness in all things, a sense of the spiritual in all aspects of life, and an inherently religious element in even the smallest action seemingly unrelated to what others call religion. The Japanese live by symbols and their symbols are basically religious in meaning.

Among all the cultures of the world, Japan seems to have the mysterious ability to transform even the humblest task or gesture into an act of exquisite spirituality.
—Columban Mission Magazine, June/July, 1982, page 16

The most widely practiced religion in Japan can best be called "Shinto/Buddhism." Although each is a religion distinct in itself with many adherents in Japan, most Japanese people practice a combination of both Shinto and Buddhism.

Shintoism,[8] which is distinctly Japanese, is a continued form of a primitive religion called "animatism" which proposes that there is a force, power, spirit, or god in all things which people encounter at every point in their lives. This belief is common among the Japanese, and accounts for the fact that most Japanese practice some form of nature worship, believe in an untold number of gods or spirits, and practice a highly developed form of ancestor worship, manifested by their elaborate burial services and care for their graves.

The Buddhism practiced in Japan is, as we said, an import from China. Its most widely known form is Zen (from the Chinese *Ch'an*, meaning religious meditation) which has uniquely Japanese characteristics.

Japanese Zen, a blend of Hindu mysticism and Chinese pantheism, continues the original Hindu tradition that the true light of the mind will appear only when greed, lust and craving have passed away.

Zen devotees accept a three-stage approach to life—virtuous living, mental culture and wisdom. So, Zen is a way of life, a full rapport with all life, accepting persons, events and things as they really are; an outlook not distorted by one's own desires, ideas or pre-conceived judgments.

8. *Shinto* is a Japanese form of the Chinese *shin tao* meaning "the way of the gods."

The Rinzai Zen sect founded by Eisai (1141–1215) has 6,000 temples and its three million members make use of *koans*—paradoxes—arresting questions which tend to halt one's "thinking about things," to create doubt and anguish in order to awaken a deeper level of the mind beyond the discursive intellect. A typical *koan* is:

"*We all know the sound of two hands clapping; but what is the sound of one hand clapping?*"

A Zen monk may meditate on this *koan* for several years before finding an answer, that to an outsider would be just as paradoxical. Yet to the monk, the solution may solve the most basic problems of his interior life.

Zazen[9] helps to break through the layers of sense, feelings and thought processes to the silent depths of the core of being . . . the pure-mind level.

The body position is important: "Sit down, fold the legs in the lotus position, straighten the back, hold arms just so and breathe in and breathe out." When the cracking kneecaps and aching backs cause discomfort take solace in the thought that for over 5,000 years humans have used this yoga posture for meditation.

Fr. Hugo Lasalle, S.J., in his book, *Zen—Way to Enlightenment,* mentions benefits that one obtains from the use of *Zazen* in the Christian life of prayer: the ability to recollect oneself more easily no matter what the distractions of everyday life may be; the ability to hold on to an interior quiet and self-control in all adversities; the gradual disappearance of annoying doubts, spiritual depression, fear and other disturbing feelings; the gradual appearance of interior harmony and joy which gives permanent satisfaction and which permits one to enjoy all good and beautiful things with one's whole being.

Satori or Enlightenment is the aim of all Buddhist meditation. This contact with puremind is not a permanent state. It must be reached again and again until a whole new attitude to life affecting the diet, clothes, sleeping habits, and life style develops. A truly enlightened Zen man is a whole person.[10]

Zen Buddhism is the most widely known form of Japanese Buddhism because it was "imported" from Japan to the United States during the late 1960s and early 1970s. It answered a spiritual need of the time which was brought on by the activist responses to the mysteries of life preached by many Western religious figures. It offered specific techniques for meditation, required periods of silence and repose, and called

9. Zazen is a meditation technique used by Zen Buddhists in Japan.
10. Fr. Kevin Flinn, *Columban Mission,* June/July, 1982, p. 17.

for self-discipline and temporary removal from the hectic pace of life. Its better-known disciplines involved judo, karate, flower arranging, calligraphy (the art of fine handwriting or printing), the composing of haiku, transcendental meditation, the tea ceremony, and biofeedback. They all became part of the American scene as many Americans turned to the Orient for its wisdom.

As we have said, however, the predominant religion in Japan itself is Shinto/Buddhist because most Japanese combine the two into one way of responding to life's mysteries. They have incorporated the Shinto gods into the Buddhist deity system, theology, and worship services, and the Buddhist deities were adopted by the Shintoists—the Buddhas and the bodhisattvas were, for the Shintoists, human forms of the Shinto gods.

Both religions have been highly influenced by Confucian and Taoist doctrines. This accounts for the manners and morals characteristic of Japanese family life, social world, and political structure.

Western religions have made some headway among the Japanese, and Western ways have influenced Japanese thinking, but by and large, the Japanese have clung to their ancient religions and practice them with a fervor that is the envy of other religious people.

Haiku

Haiku, a traditional form of Japanese poetry developed under Zen influence from the older and longer *tanka*, is composed of seventeen syllables divided into three lines, and generally deals with themes of nature. Today in Japan there are annual *haiku* competitions in which thousands of aspiring *haiku* writers take part. Mount Fuji, a symbol of Japan, is a favorite theme . . .

Springtime and winter
Fujisan changes her face . . .
yet she stays the same.

Source: *Columban Mission,* June/July, 1982, p. 49.

The Wisdom of the Orient

We see that no man is without a sense of compassion, or a sense of shame, or a sense of courtesy, or a sense of right and wrong. The sense of compassion is the beginning of humanity; the sense of shame is the beginning of righteousness; the sense of courtesy is the beginning of decorum; the sense of right and wrong is the beginning of wisdom. Every man has within himself these four beginnings, just as he has four limbs. Since everyone has these four beginnings within him, the man who considers himself incapable of exercising them is destroying himself.

—*The Book of Mencius*

The Great Tao flows everywhere. . . .
Always without desires, it may be called
    The Small.
All things come to it and it does not
    master them; it may be called
    The Great.
Therefore [the sage] never strives himself
    for the great, and thereby the great is
    achieved.

—*The Eternal Way (Tao Te Chung)*

Those who are born wise are the highest type of people; those who become wise through learning come next; those who learn by overcoming dullness come after that. Those who are dull but still don't learn are the lowest type of people. . . . I won't teach a man who is not anxious to learn, and will not explain to one who is not trying to make things clear to himself. If I hold up one corner of a square and a man cannot come back to me with the other three, I won't bother to go over that point again.

—*Confucius in the Analects*

The superior man does what is proper to his position and does not want to go beyond this. If he is in a noble station, he does what is proper to a position of wealth and honorable station. If he is in a humble station, he does what is proper to a position of poverty. . . . If he is in the midst of barbarian tribes, he does what is proper in the midst of barbarian tribes. In a position of difficulty . . . he does what is proper to a position of difficulty. . . . He can find himself in no situation in which he is not at ease. . . . He rectifies himself and seeks nothing from others, hence he has no complaint to make. He does not complain against heaven above or blame men below. Thus it is that the superior man lives peacefully . . . and waits for his destiny, while the inferior man takes to dangerous courses and hopes for good luck.

—*The Mean (Chung Yung)*

Mount Fuji seen across
Lake Hakone, Japan

Summary

1. Oriental religions are generally concerned with ordering life to achieve happiness.

2. Oriental religions include many gods and many forms of early religious awareness.

3. The two principle Chinese responses to the mystery of life are Confucianism and Taoism. The principle Japanese response is Shinto/Buddhism.

4. The religions of both China and Japan call for great self-discipline, meditation, and the acceptance of life as it is.

For Review

1. What seems to be the basic difference between the East and the West as far as response to the mystery of life is concerned?

2. Explain the history and nature of Confucianism.

3. Explain the history and nature of Taoism.

4. Explain the Chinese "principle of life."

5. Why is it true to say that the Chinese and the Japanese people are not truly a religious? How would you characterize the Chinese religious sense?

6. What seems to be the predominant Japanese religion? Explain.

7. Why do the Chinese and the Japanese have such respect for family life?

For Discussion

1. Discuss the pros and cons of the Chinese principle of life.

2. Discuss whether the principles of Confucius would apply to people living under any form of government.

3. Discuss why the Chinese and Japanese always seem so polite.

For Research

1. Prepare a brief report on Marco Polo.

2. Look up some information on the early history of China.

3. Prepare a report on the early history of Japan.

4. Prepare a report on the poetry and art of Japan.

5. Find out what you can about the origins of judo and karate.

6. Look up information of the communist revolution in China.

Words You Should Know

If there are any words given below that you are not sure of, look them up in the Word List at the end of the book.

animatism	haiku	Taoism
bodhisattva	hari-kari	yang/yin
Confucianism	rapport	Zen
esoteric	Shinto	

part three

The Question of Atheism

All beliefs on which you bet your life are fundamentally religious beliefs, and atheism can be as much a religion as theism.

—H. M. Kallen

chapter 10

The Absence of God

Atheism is rarely thought of as a "religion" in the usual sense of the word religion. It is a religion, however, if you apply to it the same criteria used to define religion. It is a response to the mystery of life. Instead of having a "God" response to the mystery of life, atheists have a "no god" response. They are as fervent in their belief as any "God people" are in theirs.

Atheism is not the same as secularism which we touched on in chapter one. Atheists reject the idea that there is a God. Secularists act as if there were no God. Secularism, as we have said, is a philosophy of life which rejects all forms of religious faith, morals, or worship in political or social affairs.

A secularist may or may not have any religious faith, but lives as if there were no God or as if the idea of a God or the practice of religion makes no difference in the real affairs of people. An atheist, on the other hand, lives in a world without a God.

Most of the great men of this world live as if they were atheists. Every man who has lived with his eyes open, knows that the knowledge of a God, his presence, and his justice, has not the slightest influence over the wars, the treaties, the objects of ambition, interest or pleasure, in the pursuit of which they are wholly occupied.

—Voltaire 1694–1778 French philosopher

There are many forms of atheism, various degrees of unbelief, many ways of expressing this unbelief, and many different reasons for not believing in some kind of God. It is impossible to discuss each and every mental attitude which is based on a no-God response to the mystery of life, but some distinctions and certain generalizations can be made about the faith of those whose response is non-God oriented:

1. An *atheist* is a person who believes that there is no God, Supreme Being, Ultimate Force, an Unknown, or any other being or "thing" responsible for this world, its affairs,

or its destiny. Such a person believes there is no other Existence outside of the known.

2. An *agnostic* is a person who believes one cannot know whether or not there is a God, Supreme Being, Ultimate Force, or Existence outside of the known.

3. A *materialist* is one who believes that nothing spiritual exists. Such a person believes that only matter or forms of matter exist.

4. A *pseudo-atheist* is one who is not a true atheist, but rather an atheist "of convenience" or one who, for one reason or another, has given no thought to the question of whether there is a God or not.

5. Not all atheists are materialists since some persons who do not believe in a God still believe that people have a mind or even a soul that is more than material. And not all materialists are atheists, since some persons who believe that matter is everything believe that such "spiritual" things as beauty, mind, virtue and so forth, are in reality very subtle states of matter. They believe in using the word "God" to stand for the Mysterious Totality of Material Things, or the Life-Force, or something similar.

Like those who profess some kind of religious belief based on the acceptance of a God as the answer to the mystery of life, most atheists, agnostics, and materialists are sincere, thoughtful people who see no conclusive proofs that there is a God. Some are more or less indifferent—they couldn't care less whether there is a God or not. Some are "sociological" atheists or agnostics—they grew up in a society that was atheist or agnostic oriented. All have faith that there is no God. This is their religion.

Some Probable Causes for Atheism

Aside from the sociological causes for atheism, one of the most common causes for atheism is what is called "a proof mentality." Seeing no "proof"—that is, physical, tangible evidence—that God exists, this kind of atheist says there is no God. Not accepting the idea that there can be a God, this kind of atheist looks for answers to the mystery of life everywhere but in the God idea. Such a person says, in effect, "You can't prove it to me; therefore there is no God."

Another common cause for atheism is a reaction against certain features of some God-centered religions.[1] Some atheists reject ideas of God or habits and practices of current religions or of "religious people" which they feel go contrary to the thrust of human society or to the discoveries of modern science, psychology, politics, and economics. The reaction is caused, on the one hand, by the existence of religions which do in fact contradict modern knowledge, and on the other, by ignorance of the development of religious awareness in response to modern knowledge. Having misconceptions about what modern religious awareness consists in, they look outside of "religion" for the answers to the mysteries of life.

A third common cause for atheism is the existence of evil. Some people, unable to explain the existence of pain, suffering, and death in "innocent" people, refuse to believe there is a God because "if there were, He would not allow such evil to exist."

There are, of course, other causes for atheism such as repressed religious feelings, neglect of religious practices, traumatic religious experiences, dislike of or hatred for certain religious persons or things, superstition, peer-group pressure, or social fashion. For the most part, people with these motives are not convinced atheists; they are "emotional" atheists. For them the denial of God fulfills some psychological need, like getting even with God or someone who represents God, punishing themselves for not being more religious, or fear that if they say they believe in God or show any sincere conviction that God exists, they will be laughed at or considered "square" or "different."

Some Commonly Expressed Reasons for Not Believing in a God

It is impossible, of course, to discuss the particular thoughts of every individual atheist or agnostic, but it is possible to chart the drift of thinking that can be found among many atheists and agnostics for their denial of the existence of God or their doubt about whether any God exists at all. Not every one of them thinks all these thoughts, but most people of an agnostic or atheistic frame of mind think some of them. (Many God-oriented people have thoughts like these also, but instead of looking outside of God for answers to their problems, they search more deeply into their religious heritage.)

---

1. Atheism is not a new phenomenon. In ancient days, people who could not accept ideas of the gods were called "a-theists"—people "without gods."

Jerusalem's Yad Vashem memorial in memory of the Holocaust

Among the reasons given by many atheists and agnostics for the denial of God or for doubt that any God really exists are these:

1. The concept of God is a threat to people's independence.

Modern psychology has revealed that a person does not truly become an adult psychologically until he or she is no longer dependent upon what his or her parents (parent substitutes) think. Some persons may be in their thirties or forties, but they still haven't "untied the apron strings"—they are always looking over their shoulder for someone older or bolder to tell them what to think or do.

For some people, "God" seems to function in their lives as an invisible father-image, a Person who has their lives so well planned for them that they are constantly insecure about doing the wrong thing. They scrupulously fear His judgment and punishments, which they imagine are ready to leap out at them from behind every corner.

Besides these obviously distorted images of God, the very notion of God Himself as the Lawgiver of the universe seems to be an obstacle to people's freedom in the eyes of many thoughtful atheists. They notice that many people obey the moral law, not because things are in themselves right or

The Question of Atheism

wrong, but because they fear the punishment of God. The concept of a rewarding or punishing God seems (to atheists) to be an infantile need for directions from a Super-Parent, and an escape from real adult responsibility.

2. Recognition of myths as poetic truth

In recent times, scholars have become able to "crack the code" of many ancient myths. Although ancient people may have taken their myths literally, we now recognize them as *symbolic* stories telling in picture form what ancient people were not able to express in abstract scientific language, which they had not yet developed. Thus, in many ancient religions the sacredness of responsibility for obeying the laws of the community is assured by their being represented as coming from God or from the gods in a miraculous manner. In the Judeo-Christian tradition, for example, the Ten Commandments are pictured as being carved in stone by God on Mount Sinai amidst lightning and thunder.

Today, we look for the meaning in these myths without taking every detail of the myths literally. Thus, while we may not literally believe that the social code of Moses' desert people was inscribed on stone tablets by lightning bolts, we recognize that the sacredness of law is enshrined in such a poetic story.

Atheists carry this demythologizing[2] process a step further, applying it not only to legends like those concerning how human laws got started, but to the very concept of God Himself. They say that the notion of a Super-Person ruling the universe is really only a poetic way of saying that *persons* should rule things; things should not rule persons. In the primitive world where nature seemed to rule over people, they needed an imaginary Super-Person, or Super-Persons in control of nature. In today's world where people, through science, are learning to harness nature, people are able to rely on themselves and no longer need confidence in a mystical Super-Power. Therefore, they proclaim that such a concept of God has outlived its usefulness and now "God is dead."

3. Historical selectivity

As the old saying goes, "There are three sides to every story: my side, your side, and the truth." We all know how different people who were present at the same event will tend to describe it differently, especially if their advantage is in one way or another connected with the event. (One has only to

2. "Demythologizing" means translating an ultimate divine truth from mythical language into literal, scientific language.

watch or read about the most recent UN debates over the latest international incident.)

We have always realized this about ordinary history—that it is written differently according to who writes it—but until recently we thought biblical history was exempt from this general condition. Scriptural studies popularized within the last seventy years, however, have shown that "God's inspiration of the Bible" can no longer be interpreted as some kind of "hot line" whereby God dictated exactly what was to be written. We know that the Bible contains historical facts, but they are interpreted from the Jewish religious point of view, and sometimes exaggerated or embellished and legendized or told in the form of epic poetry in order to emphasize the sacred meaning of the event.

Many modern people have become very skeptical about historical objectivity, and it is not surprising that some of them are skeptical about any historical arguments offered to prove the existence of God or to prove that He intervened in history to reveal Himself.

4. Unresolved theological problems

Some persons are atheists because they find that the concept of "God" raises theological problems to which they can see no solution.

One such problem is that of divine causality and human freedom. How can a person be truly free if the source of his actions is really God?

Another is that of providence versus the natural laws of the universe. Why should God make natural laws to run the universe if He is always going to be interrupting them in answers to prayers? Or if He already has the answer to someone's prayer "programmed into" the laws of the universe from the beginning, then why pray for what's already going to happen?

5. The existence of evil

If a good God exists, how come there's so much evil in the world? This serious question bothers a lot of sensitive people. Looking at life to see if they can discern the hand of a Person behind it all, they are stumped by what they see—family quarrels, international wars, daily murder and robbery, race riots, broken hearts and wounded bodies due to both human causes and natural causes. "Where is the hand of God in all this?" they ask. "Either there's no God or else God is powerless. One way or the other, He's not worth taking into account."

The Question of Atheism

6. Failure of religious people and communities to live up to their beliefs

Most believers in God have received their faith within a Church community. Although they believe the existence and nature of God can be proved from reason, they in their own lives have not reasoned this out but have accepted it because the Church they belong to seemed believable to them.

Likewise, many atheists disbelieve in God, not because of philosophical arguments, but because the Churches they see do not convince them. A community which says God established it to spread love on earth is not believable to people who say they see it showing little or no love within its own ranks.

Again, a Church which says it stands for human progress is the laughingstock of many atheists, who believe it repeatedly uses out-of-date techniques and ideas and political methods within its own institutions. A community which says God loves the poor is a blasphemy in the eyes of many humanitarian atheists who love their fellow human beings and who see "God" as the Super-Defender of the status quo, when, as far as they can tell, a Church is rich in its buildings and leaders, and supports political regimes which favor the wealthy over the starving poor.

7. Closed-mindedness of "true believers"

In the face of modern discoveries and the questions they raise, some atheists say, a person who wishes to retain his or her religious faith can do so in one of two ways: (1) open his or her mind to the discoveries, let the questions speak themselves in his mind, and reinterpret what has been inherited in a way that makes sense; or (2) close his or her mind to the discoveries, squelch questions before they are bothersome, and think that any kind of reinterpretation is a form of blasphemy.

Many atheists believe that the first way is a "nice try" but it can't be kept up for any length of time because a completely honest reinterpretation could only lead (so they say) to atheism. They believe that the only way a person can retain religious faith is to adopt the second way, that of closed-mindedness, of refusing to consider the evidence. There are enough religious believers of this type around to convince them that religious faith creates a closed mind.

8. Vested interests

Many nonbelievers feel that religious faith (which to them is a form of closed-mindedness) could not be maintained by ignorance alone, but must also be the result of selfish leadership in a Church. They believe that persons in power maintain a system which promotes their own position of authority, using moral fear to make people conform.

9. Materialism

Finally, there are those who cannot believe in God because they cannot believe in anything that is not material. They realize, of course, that there are many things about people which cannot be located or defined physically—for example, they believe in "truth" and "love" and they realize that a surgeon cannot cut a man open and extricate an organ named "truth" or a tissue called "love." But they believe that such "spiritual" things are in reality *expressions* of matter. As an example of this point of view, one might consider a dance or a song. The dance is not the body, but it is artistic motions of the body; the song is not the vocal chords, but it is the vocal sound arranged artistically. You cannot operate on the body and amputate a dance, nor can you label any particular organ the song. The dance and the song are not physical things, they are *expressions* of physical things; yet they are not spiritual "things" existing in their own right. Following this line of reasoning, materialists say that there is no spiritual substance called a soul or called God—there is only matter and its various expressions.

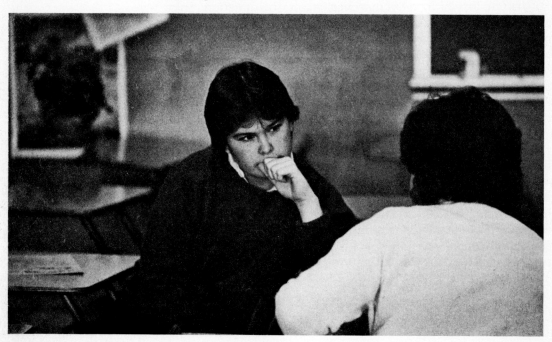

For the most part, atheists live in God-oriented societies as individuals seeking answers to life's mysteries in their own ways, seldom banding together to form any community of believers. They have only one common denominator: belief that there is no God, and only one thing to celebrate—this life's meager triumphs. Their vision is limited to what life has to offer, and their hope is circumscribed by their own death.

Atheism, like religious faith, is a way of looking at the world, human experience, and the mysteries of life. For some people, it is the only way. They are as secure in their faith as many religious people are in theirs.

Summary

1. Atheism is a religion because it is a response to the mystery of life.

2. Most atheists reject the idea that there is a God because they can find no physical proof that there is a God.

3. Some people are atheists because they are disappointed or disenchanted with the religious faith and actions of established religions.

For Review

1. What is the difference between an atheist and an agnostic?

2. What are three probable causes for some atheism?

3. Examine each of the reasons given why some people reject the idea of a God and prepare a response that you think might come from someone who truly believes in God. Are there any you do not have a good response for?

4. Is it correct to say that atheists and agnostics are really religious? Why? Why not?

For Discussion

1. Discuss whether or not it is realistic to blame God for the faults of some God-oriented people.

2. Discuss why some religious people attack people who do not believe in God.

3. Discuss why some atheists work so hard against religion and/or religious institutions.

4. The First Amendment of the Constitution of the United States states: "Congress shall make no law respecting the establishment of religion, or prohibiting the free exercise thereof. . . ." What does this mean? Do you think this is a good idea? Why? Why not? Is making laws forbidding prayers in the public schools "prohibiting the free exercise of" religion? Exchange your thoughts with your classmates in an open forum.

5. Discuss the quotation from Voltaire on page 229. Do you think it is generally true? What effect does it have on world affairs? Do you think it applies to people in general and not simply to people in power? Why? Why not?

6. Discuss what things in established religions discourage people from practicing religion. How do you account for the great surge toward fundamentalism?

For Research

Karl Marx and Friedrich Engels, the "fathers" of modern communism, said, "Religion is the sigh of the oppressed creature, the feeling of a heartless world, just as it is the spirit of unspiritual conditions. It is the opium of the people." What do you think they meant? Do some research on the origins of modern communism, trying to determine why it was called "atheistic" communism. Is there any other kind?

Words You Should Know

Be sure that you can define the words given below. If you cannot, look them up in the word list at the end of the book.

agnostic	embellish	nihilist
atheist	freethinker	rationalist
criteria	legendize	secularist
deist	materialist	squelch
demythologize		

Places and Dates Associated with the Origin of the Principal Expressions of Religious Awareness

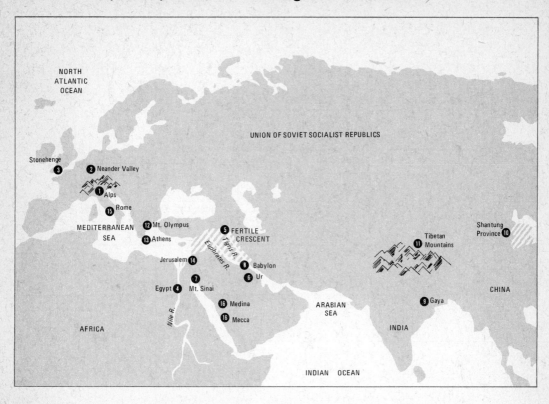

① 180,000–50,000 BC: totems (bear shrines) caves.

② 50,000 BC–10,000 BC: cave paintings.

③ 5000–2000 BC: stone arrangements for sacred worship places.

④ 3100 BC: Egyptian religion flourishes.

⑤ 3000 BC: Babylonian religion flourishes.

⑥ 1900 BC: Biblical "Abraham" migrates to Promised Land.

⑦ 1285 BC: Moses establishes the Covenant with Yahweh after the Exodus.

⑧ 587–536 BC: Babylonian Exile of the Jewish people.

⑨ 500 BC (roughly): Buddha becomes "awakened" under the Bo tree.

⑩ 500 BC (roughly): Confucius edits the Chinese classics.

⑪ 500 BC (roughly): Legendary Lao-Tzu is said to write *Tao te Ching* before crossing Tibetan border.

⑫ 900 BC: Greek gods "established" on Mount Olympus.

⑬ 500–300 BC: Golden Age of Greek philosophers.

⑭ 29 AD: Jesus of Nazareth crucified near Jerusalem.

⑮ 1st century AD: St. Peter establishes focus of Christianity at Rome.

⑯ 622 AD: Mohammed flees from Mecca to Medina.

Comparison of Religions

		PRE-HISTORIC	BABYLONIAN	EGYPTIAN	GREEK	JUDAISM
ROOT AWARENESS OF MYSTERY	BEGINNING OF LIFE		Marduk vs. Tiamat	various myths of man fashioned by gods	various myths	Adam and Eve
	DEATH: END OF LIFE	special arrangements of bones	uncertain view	life after death	uncertain	Resurrection
	GOD(S): POWER OVER LIFE AND DEATH	world of spirits totems	total powers	Re and Osiris the chief gods Short-lived attempt to proclaim Aton One God	half-human half-divine hero-gods	Yahweh the One God
SYSTEMATIC EXPRESSION OF THIS AWARENESS IN . . .	THOUGHT: DOGMA THEOLOGY		myths (general) astrology	myths fixity of belief	rational math, science, philosophy	no creed One God creating His People
	RITUAL: WORSHIP	hunting, fertility, death, puberty rites ceremonial animals carved figures of women definite places of worship	rites to ward off the evils planned by the gods	burial rites (mummies)	ceremonies for many gods	Dialogue with God's Word Major Feasts
	ACTION: MORALS, ETHICS, LAW	taboos	Code of Hammurabi		the good life	The Torah Covenant Sin and Redemption
COMMUNITY STRUCTURE FOR MAINTAINING THIS AWARENESS AND EXPRESSION	FOUNDER					1285 BC: Moses
	AUTHORITY SYSTEM			Pharaoh as divine		prophets rabbis
	TRADITION	word of mouth	oral and written	oral, written, and symbols	song, drama	Jewish interpretation of salvation history
	SACRED BOOKS					Old Testament Bible Talmud
	PROPHECY					Prophets
	PRIEST-HOOD	shamans,	priestly clan		priests, vestal virgins	

CHRISTIANITY	ISLAM	HINDUISM	BUDDHISM	CONFUCIANISM	TAOISM	ATHEISM
Breath and word of God in creation	Allah the Creator	Song of Creation cycle of creation The One Existence becomes many				
Share in Christ's Resurrection	Heaven or hell	re-incarnation Nirvana		heritage of many gods		
Trinity	Allah	Brahman Brahman's many manifestations		no single God-Above-All		
Creed	simple theology four major themes	openness of mind	The Four Noble Truths	basic yang-yin mentality	[1]Wu wei	various explanations of the reaction against the God-concept
Sacraments	five pillars	worship, sacraments, sacred cows		Li (The Right Pattern)		
Love in Christ		discovery of the "self" or Atman 4 yogas	The Eightfold Path	The Five Principles	Wu wei	
29 AD: Jesus	622 AD: Mohammed		500 BC: The Buddha	500 BC: Confucius	500 BC: Lao-Tzu	
successors of apostles	successors of Mohammed					
		caste system				
New Testament community memories of Jesus	Koran			Confucian edition of the Chinese classics	Tao-te-Ching	
	Moses, Jesus, Mohammed					
participation in Jesus' worship of the Father			Buddha forms an order of Monks			

The faithful of yesterday,
today and tomorrow

Adherents in millions and as a % of world population

Religion	1900	%	1980	%	2000	%
Christian	558	34.4	1,433	32.8	2,020	32.3
Roman Catholic	272	16.8	809	18.5	1,169	18.7
Protestant & Anglican	153	9.4	345	7.9	440	7.0
Eastern Orthodox	121	7.5	124	2.8	153	2.4
Other	12	.7	155	3.6	258	4.1
Non-religious & atheist	3	.2	911	20.8	1,334	21.3
Muslim	200	12.4	723	16.5	1,201	19.2
Hindu	203	12.5	583	13.3	859	13.7
Buddhist	127	7.8	274	6.3	359	5.7
Chinese Folk Religion	380	23.5	198	4.5	158	2.5
Tribal & Shamanist	118	7.3	103	2.4	110	1.8
"New Religions"	6	.4	96	2.2	138	2.2
Jewish	12	.8	17	.4	20	.3
Other*	13	.8	36	.8	81	1.0
World population	1,620		4,374		6,260	

*including Sikh, Confucian, Shinto, Baha'i, Jain, Spiritist, Parsi

Due to rounding off, percents may not equal 100

Source: *World Christian Encyclopedia* as quoted in TIME, May 3, 1982, p. 66.

MAJOR WORLD RELIGIONS

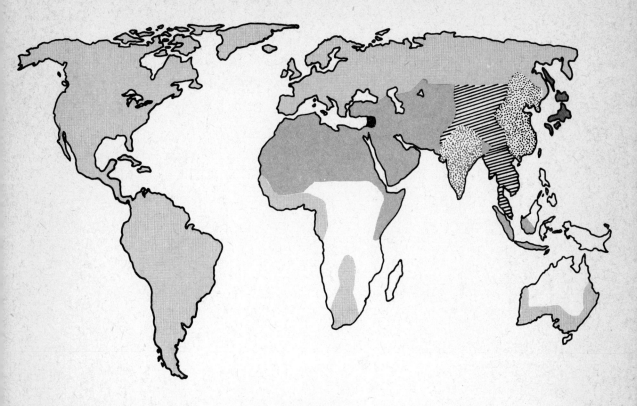

This map gives a general idea of the areas where the world's major religions have exerted their strongest direct influences.

☐ Christianity	☐ Hinduism
☐ Islam	☐ Shintoism
☐ Buddhism	☐ Judaism
☐ Confucianism and Taoism	☐ Primitive Religions or sparsely populated regions

Word List

Aborigines the primitive native inhabitants of a region, in contrast to invading or colonizing people

Absolutely Other a state of being totally removed from the human dimension

Accretions additions; growth in size or extent

Acts of the Apostles the New Testament book by St. Luke which describes the origin and development of the early Christian Church

Adonai a Hebrew name for God meaning "Lord"

Agnostic one who holds that God is not knowable

Alienation separation from; estrangement

Allah *the* God, in Islam

Amalgam joining together; union of items into a single whole

Amorphous formless; lacking definite shape or outline

Analetics collected writings of Confucius

Ancestor worship the practice of venerating one's ancestors through ritual and prayer

Angel a messenger; one who does good things for another

Animatism belief that attributes consciousness to inanimate objects

Animism belief that a soul inhabits *every* living being

Anthropologists scientists who deal with the origins, and the physical, cultural, developmental, racial characteristics, and social customs of people

Anthropomorphic giving human characteristics to the nonhuman

Apostle one chosen and taught by Jesus, sent forth by Jesus to preach Christianity

Archeologists scientists who deal with the study of historic and prehistoric people and their cultures by analysis of artifacts and other remains

Areligious without or lacking religion

Artifacts various items used; materials associated with a particular culture or archeological dig

Ascetic one who dedicates his or her life to the pursuit of contemplative ideals and who practices extreme self-denial for religious reasons

Astrology the art or practice which professes to interpret the influence of the stars and planets on human affairs

Astronomy the science which deals with the material universe beyond the earth's atmosphere

Atheist one who denies the existence of God

Atman Hindu word for true self, or soul

Auguring trying to tell the future; divination

Baptism initiation into; ceremony introducing a person into a Christian sect; a cleansing action

Bhagavad-Gita one of the Hindu scriptures

Bodhisattva in Buddhist thought, one who is at the threshold of Nirvana but postpones his or her own entry to help others to salvation

Book of Revelation the final book of the New Testament which describes in symbolic language the final triumph of Christ

Brahman or Brahma for Hindus, the impersonal supreme being and the primal source and ultimate goal of all people

Brahmin highest caste in Hinduism

Buddhism religion which arose from spiritual insights of Siddhartha Gautama

Caliph a successor to Mohammed

Calligraphy the art of beautiful handwriting

Caste a division in Hindu society based on one's position in life

Categorize to put into a class; to label

Charismatic attractive; unusually persuasive

Chronicler an individual who records events in history

Chun-tzu being the ideal person, in Confucianism

Church a group of people with similar belief banded together for worship

Circumvent to get around; to avoid

Codify to classify according to a particular system; to put in order

Communism a philosophy based on the writings of Marx and Engles which attributes ownership to the State

Confucianism a moral/ethical system developed by the Chinese philosopher Confucius, emphasizing forbearance and moral acting in its teaching

Conservative Jew one who adheres for the most part to the orthodox principles and practices of Judaism, but modifies them according to circumstances

Contemplation private spiritual or mystical thought

Covenant an agreement or testament between two parties

Creed an official formula of religious belief

Criteria standard of judgment

Curry to seek favor; to fawn

Deductive to arrive at a conclusion from given data; to infer

Deist one who belongs to a religion based on reason, not revelation

Demythologize to get to the facts; to seek the reality behind a story or myth; to take apart

Dhamma essential quality of Buddhism; similar to dharma

Dharma the duty one has in life as designated by one's position

Divination the practice of attempting to tell the future or to discover hidden knowledge by magical means

Dogmas church doctrines, formally stated and authoritatively proclaimed

Dome of the Rock Islamic shrine in Jerusalem; according to Islamic belief, the site of Mohammed's ascent into heaven on horseback

Dynasty ruling family or group

Eke to squeeze out; to barely make it

Embellish to add to; make more than it is

Enclave a group entirely surrounded by some other group or territory

Enlightenment Buddhism, a final state of being where neither desire nor pain are felt

Epistles New Testament letters written to the early Christian communities

Esoteric not simple, not for the unlettered

Experiential learn by experience

Exploit to take advantage of

Exodus Old Testament book detailing the removal of the Israelites from Egypt to Palestine

Fratricide the act of killing one's own brother

Fetishism belief in the power of magical charms or superstitious objects

Freethinker one who doubts religious teaching or authority

Galaxy a collection of stars

Galvanize bind together; to spellbind

Genesis the first book of the Old Testament, containing accounts of creation and the origin of the Jewish people

Golgatha small hill outside Jerusalem where Christ was crucified

Gospels the accounts of Christ's life and teachings attributed to the four evangelists: Matthew, Mark, Luke, and John

Guru a teacher or guide in the Hindu religion

Hadith a collection of Mohammed's teachings

Haiku a form of Japanese poetry

Hanukkah Jewish "Feast of Dedication"

Hari-kari Japanese suicide rite

Hegira Mohammed's flight from Mecca to Medina

Hierarchy a ranking based on one's station in life

Hinduism the basic religion in India, marked by contemplation and self-denial for religious reasons

Horoscope a chart supposedly telling the future by the position of the stars

Hypothesis an assumption based on known data; calculated guess

Imam a Moslem leader

Inductive a form of reasoning; arriving at a conclusion from limited data about something

Infantilism acting like an infant; babyish

Inspired moved to action by someone's words or acts; influenced

Instigate to start; to prompt to action

Islam the religion of the Moslems

Jen humaneness, Confucian supreme virtue

Jinns according to Moslems, a class of spirits capable of taking on human form and influencing human beings for good or evil

Judaism the religion of the Jewish people characterized by belief in one God and the living out of His law as expressed in their scripture

Judo oriental art of weaponless fighting, emphasizing defense

Ka'ba   the rectangular sacred shrine of Islam which contains the sacred black stone of Moslem veneration

Karate   oriental art of weaponless fighting, emphasizing offense

Karma   the Hindu connection between how one acts and the consequences for the actions

Koran   Moslem book of sacred writings

Krishna   a popular Hindu god

Legendize   to make a legend out of

Li   following the right, or Confucian, pattern

Linguists   specialists in the sounds, meanings, history, and uses of words and languages

Lord's Supper   in Christian Churches, the Eucharist

Magic   supernatural influence over natural objects

Mammoths   prehistoric animals of immense size, shaped like elephants

Mana   Polynesian concept of a "power"

Mantra   in Hinduism a prayer, invocation, or incantation associated with meditation

Materialist   one who believes that nothing spiritual exists

Matzoth   unleavened bread

Mecca   sacred city of Islam; a special place

Messianic Age   the period in history when the Messiah will come to save

Minaret   Moslem tower with balconies used for the announcement of prayers

Monotheism   belief in one God

Moral   conforming to a standard of right behavior

Moslem   an adherent or believer in Islam

Mosque   Moslem house of prayer and worship

Muezzin   an Islamic prayer announcer

Mummification   to make a mummy out of; to bury in materials intended to preserve the body

Muslim   one who follows the way of Islam

Myth   story or tradition with loose historical basis

Neti, neti   "not this, not that": God is incomprehensible

New Testament   second part of the Christian scriptures

Nihilist   person or thought that denies objective truth

Nirvana   a Hindu state in which a person is united with his or her deepest God-self

Noa   Polynesian name for "positive force"

Nuances   shades of meaning

Om   most sacred Hindu religious symbol or mantra

Orthodox Jew   one who adheres faithfully to the principles and practices of Judaism

Pantheism   the belief that all the universe is God

Passover   the Jewish feast commemorating Hebrew liberation from slavery in Egypt

Patriarchs   revered founders or ancestors

Pentateuch   the first five books of the Bible (see also *Torah*)

Pentecost   the Christian feast which celebrates the descent of the Holy Spirit on the apostles

Pesah   Jewish Passover

Placate   please; to seek the favor of

Polygamy   religious practice that allows a man to take more than one wife

Polytheism   belief in many gods

Postulate   propose; take for granted; assume

Prehistory   events occuring before records were kept

Preternatural   above or beyond the natural; not in accord with nature

Primitive   early; first; not sophisticated; without pretense

Proliferation   overabundance, spread widely

Prophet   one through whom God reveals Himself

Pseudo-atheist   one who is not a true atheist; rather an atheist of convenience, who gives no real thought to whether God exists

Pseudo-Buddhist   one who has adopted certain Buddhist practices, but does not embrace "The Way"

Puberty   coming of age; able to produce offspring

Purim   Jewish "Feast of Lots"

Quasi-religious   resembling religion

Ramadan   the ninth lunar month of the Moslem year devoted to fasting

Ramayana   Hindu sacred religious epic or myth

Rapport   harmonious relationship; feeling of mutuality

Rational   reasonable

Rationale   give a reason for

Rationalist   one who relies on reason as the basis for determining religious truths

Reform Jew   one who practices a system of ethics and religious rituals which are meaningful in light of contemporary conditions

Reincarnation   rebirth in new forms of earthly life

Relevant   appropriate; suitable; fitting

Religion   the human response to whatever the answer to the mystery of life is for a person

Revelation   knowledge given by God concerning Himself

Risen dimension   the dimension of existence attained after resurrection; state of being in the afterlife

Ritual   practices or traditions relating to religion and worship

Rosh Hashana   Jewish New Year's Day

Sabbath   a day set aside for religious worship; specifically, from Friday evening to Saturday evening for Jews, and Sunday for most Christians

Sacrament   a religious action done to participate in a special way in the benefits of religion; in Christianity an action of the Church designed to produce a result

Salam   Arabic for "peace," source of name, Islam

Salvation history   awareness among people of God's saving works in time

Samadhi   in Buddhism deep contemplation

Samskara   Hindu sacrament

Sangha   Buddhist ideal of the brotherhood among monks

Sanskrit   ancient Indic language

Satellite   anything that depends on, serves, or accompanies something else

Satori   the Buddhist moment of truth or enlightenment

Secular   worldly or without regard to religious elements

Seder   Passover dinner; seder means "order"

Seer   a person who prophecies future events; a wise person

Shaman   one who acts as both priest and doctor

Sharia   Koranic law

Shavuoth   Jewish "Feast of Weeks"

Shinto   Japanese form of the Chinese *shin tao* meaning "the way of the gods"

Shiva   Hindu god of destruction

Shophar   ram's horn used in Jewish synagogues at Rosh Hashana and Yom Kippur

Shruti   Hindu scripture divinely revealed to seers in each world cycle

Smriti   Hindu scripture, "that which is remembered"

Speculative   thoughtful; given to reflection; reflective; a reasoned guess

Squelch   suppress

Subsequent   following; coming in order; after

Sufism   Islamic mysticism

Sufiturug   Moslem mystical guilds, led to the development of Sufism

Sukkoth   Jewish "Feast of Tabernacles"

Swami   Hindu religious teacher

Symbol   a thing which stands for something else

Synagogue   Jewish building for religious services, from the Greek word for "the gathering of people"

Syncretism   reconciling and absorbing opposing principles

Taboo   forbidden; from the Polynesian word for "negative force"

Talmud   authoritative collection of Jewish tradition

Tangible   feelable; real; capable of being seen or felt

Tantric   branch of Buddhism which incorporates magic rituals and polytheism

Tao Te Ching   contains message of Taoism: importance of union with nature

Taoism   teaches importance of union with nature, which is self-sufficient and does not need God

Tat tvam asi   "That art thou" expresses human relationship with God

Te   Confucian government by moral power

Theism   belief in the existence of God

Torah   the collection of law in Jewish scripture, including the first five Old Testament books: Genesis, Exodus, Leviticus, Numbers, and Deuteronomy

Totemism   belief in kinship and/or patronage of a revered symbol

Transcultural   passing from one culture to another

Transmigration   the movement of the soul at death from one being or body to another

Tribulation   suffering; sorrow

Triune   threefold; consisting of three things

Unencumbered   not weighed down; free; loose; unattached

Upanishads   a collection of Hindu philosophical commentaries dealing mostly with Indian deities

Vedanta   Hindu collection of speculative religious thought

Vedas   four collections of Hindu religious material containing prayers, ritual, liturgy, hymns, spells, and charms of a popular nature

Viable   alive; having life

Vishnu   a Hindu deity

Wen   Confucian cultivation of the peaceful arts

Worship   religious acts directed toward God

Wu wei   the Taoist principle that states that all people should act in harmony with the nature of what they are dealing with

Yahweh   God's personal name, given by Him to the Israelites in the Old Testament

Yang   general Chinese term referring to any active or positive principle

Yin   general Chinese term referring to any receptive or negative principle

Yoga   a system of physical discipline designed to achieve a spiritual purpose

Yogi   a practicer of yoga

Yom Kippur   "Day of Atonement" most holy of Jewish days

Zen   major division of Buddhism in which, under the direction of a master teacher, one attempts to arrive at Satori—the moment of truth

Zoomorphic   ascribing animal form to primitive gods

Index

Photo Credits

American Museum of Natural History—29
Kate Bader—160, 162, 166, 170
Hal Bergsohn—86
Grover Brinkman—25
Dorothy Loa Bruegger—9, 206
Camerique—34, 34
Alan Cliburn—122
Bob Coyle—6, 120, 132
Danish Information Office—24
Vivienne della Grotta—27, 204
Documerica—228
Stephen Emery—10, 146, 173
Ruth Feldman—142
Field Museum of Natural History, Chicago—
    58, 59
David Frazier—127
Free Lance Photographers Guild—200
Charles Gatewood—152
Luke Golobitsh—4, 168, 174, 176, 179, 193,
    196
The Granger Collection—20, 40, 48, 65
Jeff Halvorsen—223
J. L. Hamar—60
Israel Ministry of Tourism—14, 80, 107,
    112, 136
Doranne Jacobson—18, 156, 164, 175, 182,
    184, 199, 210, 224
Yoram Kahana—24, 28
Isaiah Karlinsky—74, 98
Ellen Knudsen—195, 208, 214, 215
Jerg Kroener—37
Anne P. Layman—192
Lick Observatory—7
Liedtkes of Dubuque—50
Carolyn McKeone—83
Metropolitan Museum of Art—49, 66
Museum of Fine Arts, Boston—180, 213
National Aeronautics and Space
    Administration—38
Richard Nowitz—8, 39, 71, 79, 85, 101, 102,
    103, 110, 130, 230
Chip and Rosa Peterson—207, 218
Religious News Service—104, 125, 128, 209
Reynolds Photography—165
James Shaffer—13, 229, 230, 236
Florence Sharp—221
David Strickler—188
United Press International—46
William Updike—136
Betty Zoss—147, 154